SIXTH EDITION
GRAMMAR 3
IN CONTEXT

TEACHER'S EDITION

SANDRA N. ELBAUM

NATIONAL GEOGRAPHIC LEARNING | CENGAGE Learning·

Australia • Brazil • Mexico • Singapore • United Kingdom • United States

Grammar in Context 3, Sixth Edition
Teacher's Edition
Sandra N. Elbaum

Publisher: Sherrise Roehr
Executive Editor: Laura Le Dréan
Managing Editor: Jennifer Monaghan
Senior Development Editor: Claudi Mimó
Executive Marketing Manager: Ben Rivera
Product Marketing Manager: Dalia Bravo
Senior Director, Production: Michael Burggren
Content Project Manager: Mark Rzeszutek
Manufacturing Planner: Mary Beth Hennebury
Interior Design: Brenda Carmichael
Compositor: SPi Global
Cover Design: Brenda Carmichael

ISBN 13: 978-1-305-07557-3

National Geographic Learning
20 Channel Center Street
Boston, Massachusetts 02210
USA

Cengage Learning is a leading provider of customized learning solutions with office locations around the globe, including Singapore, the United Kingdom, Australia, Mexico, Brazil, and Japan. Locate our local office at international.cengage.com/region

Cengage Learning products are represented in Canada by Nelson Education, Ltd.

Visit National Geographic Learning online at **ngl.cengage.com**
Visit our corporate website at **www.cengage.com**

Printed in the United States of America
Print Number: 01   Print Year: 2015

CONTENTS

Grammar in Context 3, Sixth Edition

Welcome to *GRAMMAR IN CONTEXT,* Teacher's Edition!

Grammar in Context, Sixth Edition, contains a rich variety of material, making it easy to customize to any program's needs. This new *Teacher's Edition* will help you take full advantage of the National Geographic images and content in the *Student Book.* It includes extra resources to make planning your syllabus and preparing lessons easier than ever before. It also reinforces an active inductive approach to instruction that will encourage your students to discover answers and rules for themselves. Here's what the *Grammar in Context Teacher's Edition* offers you:

New suggestions for teaching a lesson (see page vi).

New Lesson Opener activities that include helpful background information for instructors on the opening thematic photos and quotations.

Ten easy solutions for customizing *Grammar in Context, Sixth Edition,* to meet your classroom needs (see page v).

Revised Presentation Ideas suggest alternative ways of presenting select grammar charts and checking students' understanding of the target grammar. They also provide suggestions for more detailed examination of select complex grammar points.

Updated Practice Ideas include ways to adapt grammar exercises to target specific skills: reading, writing, listening, and speaking.

Clearly identifiable "Fast Track" icons ⭐ highlight essential readings, charts, and exercises for courses that don't have the time to present and practice the full range of readings, grammar charts, and exercises available in *Grammar in Context, Sixth Edition.* Teaching these essential items gives students a basic understanding and practice of the most important grammar in each lesson.

Useful pacing guides for every activity provide a timing framework for lesson planning.

Supplemental activities provide students with additional practice, reinforcing their skills and building their confidence as language learners.

Ten Tips for Customizing *GRAMMAR IN CONTEXT,* *Sixth Edition,* to fit your program

1. Work within your curriculum.

Let your curriculum guide you on what to cover from this rich, comprehensive series. For example, if your program doesn't expect students to learn about nonessential adjective clauses at this level, a teacher could skip the chart about nonessential adjective clauses. Also, it may be enough for your program to teach unreal conditions in the present without getting into unreal conditions in the past.

2. Do the Test/Review section at the start of each lesson.

One way to find out how much practice your students need is to give them the Test/Review section at the beginning of the lesson. If you find that most of your students can do this with relatively few errors, then you can skip the lesson altogether or focus only on the points that your students find difficult.

3. Assign the readings as homework.

All the readings are important in introducing the grammar in context and should not be skipped. To save class time, however, the readings can be done at home. The reading level is low enough that classroom instruction on how to read should not be necessary. The reading is not meant to challenge and improve students' reading skills; it is meant to illustrate the grammar in a stimulating context. Additionally, using the context notes, glossed words, and guided pre-reading activities in the *Teacher's Edition* can help ensure that students process the ideas and allow them to focus on relevant grammar functions.

4. Set time limits for each fill-in-the blank exercise.

Set a maximum time limit for each exercise. Suggested times are given in this *Teacher's Edition*. Once the time limit has expired, ask students to put down their pens and move on to the next exercise. Students can complete the rest of the exercise at home.

5. Assign audio-based exercises for lab time.

Many exercises contain audio tracks (indicated with a listening icon 🎧). These exercises can take time to set up and run, so you may wish to assign these for lab credits or homework. You may also decide to do only one of these per class to add variety.

6. Use one of the "About You" exercises per class.

These exercises are fun to do; if you find your students' attention waning, you can insert one of these activities per lesson. If your students attend another class for speech and conversation, these exercises may be skipped.

7. Use Expansion Activities if there is time.

The Expansion Activities are fun, but time is limited. If you do have extra time, choose the activity that seems the most enjoyable. Students are likely to remember the lesson better if there is an element of fun.

8. Assign exercises for extra credit.

Students can go beyond the basic curriculum and do more of the exercises at home for extra credit.

9. Let students check answers at home.

Print the answer key for each lesson from the Cengage Learning website (NGL.Cengage.com/gic). You may wish to give the answer key to students at the start of each lesson so that they can check their answers at home. Set aside ten minutes every week to do a quick troubleshooting of particular grammar points.

10. Use this *Teacher's Edition*.

Each level of the student book has an accompanying *Teacher's Edition,* which offers comprehensive teaching suggestions on how to present and teach each grammar point.

Suggestions for Teaching a Lesson of
GRAMMAR IN CONTEXT, Sixth Edition

1. How to use the lesson opener photo and quote

Use the photo, caption, and quotation to interest students in the topic. Provide background information on the photo and person who is quoted. Have students look through the lesson to find out how the lesson opener photo and quote connect to photos and illustrations throughout. Have them identify reading topics and discuss what they know about them in pairs or small groups. Tell students the grammar functions they will practice in the lesson and elicit prior knowledge about them. Provide example sentences to model usage of the functions. Use Expansion Activities to stimulate interest, activate prior knowledge, and provide additional preparation.

2. How to approach the pre-reading activities

Use photos, captions, graphs, titles, and other special text features to guide students to predict main ideas in the reading. Set up a short discussion to activate students' knowledge of the reading topic. Have students discuss questions in pairs or small groups. Try to pair or group students of similar or different cultures together, depending on the questions. Ask for a few volunteers to share their answers with the class.

3. How to handle the reading

Have students first read the text silently. Tell them to pay special attention to the words and phrases in bold. Pre-teach essential terms students may not know. Play the audio and have students listen and read along silently. Encourage students to read for key ideas the first time and then to read or listen for details. In class, ask questions about the reading or the vocabulary to ensure that students read and understood the text. Ask *Additional Comprehension Questions* as follow up. Use *Context Notes* to clarify idiomatic language, provide bytes of culture background, and add interest. Before or after the reading, as appropriate, introduce materials for expansion, if desired.

4. How to teach the grammar charts

Use a variety of presentation approaches to hold students' interest. In addition to the suggestions included in this *Teacher's Edition*, you can use the Presentation Tool. When the material permits, guide students to discover rules and explanations for themselves. Clarify vocabulary students do not understand in the chart. Have students review examples, explanations, and Language, Pronunciation, and Punctuation Notes. Elicit example usages in complete sentences from students to check understanding, and provide models when needed. Use *Additional Practice* activities to concretize difficult target functions.

5. How to teach the exercises in general

Tell students what the exercise is about. Have students read the direction line. Direct students to the example. Elicit the grammar point being practiced. Complete the first item with the class. Have students complete the rest of the exercise individually. Remind them to review the grammar chart if necessary. Then have them check their answers in pairs or small groups, depending on the exercise. Monitor pair/group work. If necessary, check the answers as a class. Use *Additional Practice* ideas to help students further synthesize the material and practice language.

6. How to handle writing activities

Encourage students to prepare before writing. In opening lessons of your course, review brainstorming, mapping, and simple coherence and transition devices (e.g., *first, second, third, next, last*). Where appropriate, have students first discuss the topic with partners or a group. Periodically, model clear topic statements and conclusions. Collect assignments for assessment as desired.

1 LANGUAGE

GRAMMAR CHARTS

LESSON OPENER

Have students look at the photo and read the caption. Elicit or say that a petroglyph is a type of rock art, especially prehistoric, and petroglyphs are icons or pictograms carved into rock. Ask students to share their ideas about the meaning and purpose of the petroglyph in the photo. Have them read the quotation. Ask: *What does it mean? Think about rock art. Is it limited as a language?*

Background: Petroglyphs, or picture writing, includes animal, art, body, dream, and mathematical language as well as traditional languages. Rock art was carved by many ancient peoples. Artists depicted animals, hunts, and other aspects of ancient life. They often carved their pictures close to waterways and crossroads where migrating tribes could easily see them.

The Ute were once a powerful and rich American Indian nation. For hundreds of years, they controlled a great territory that covered much of the northwest United States. By 1882, outsiders had pushed the Ute off their land, threatening the existence of their language and traditions.

CONTEXT

This unit is about language. Students will read about a young man who speaks many languages, a project that records speakers of dying languages, and an animal who learned to speak a sign language.

1. Give students a few minutes to look through the lesson. Have them look at the photos and titles. How do they relate to the context?

2. Elicit the topics that will be discussed.

3. Have students discuss their ideas about language and types of language in pairs or small groups.

GRAMMAR

Students will review basic verb tenses: the present of be, the simple present, present continuous, future, simple past, and the present continuous versus the simple present.

1. To activate students' prior knowledge, have students name as many of these verb tenses as they can. Then ask what students know about the purpose or use of each tense they are going to review.

2. Give several examples of sentences in the different tenses (e.g., *I am tall. / We like pizza. / He is taking a shower. / She will be an artist. / He is going to his first class tomorrow. / They live in New York, and she is working at a library. / We walked in the park yesterday.*).

3. Have volunteers give additional example sentences and write them on the board.

EXPANDING ON THE CONTEXT

The context for this lesson can be enhanced with the following items:

1. Timeline of the development of human language
2. Family tree of human languages
3. Examples of hieroglyphic writing
4. Photo of Walnut Knob showing its high-visibility location
5. Images of graffiti on overpasses shown in contrast with surrealistic art in a gallery, such as by artist Salvador Dali
6. Articles about animal language

The Amazing Timothy Doner,
page 4

PRE-READING

⏱ Time: 10–20 min

1. Have students look at the photo and read the title. Ask: *What do you see in the picture?* (a young man and many books, including many language books) *Who is the man?* (Timothy Doner)

2. Have students look briefly at the reading. Ask: *What is the reading about? How do you know?* Have students make predictions.

3. Pre-teach any essential vocabulary words your students may not know, such as *amazing, average, equally, video chats,* and *memorizes.*

4. Ask: *Why does Timothy study other languages?* Have students discuss in small groups. When they are finished, have each group share their ideas with the class.

ADDITIONAL PRACTICE

During pre-reading, have students skim the first and last sentences of each paragraph to find the article's main idea. Help students with vocabulary, if needed.

READING GLOSSARY

amazing: favorably impressing or surprising
average: ordinary
equally: to the same extent or degree
video chat: a face-to-face conversation over the Internet
to memorize: to remember something exactly

READING CD 1 TR 2

⏱ Time: 10–15 min

After students have read the article, go over the answers to the Comprehension Check on page 5: **1.** F; **2.** T; **3.** F

ADDITIONAL COMPREHENSION QUESTIONS

How many languages does Timothy Doner speak? (twenty) *How can people see and hear Timothy on the Internet?* (videos and video chats) *Where can Timothy practice Russian?* (video store in New York) *How do songs help him learn a language?* (He memorizes the lyrics.) *Why does he learn new languages?* (to connect with other people, to feel good, to feel like a different person)

EXPANDING ON THE READING

The topic for this reading can be enhanced with the following items:

1. Maps identifying languages and their countries

2. Pie charts identifying numbers of speakers of languages

3. Biography of Timothy Doner from the Internet

4. Poster of the same sentence in many different languages for students to analyze

5. Video clips of other polyglots (speakers of multiple languages)

PRACTICE IDEA: SPEAKING

Have students work in small groups to share which languages they speak. After a student shares with the group, have him or her introduce the previous person. Write this example on the board: *I'm Li Xu. I speak two languages, Mandarin and English. . . . This is Mi Son. She speaks three languages, Korean, English, and Italian.* Provide additional statement examples, such as *I study Italian. He likes to study French.*

1.1 The Present of *Be,* page 5

⏱ Time: 10–15 min

1. Have students close their books or cover grammar chart **1.1.** Write on the board: *The verb* Be. Ask volunteers to conjugate *be* and write the forms on the board.

2. To activate students' prior knowledge of *be,* have students identify uses and provide example sentences (e.g., use: state the weather; example: It is sunny today.). List on the board: state a habit, routine, fact; use with description, classification, location; give time and age; state a subject. Ask: *Which is incorrect?* (state a subject)

3. Have students uncover and look at the chart. Review the examples and explanations.

4. Direct students' attention to the Language Note. Point out that contractions are used in conversational English but avoided in formal and academic writing.

5. Have students cover the chart again. Write on the board: *a) The house's white. b) Mary's three years old. c)*

We am hungry. d) It has 3:00. Ask: *Are these sentences correct? Why or why not?* a) no—incorrect contraction, b) yes for conversational English, c) no—incorrect verb form, d) no—incorrect verb. Ask volunteers to come to the board and rewrite the incorrect sentences *(a) The house is white. c) We are hungry. d) It is 3:00.*)

ADDITIONAL PRACTICE

Have students work as a class to contract question words with *be* in additional ways. List these combinations on the board: *what are, why are, when is.* Elicit answers from the class and write them on the board. (what're, why're, when's)

PRESENTATION IDEA: LISTENING

Have students practice distinguishing contractions. Tell students to close their books and have a pen and piece of paper ready. Say these questions: *What're you doing? When's dinner? Why's he going home? What time is it? What's the time? Why're you sad?* Pronounce the words distinctly at a normal speed. Have students write the full forms. Repeat the questions if needed. Have students compare their answers as a class.

ADDITIONAL PRACTICE

Divide students into pairs to write questions and answers with *be*. Provide cues such as *what's, when's, French, 15 years old, 8:00, easy/difficult, where's/it's in.* If needed, provide this model: *Q: What's your French teacher's name? A: Her name is Dr. Miller.* After students are finished, ask several pairs to share their answers with the class.

EXERCISE 1 page 6 CD 1 TR 3

🕐 Time: 10–15 min

Answers: 1. 's your native language; **2.** language is; **3.** Are you from; **4.** I'm not; **5.** I'm; **6.** Where's; **7.** It's; **8.** is it in; **9.** Is French; **10.** it isn't; **11.** There are; **12.** are

EXERCISE 2 page 6

🕐 Time: 5–10 min

Answers: 1. are there; **2.** are; **3.** is; **4.** is; **5.** Is it; **6.** isn't; **7.** 're; **8.** are; **9.** There are; **10.** it's; **11.** is; **12.** 's; **13.** Is Cameroon; **14.** are; **15.** 's; **16.** 'm; **17.** 'm; **18.** Are you; **19.** am

1.2 The Simple Present, page 7

🕐 Time: 10–15 min

1. Have students look at the Form section of grammar chart **1.2**. Elicit or say the reasons that verbs in English change form. (to show number and tense or time) Write several pairs of base/s-form verbs on the board (e.g., *speak/speaks, go/goes, do/does, say/says*). Ask: *What does the -s form show?* (that the subject is singular and the verb is in present tense)

2. Review the examples and explanations. Remind students of synonymous terms they may hear such as: the *to* form (infinitive), first-person (base form), third-person singular (-s form).

3. Draw students' attention to the sentence patterns and Language Notes. Ask: *Where does the subject go in a question?* (after the question word or between the auxiliary and main verbs) *What is the s-form of have?* (has)

4. Have students look at the Use section on page 8. Elicit uses of the simple present (to state facts, routines, repeated actions) and the locations of frequency adverbs in sentences.

ADDITIONAL PRACTICE

Have students look at the 15 frequency adverbs on page 8 and then close their books. Tell them to list as many frequency adverbs as they can think of, including ones that are not on the list. If appropriate, set a time limit (about 3 minutes) and have them compete to write the longest lists. Provide cues such as the initial letters of the adverbs if needed.

PRACTICE IDEA: WRITING

1. Bring in a few lists of four or five jumbled sentences in the simple present with adverbs. Be sure the sentences vary in length and include questions and statements. Have students close their books and work in pairs to unscramble the sentences.

2. When they are finished, ask volunteers to write the sentences on the board.

3. As a timesaver, have students work in small groups.

EXERCISE 3 pages 8–9

🕐 Time: 10–15 min

Answers: 1. Does he live; **2.** doesn't speak/does not speak; **3.** Does he speak, does; **4.** Does he memorize; **5.** uses, does; **6.** Does he take; **7.** has, Does, does; **8.** have, Does; **9.** does he feel; **10.** isn't/is not, isn't he; **11.** doesn't challenge/does not challenge; **12.** feels, Does he, does; **13.** Do they speak; **14.** isn't/is not; **15.** Does he study, does; **16.** does he practice; **17.** speak

EXERCISE 4 pages 9–10
Time: 10–15 min
Answers: 1. Do you speak; **2.** say; **3.** speak; **4.** has; **5.** speak; **6.** has; **7.** Do you know; **8.** don't/do not; **9.** speaks; **10.** call; **11.** do you use; **12.** use; **13.** write; **14.** Do you want to see; **15.** do; **16.** does Chinese have, **17.** doesn't have/does not have; **18.** has; **19.** represents; **20.** seems; **21.** takes; **22.** looks; **23.** looks

EXERCISE 5 page 10
Time: 10–15 min
Answers will vary.

EXERCISE 6 pages 10–12
Time: 10–15 min
Answers: 1. 's; **2.** are you from; **3.** do you spell; **4.** Do you speak; **5.** is; **6.** speak; **7.** is; **8.** don't know/do not know; **9.** Does Vietnamese use; **10.** does; **11.** Do you see; **12.** do; **13.** looks; **14.** Is it; **15.** does "tonal" mean; **16.** means; **17.** are; **18.** means; **19.** has; **20.** has; **21.** doesn't have/does not have; **22.** speaks; **23.** do you spell Cocama; **24.** speak; **25.** don't know/do not know; **26.** want to learn; **27.** takes; **28.** do you say

EXERCISE 7 page 12
Time: 10–15 min
Answers will vary.

1.3 The Present Continuous,
page 13
Time: 5–10 min

1. Write on the board a few verbs in the present and the present continuous tenses. Ask: *Which verbs are in present continuous? How do you know?* (the form of the verb: auxiliary verb *be* plus the *-ing* form of the main verb)

2. Elicit or say the differences in use of the two tenses (simple present: to state facts, routines, customs; present continuous: to show action in progress).

3. Review the example sentences and explanations in both sections. Write these uses of present continuous on the board and elicit example sentences: *to describe a trend* (Everyone is reading J. K. Rowling's new book.); *to describe a video/picture* (He's practicing Russian with a neighbor.); *long ongoing action* (He's going to NYU now.)

4. Draw students' attention to the use of the present continuous with *live* to convey a temporary situation, and with certain nonaction verbs (e.g., *is sitting* or *is standing*).

ADDITIONAL PRACTICE

1. Have students read paragraphs 2 and 3 of the reading on page 4. Have them switch the tenses, changing present tense into present continuous and vice versa. Then tell them to analyze the paragraph to see if the meaning changes.

2. Ask: *What kind of information do the paragraphs give?* (Paragraph 2 describes actions in videos people are watching. Paragraph 3 states facts about Timothy, some of his routines, and ways that he learns.) *Can you change the tenses and keep the same meaning?* (No, paragraph 2 becomes a list of facts instead of ongoing actions people are watching. Paragraph 3 becomes ongoing actions that are no longer facts and methods of learning.)

EXERCISE 8 page 14
Time: 5–10 min
Answers: 1. they're talking; **2.** are they doing; **3.** Are they spelling; **4.** 're using; **5.** I'm beginning; **6.** are you studying

EXERCISE 9 page 15
Time: 5–10 min
Answers: 1. 'm taking; **2.** 're getting; **3.** 's learning; **4.** 's wearing; **5.** 'm knitting

EXERCISE 10 page 15
Time: 10–15 min
Answers will vary.

EXERCISE 11 page 15
Time: 5–10 min
Answers will vary.

CONTEXT NOTE

The word *tense* in English is related to an Old French word for time. While some languages, such as Chinese, do not have tenses, others may have two or many. English is the latter type and uses verbs to show different kinds of action in time. Elicit from students how their native languages show ongoing actions. Have students discuss why a language does or doesn't have tenses and explore how this might be connected to the culture.

1.4 The Present Continuous vs. The Simple Present— Action and Nonaction Verbs, page 16

Time: 5–10 min

1. Have students cover grammar chart **1.4**. Tell students that this is an important chart because it shows how to accelerate their mastery of English.

2. Write example pairs on the board: *see* versus *looking*, *look* versus *looking*. Say: *The verb* see *indicates a one-time act of recognition or of 'seeing' something.* Elicit which is correct: *I see the pencil* or *I am seeing the pencil.* (*I see the pencil.*)

3. Say: *The verb* look *can mean a one-time act or an ongoing action.* Elicit which is correct: *Jim looks tired* (appears), *Jim looks at the car* (glances), or *Jim is looking at the painting* (studying, observing, watching). (All three are correct.) Note that in the continuous tense, Jim is actively observing (the painting), even though he might be standing in one place.

4. Have students uncover the chart. Review the examples and explanations. Direct students' attention to the Language Notes. Tell students that when they master this chart, they will speak like native speakers.

ADDITIONAL PRACTICE

Assign pairs different lists of five or six nonaction verbs from those in grammar chart **1.4**. Tell students to close their books. Have each pair write two brief sentences for each verb—one in simple present, one in present continuous—and discuss if they are correct. When everyone is finished, have each pair share a few sentences and defend their answers.

EXERCISE 12 page 17

Time: 10–15 min

Answers: 1. are you looking; **2.** is he speaking; **3.** don't recognize/do not recognize; **4.** Do you understand; **5.** 'm watching/am watching; **6.** 'm listening/am listening; **7.** hear; **8.** sounds; **9.** knows; **10.** looks; **11.** 's he talking/is he talking; **12.** are they talking; **13.** 's talking/is talking; **14.** 're introducing/are introducing; **15.** look; **16.** takes; **17.** loves; **18.** 's having/is having; **19.** 's laughing/is laughing; **20.** joking; **21.** think; **22.** doesn't like/does not like; **23.** 's he planning/is he planning/does he plan; **24.** 's thinking/is thinking; **25.** think

EXERCISE 13 page 17

Time: 5–10 min

Answers will vary.

The Enduring Voices Project,
page 18

PRE-READING

🕐 Time: 10–15 min

1. Have students look at the photo and read the caption. Ask: What is happening? (A man is recording a woman's voice while a boy watches.)

2. Have students look quickly at the reading. Ask: *What is the reading about? What does it tell us about languages? How do you know?* Have students use the title, photo, and information from the reading to make predictions.

3. Pre-teach any vocabulary words your students may not know, such as *endangered, disappearing, dominate, permit, preserve, linguists.*

4. Activate students' prior knowledge about dying languages. Ask: *Are any languages in your country endangered? What will happen to them?* Have students discuss the questions in pairs or small groups. If possible, put students of different cultures together.

5. Ask a few volunteers to share their answers with the class.

PRESENTATION IDEA

Briefly discuss this question: *What happens if your language dies?*

READING GLOSSARY

endangered: in danger or a harmful situation
disappearing: going out of sight or existence
to dominate: to have the most important place or greatest influence
to permit: to allow
to preserve: to guard; protect from harm or change
linguists: people who know or study languages and their structures

EXPANDING ON THE READING

The topic for this reading can be enhanced with the following ideas:

1. List of some endangered languages
2. Talking dictionaries of endangered languages on the Internet
3. Discussion about cultures with threatened languages
4. Video clip about the Enduring Voices Project

READING

🕐 Time: 10–15 min

After students have read the article, go over the answers to the Comprehension Check on page 19: **1.** F; **2.** T; **3.** T

ADDITIONAL COMPREHENSION QUESTIONS

What is the Enduring Voices Project (a project to save dying languages) *What is Ojibwe?* (an American Indian language) *Are languages with many speakers going extinct?* (no) *Which are dying languages: Hindi, Seri, Arabic, English, Koro?* (Seri and Koro) *What happens when a language dies?* (A culture dies with it.)

PRACTICE IDEA: LISTENING

To practice listening skills, have students first listen to the audio alone. Ask a few comprehension questions such as: *How many languages could disappear by the year 2100?* (more than 3,550) *How old are the speakers of Ojibwe?* (most are older than sixty-five) *Who is recording endangered languages?* (linguists) Repeat the audio if necessary. Then have students open their books and read along as they listen to the audio.

1.5 The Future—Form, page 19

🕐 Time: 10–15 min

1. Ask: *When do the main events in the reading happen? When do 3,550 languages die?* (in the future). Elicit or say that we know the time of the event by the form of the verbs.

2. Demonstrate how to form the future. Point out the parts of the form (the auxiliaries *will* and *be going to* with a main verb). Write on the board two future verbs from the reading and underline the auxiliary once and the main verb twice (e.g., <u>will</u> probably <u>disappear</u>, <u>are going to</u> <u>become</u>).

3. Write verb pairs on the board such as: *be going to + survive, will + memorize, be going to + eat, will + go*. Conjugate the verbs in the future (am/is/are going to survive; will memorize; am/is/are going to eat; will go). Ask: *What changes in future forms: the main verb, will, be, or going to?* (*be*) *What form of the main verb is used in the future?* (the base form)

4. Review the example sentences and explanations in grammar chart **1.5**. Draw students' attention to the future in the negative. Demonstrate how to form the negative future with contractions (will/be + not: *won't go, isn't/aren't going to*). Point out negative short answers. Say: *In conversational English, you may answer with* will + main verb *to stress your answer* (*No, I will not.*), *but normally contractions are used* (It won't disappear. No, we aren't.).

5. Direct students' attention to the Language Notes and the types of contractions possible with *will* and *be*. Write pairs of subjects with *will/be going to* on the board such as: *where + is, who + is, you + be going to, they + be going to*. Elicit contractions from students and list them on the board underneath the relevant pairs (where's, who's, you're going to, they're going to).

PRESENTATION IDEA

Begin by having students skim the reading to locate future tense verbs. Elicit examples and write them on the board (e.g., *will probably disappear, are going to become, will survive*).

PRACTICE IDEA: LISTENING

1. Discuss with students some negative contractions that can be difficult to understand. This can be caused by mispronunciations (M), ellipsis (E), and colloquialisms (C). For example, *why's* (why + is) can sound like *wise* (M), *he'll* (he + will) like *hill* (M), and *who're* (who + are) like *who ya* as in *Who ya going with?* (E, C)

2. Say these common pronunciations of contractions /wise/ (why's), /shill/ (she'll), /where ya/ (where're you), /when ya/ (when're you), /gonna/ (going to) in sentences.

3. Have students guess the contracted words. Then have them pronounce the contractions and use them in sentences of their own.

PRACTICE IDEA: SPEAKING

Brainstorm with the class a list of future plans such as: get a PhD degree, marry, go back to your native country, live in the United States, teach, have kids, make a lot of money. Have students work in pairs to ask and answer questions about themselves with *will* and *be going to* (e.g., *Are you going to teach? No, I'm not.*).

EXERCISE 14 page 20 CD 1 TR 6
🕐 Time: 10–15 min

Answers: 1. 'm going to change; **2.** are you going to study; **3.** 'm going to get; **4.** 's going to prepare; **5.** go; **6.** 'm going to be; **7.** 'll be; **8.** will it be; **9.** practice; **10.** 'll be; **11.** 'm going to room; **12.** 'm going to speak; **13.** will improve; **14.** 're going to learn; **15.** teach; **16.** 'm going to start

EXERCISE 15 page 21
🕐 Time: 5–10 min

Answers: 1. will teach; **2.** die; **3.** will be able to hear; **4.** will learn; **5.** will have; **6.** will make; **7.** will continue; **8.** visit; **9.** will hear

EXERCISE 16 page 21
🕐 Time: 10–15 min

Answers: 1. are going to have; **2.** 're going to switch/are going to switch; **3.** are you going to do; **4.** 's going to have/is going to have; **5.** 're not going to be living/are not going to live; **6.** aren't going to be/are not going to be;

7. 's going to lose/is going to lose; **8.** is going to confuse;
9. 's going to open/is going to open; **10.** 's going to have/
is going to have

EXERCISE 17 page 22

 Time: 5–10 min

Answers will vary.

1.6 Choosing *Will, Be Going To,* or Present Continuous for Future, page 22

🕐 Time: 5–10 min

1. Have students cover grammar chart **1.6**.
   Write example sentences on the board: *1) I'm having dinner at 8:00; 2) Dying languages will disappear; 3) She's going to start an online business; 4) Will you help me? Sure I'll be glad to do that.* Elicit or say the use of the future in each example. (1: a definite plan; 2: prediction; 3: existing plan; 4: asking for help/a comment of reassurance)

2. Review the examples and explanations in the grammar chart. Draw attention to the use of *won't* for *refuse to* (*won't support me*).

ADDITIONAL PRACTICE

1. Have students work in small groups. Have them develop examples of each use of the future: (1) stating a definite plan; (2) making a prediction; (3) stating a pre-existing plan; (4) using *will* for promises, requests for help, offers to help, comments of reassurance; (5) using *won't* for *refuse to.* When the groups are finished, have each group share some of their examples with the class. Help students analyze incorrect choices and correct the errors.

2. Write these sentences on the board. Have students match them with uses of the future: promise, previous plan, reassurance, prediction, definite plan, refuse to.
   a. *Don't worry. I'll help you.* (reassurance)
   b. *He's going to apply this spring.* (definite plan)
   c. *Yes, she'll wash the dishes.* (promise)
   d. *We're going to open a bookstore in Atlanta.* (previous plan)
   e. *My Dad's mad. He won't help me.* (refuse to)
   f. *Many people will get sick.* (prediction)

EXERCISE 18 page 23

🕐 Time: 10–15 min

Answers: 1. 'll go; **2.** 'm going to get/am going to get;
3. are you going to use; **4.** 'm just going to google/am just going to google/'ll just google/will just google; **5.** are you going to write; **6.** 'm going to look/am going to look; **7.** 'll go/will go; **8.** won't bother/will not bother; **9.** 'll just get/will just get; **10.** 'll check/will check; **11.** will you help; **12.** will; **13.** won't do/will not do; **14.** 'm not going to do/am not going to do/won't do/will not do; **15.** 'll do/will do; **16.** 'll buy/will buy; **17.** 'll be/will be

---

PRACTICE IDEA: WRITING

Have students write their plans for tomorrow and the next week. Tell them to include predictions and *won't* for *refuse to,* if logical, as well. Divide the class into pairs or small groups. Have students exchange papers and provide feedback.

READING

An Unusual Orphan, page 24

PRE-READING

🕐 Time: 5–10 min

1. Have students look at the photo, caption, and title. Ask: *Who is in the picture?* (Washoe and Loulis) *What kind of animal are they?* (chimpanzees, or chimps) Have students use the title and photo to predict the topic of the story (a chimpanzee, Washoe, who does something interesting)

2. Have students skim the reading. Ask: *Why is Washoe unusual? Why do you think so?*

3. Pre-teach any vocabulary words your students may not know, such as *orphan, avoided, deaf, catalogs,* and *bugs.*

4. Ask: *How did Washoe learn sign language? How many signs did she learn?* Elicit the answers and discuss as a class.

READING GLOSSARY

orphan: a child without parents
to avoid: to stay away from
deaf: unable to hear
catalogs: booklets with information about products, school courses, etc.
bugs: insects

READING CD 1 TR 7

🕑 Time: 10–15 min

After students have read the article, go over the answers to the Comprehension Check on page 25: **1.** F; **2.** F; **3.** T

ADDITIONAL COMPREHENSION QUESTIONS

Where was Washoe born? (West Africa) *Who taught Washoe sign language?* (the Gardners) *What happened at the University of Oklahoma?* (Washoe met other chimps and "talked" to them through sign language.) *How is Loulis related to Washoe?* (Washoe adopted him.)

PRACTICE IDEA: LISTENING

To practice listening skills, have students first listen to the audio alone. Have students write all of the past tense verbs they hear. Repeat the audio if necessary. Then have students open their books and read along as they listen to the audio.

CONTEXT NOTE

1. Could Washoe really communicate? The topic is controversial. More recent research has indicated that chimps may only be giving back what is given to them. One observer noted that Washoe, for example, never asked questions. After the discovery that chimps may not be communicating, different teaching methods were developed.

2. Direct students' attention to the last statements in paragraph 3: *She called them "black cats" or "black bugs. "Eventually she started to interact and "talk" to them* [the other chimps]. Point out the different uses of quotation marks. In the former sentence, the

marks indicate Washoe's exact words. In the second statement, however, the marks indicate that *talk* is being used in an unusual way.

3. Ask: *Is the author saying that Washoe did not "talk" as we understand talking?* Have students share their ideas about what "talk" could mean.

PRACTICE IDEA: SPEAKING

Have students work in pairs and retell Washoe's story in their own words. Tell them to close their books but refer to the list of verbs from the reading that they developed in the Listening activity. After each partner has retold the story, ask for a few volunteers to retell different parts of the story to the class: Part I: Learning Sign Language, Part II: Meeting Other Chimps, Part III: Washoe and Loulis.

1.7 The Simple Past, pages 25–26

🕑 Time: 10–15 min

1. Have students look at the Form section of grammar chart **1.7**. Elicit simple past verbs from the reading and write them on the board. Ask students to tell you the base form of the verbs and write them next to the past tense. (*be/was, adopt/adopted, understand/understood,* etc.)

2. Elicit the form of the simple past of regular verbs (add *-d/-ed* to the base form). Remind students that the past of irregular verbs occurs in different ways: the spelling may change internally (*begin/began/begun*) or the words can be different altogether (*go/went/gone*). Then review the examples and explanations.

3. Remind students that question forming is the same in simple present and simple past.

4. Have students look at the Use section of grammar chart **1.7**. Review the example sentences, explanation, and the Language Note.

ADDITIONAL PRACTICE

Have students work in small groups to write simple past questions with *do/be* + verb. Provide cues such as: born/West Africa, go/United States, learn/ASL, meet/other chimps, adopt/baby, die/2007. When they are finished, ask volunteers from each group to share some of their sentences with the class. Provide feedback.

EXERCISE 19 page 26   CD 1 TR 8

⏱ Time: 10–15 min

Answers: 1. a. was, b. wasn't; **2.** a. liked, b. didn't like, c. didn't she like; **3.** a. Did she have, b. did, c. had, d. died; **4.** a. taught, b. taught; **5.** a. did she live, b. lived; **6.** a. didn't use, b. didn't they use

EXERCISE 20 pages 26–27

⏱ Time: 10–15 min

Answers: 1. didn't live; **2.** took; **3.** didn't start/did not start; **4.** didn't feel/did not feel, didn't she feel; **5.** did they give; **6.** did she teach Loulis/did she teach him; **7.** wasn't/was not; **8.** did Washoe die/did she die

EXERCISE 21 pages 27–28

⏱ Time: 10–15 min

Answers: 1. Did you like; **2.** did; **3.** wasn't/was not; **4.** were; **5.** saw/watched; **6.** learned; **7.** did she die; **8.** Was she; **9.** did they begin; **10.** was; **11.** Did you learn; **12.** wanted; **13.** gave; **14.** wasn't/was not; **15.** want; **16.** Did they give; **17.** did; **18.** chose; **19.** gave; **20.** ran; **21.** told; **22.** was; **23.** did she sign; **24.** gave

EXERCISE 22 page 29

⏱ Time: 5–10 min

Answers will vary.

SUMMARY OF LESSON 1

⏱ Time: 20-30 min

PART A SIMPLE PRESENT

List uses on the board and have students make a complete sentence for each one: fact, general truth, habits, customs; place of origin; time clause or if clause with the future; nonaction verbs (e.g., *I speak three languages. / People are kind. / You get up at 6:00 every morning. / The Tibetan people make jewelry with turquoise. / We are from Australia. / If many people do not speak a language, it will die. / He sees the catalog on the table.*).

If necessary, have students review:

1.1 The Present of *Be* (page 5)

1.2 The Simple Present (pages 7–8)

1.4 The Present Continuous vs. The Simple Present—Action and Nonaction Verbs (page 16)

PART B PRESENT CONTINUOUS

Provide a list of cues from the last reading, "An Unusual Orphan." Write on the board: *live/United States, stay/Gardners' home, learn/sign language, not like/other chimps, teach/Loulis.* Tell students to imagine that Washoe is alive now. Have students make statements about Washoe using the present continuous. Warn students that one cue cannot be used in present continuous.

If necessary, have students review:

1.2 The Simple Present (pages 7–8)

1.3 The Present Continuous (page 13)

1.4 The Present Continuous vs. The Simple Present—Action and Nonaction Verbs (page 16)

PART C FUTURE

Have students talk about their friends' plans for the future and include predictions. Write prompts on the board such as: *get a degree, finish college, get a job, stay in this country, go back to his or her country, save money, get a pet, buy a computer* (e.g., *Mali's going to get a business degree. / Roberto's going to get a job after college. / Kofi will succeed.*).

If necessary, have students review:

1.5 The Future—Form (page 19)

1.6 Choosing *Will, Be Going To,* or Present Continuous for Future (page 22)

PART D SIMPLE PAST

Have students retell the events of a past experience that happened to themselves or others. Model a response on the board such as: *The Utes lived many years ago. They made rock art. They were rich and powerful. They ruled a large territory in the United States. Then outsiders pushed them out. They almost lost their language and their entire culture.*

If necessary, have students review:

1.7 The Simple Past (pages 25–26)

TEST/REVIEW

⏱ Time: 15 min

Have students do the exercise on page 31. For additional practice, use the Assessment CD-ROM with Exam*View*® and the Online Workbook.

Answers: 1. are you reading; **2.** seem; **3.** 's/is; **4.** are disappearing; **5.** 're becoming/are becoming; **6.** became; **7.** died; **8.** Does that mean; **9.** didn't speak/did not speak; **10.** learned; **11.** died; **12.** speak; **13.** Did the Enduring Voices Project record; **14.** died; **15.** started; **16.** 's/is; **17.** have; **18.** 'll speak/will speak/'m going to speak/am going to speak; **19.** 're/are; **20.** 'll have/will have/'re going to have/are going to have; **21.** want; **22.** don't want/do not want; **23.** need; **24.** 'll send/will send

WRITING

PART 1 EDITING ADVICE

⏱ Time: 10–15 min

1. Have students close their books. Write the first few sentences without editing marks or corrections on the board. For example:

   What he is saying?

   When Washoe died?

   What means "enduring"?

2. Ask students to correct each sentence and provide a rule or an explanation for each correction. This activity can be done individually, in pairs, or as a class.

3. After students have corrected each sentence, tell them to turn to page 32. Say: *Now compare your work with the Editing Advice in the book.* Have students read through all the advice.

PART 2 EDITING PRACTICE

⏱ Time: 10–15 min

1. Tell students they are going to put the Editing Advice into practice. Ask: *Do all the shaded words and phrases have mistakes?* (no) Go over the examples with the class. Then do #1 together.

2. Have students complete the practice individually. Then have them compare answers with a partner before checking answers as a class.

3. For the items students had difficulties with, have them go back and find the relevant grammar chart and review it. Monitor and give help as necessary.

Answers: 1. were born; **2.** C; **3.** didn't speak/did not speak; **4.** C; **5.** C; **6.** heard; **7.** C; **8.** C; **9.** started to lose; **10.** I think; **11.** is dying; **12.** C; **13.** C; **14.** didn't try/did not try; **15.** became; **16.** C; **17.** do you want to study; **18.** don't you study; **19.** doesn't understand/does not understand; **20.** C; **21.** What does *schlep* mean? **22.** C; **23.** C; **24.** has; **25.** C; **26.** speaks; **27.** C; **28.** have; **29.** I'm going/I am going

PART 3 WRITE ABOUT IT

⏱ Time: 30–40 min

1. Review the present of *be* and each tense with its uses: the simple present, present continuous, future, simple past, and the present continuous versus the simple past with nonaction and action verbs.

2. Have students read the two writing topics on page 33. For each topic, elicit appropriate tenses for responses. (1: simple present and future, 2: simple present and past)

3. Have students brainstorm ideas for both topics. Remind students to think of general ideas and specific supporting details. Elicit ways to organize ideas for their responses, such as Venn diagrams, concept maps, timelines, or clusters.

4. If necessary, provide examples of topic sentences and write them on the board (e.g., *It is important to keep records of dying languages for ___ reasons. / There are many benefits to being bilingual.* OR *There are two main benefits to being bilingual.*). Elicit or remind students of ways to conclude their writing (e.g., by summarizing or giving results) and provide an example if needed (e.g., *Why do we need to keep records of endangered languages? There are many reasons, but in my opinion the two most important are ___ and ___.*).

5. Tell students to choose one topic and tell a partner about it. Then have them write their assignments.

PART 4 EDIT YOUR WRITING

🕐 Time: 15–20 min

Have students edit their writing by reviewing the Lesson Summary on page 30 and the Editing Advice on page 32. Collect for assessment and/or have students share their essays in small groups.

EXPANSION ACTIVITIES

1. Have students think about a friend and describe him or her in the past, present, and future. Provide cues such as the following and write them on the board: *favorite foods, music, hobbies, goals, rich/poor, right-handed/left-handed, good driver/bad driver, sports, bad experience, languages, family.*

2. Divide students into small groups. Provide students with the option of taking notes before talking to group members. Tell them to include adverbs of frequency (e.g., *always, sometimes, never, hardly ever*); nonaction and action verbs; and promises and predictions. When students have finished, ask volunteers to tell the class about their friends.

PRACTICE IDEA: WRITING

Have students write a paragraph on a topic related to this lesson (e.g., dog language, a dead language, another animal who has learned to "talk"). To save class time, have students research their topic at home and take notes. Then have them write their reports in class. Ask several students to share theirs with the class. Collect all paragraphs and provide encouragement and feedback.

---

2 RISK

GRAMMAR CHARTS

LESSON OPENER

Have students look at the photo and read the caption and quotation. Ask: *Where is the man? What is he doing? Do you agree with the quote?*

Background: Victoria Falls is the largest waterfall on Earth. Located on the Zambezi River in southern Africa, it is 1.7 kilometers (1 mile) wide and 108 meters (360 feet) high. The Falls has a long vertical drop through empty space to a gorge below, which attracts many tourists and extreme adventurers.

Also called Mosi-oa-Tunya or the "smoke that thunders," Victoria Falls is one of the Seven Natural Wonders of the World. In 1855, British explorer and missionary David Livingstone was the first European to see it, and he named it Victoria Falls after Queen Victoria. Livingstone was also the first to explore the heart of Africa.

CONTEXT

This unit is about extreme risk taking. Students will read about research on a connection between chemicals in the brain and risk taking; types of risk taking, such as mountain climbing; and people who take risks for their work, such as Paul Nicklen, Sylvia Earle, and Lonnie Thompson.

1. Give students a few minutes to look through the lesson. Have them look at the photos and titles. How do they relate to the context?

2. Elicit the topics that will be discussed.

3. Have students discuss what they know about taking risks and risk takers in pairs or small groups.

GRAMMAR

Students will learn about the present perfect, the present perfect continuous, and the present perfect versus the present perfect continuous and the simple past.

1. To activate students' prior knowledge, have students name as many verb tenses and their uses as they can. Then ask what they know about the present perfect.

2. Give several examples of sentences in the present perfect tense (e.g., *They have opened their restaurant. / I have run 5 miles. / He has bought a new computer.*).

3. Have volunteers give examples and write them on the board.

EXPANDING ON THE CONTEXT

The context for this lesson can be enhanced with the following items:

1. List of past and present explorers

2. Timeline showing important discoveries by risk takers through history

3. Biography of a famous explorer, such as David Livingstone , or other risk takers

The Mystery of Risk, page 36

PRE-READING

🕐 Time: 10–20 min

1. Have students look at the photo and read the caption on page 36. Ask: *Where do you think the photographer is?* (He is in the Arctic.) *Is his job dangerous?* (Yes, it is.) *Why does he do it?* (Answers will vary.)

2. Have students look briefly at the reading. Have them look at the title of the reading. Ask: *What is the reading about? How do you know?* Have students make predictions.

3. Pre-teach any essential vocabulary words your students may not know, such as *mystery, risk, extreme, motivated,* and *reputation.*

4. Ask: *What motivates extreme risk takers?* Have students discuss in pairs.

5. Ask for a few volunteers to share their ideas with the class.

READING GLOSSARY

mystery: an event that has no known cause

risk: a chance; danger of losing something important

extreme: severe; far from what is generally accepted

motivated: encouraged, prompted, or gave a reason to do something

reputation: an opinion about the quality of something such as a person's character

READING 🎧 CD 1 TR 9

🕐 Time: 10–15 min

After students have read the article, go over the answers to the Comprehension Check on page 37: **1.** F; **2.** T; **3.** T

ADDITIONAL COMPREHENSION QUESTIONS

What dangers do explorers face? (hunger, animal attacks, extreme weather, loneliness, and uncertainty about the future) *What did Christopher Columbus do?* (He sailed across the Atlantic in 1492.) *What are some reasons people take risks?* (financial reward, fame, saving lives) *Who are extreme risk takers?* (people who put their reputation, money, and even their lives in danger) *What chemical in the brain affects risk taking?* (dopamine) *Why is Paul Nicklen a risk taker?* (He risks animal attacks, severe weather, and his life to photograph Arctic animals.)

EXPANDING ON THE READING

The topic for this reading can be enhanced with the following items:

1. Lists of types of risk takers (puffer fish eaters; snake charmers; soldiers; immigrants; inventors; entrepreneurs [e.g., Richard Branson, Elon Musk]; extreme athletes and "daredevils" [e.g., tightrope walkers])

2. List of additional reasons that motivate risk takers (gaining knowledge, excitement, independence, helping others)

3. Video clip of one of Nik Wallenda's tightrope walks

4. A biography or profile of Paul Nicklen

2.1 The Present Perfect— Form, page 37

🕐 Time: 10–15 min

1. Have students look at Part A of grammar chart **2.1.** Elicit the form of the present perfect tense (*have/has* plus a past participle).

2. Have students cover the chart. Write this sentence on the board: *I have learned three languages.* Have students identify the present perfect form. (have learned) Ask: *Which is the participle?* (learned) Write the following sentence on the board and repeat the procedure for *has*: *She has not won a spelling contest.*

3. Have students uncover the chart. To help students understand present perfect with *there*, draw students' attention to the example sentence complements. Have a volunteer write new example sentences on the board. Ask: *What is the rule for using* there *in present perfect?* (Use *there have* with plural complements; use *there has* for singular complements.) Correct the sentences as a class if necessary.

4. Direct students' attention to the Language Notes. Point out that contractions with *has* are used in informal English. Then have students review Part B of grammar chart **2.1.** Elicit the difference between the two parts of the chart. (Part A shows how to form the present perfect tense; Part B shows how to use it in different types of sentences.) Review the example sentences and questions in Part B.

EXERCISE 1 page 38

Time: 10–15 min

Answers:

Base Form	Simple Past Form	Past Participle	Same (S) or Different (D)
wonder	wondered	**wondered**	S
think	thought	**thought**	S
endure	endured	**endured**	S
be	was/were	**been**	D
find	found	**found**	S
begin	began	**begun**	D
come	came	**come**	D
give	gave	**given**	D
survive	survived	**survived**	S

2.2 The Past Participle, page 38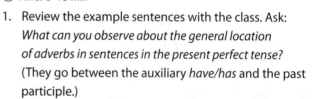

Time: 5–10 min

1. Have students identify three forms of ten or twelve verbs: base, simple past, past participle. Have them cover grammar chart **2.2**. Draw a three-column chart on the board. Elicit the base forms and write them in the left column. Then elicit the past forms and write (or have a student write) these in the middle column. Finally, elicit the past participles and write (or have a student write) these in the right column.

2. Ask students to say what they observe about the rules for forming past forms and past participles (With regular verbs, the past form and the past participle are the same, and end in *-d* or *-ed*. With irregular verbs, the past participle may or may not be the same and can be formed in several ways.).

3. Have students look at grammar chart **2.2**. Review the groups of verbs and explanations. Ask: *Which verbs have* -d *added in the past forms?* (receive, hear) *Which have* -ed *added?* (work, wonder)

4. Draw students' attention to the last section of the chart. Point out that irregular past participles like these do not conform to rules and must be learned individually.

ADDITIONAL PRACTICE

1. Have students look at the alphabetical list of irregular verbs in Appendix H. Ask students to identify the pattern in this set of irregular verbs: *drive, ride, write.*

(The simple past form changes from *i* to *o*, and the past participle adds -*en*: *drove, driven; rode, ridden; wrote, written.*) Then have them find patterns for other sets of irregular verbs.

2. Have students work in groups. Ask each group to quickly list ten new verbs on a piece of paper and then write the past form and past participle for each verb as quickly as they can. When all groups are finished, have groups exchange lists and check each other's work.

EXERCISE 2 page 39

Time: 5–10 min

Answers: 1. have read; **2.** have experienced; **3.** have begun; **4.** 've found/have found; **5.** 's been/has been; **6.** 's taken/has taken; **7.** 's won/has won; **8.** 've seen/have seen

2.3 Placement of Adverbs, page 39

Time: 5–10 min

1. Review the example sentences with the class. Ask: *What can you observe about the general location of adverbs in sentences in the present perfect tense?* (They go between the auxiliary *have/has* and the past participle.)

2. Direct students' attention to the Language Notes. Review the examples. Ask: *Where does* ever *go in a question in the present perfect?* (between the subject and past participle)

EXERCISE 3 page 40 CD 1 TR 10

Time: 10–15 min

Answers: 1. 've never thought; **2.** 've always tried; **3.** 've never jumped; **4.** 've never climbed; **5.** have never occurred; **6.** 've taken; **7.** haven't; **8.** have I done; **9.** 've always thought; **10.** 've given

EXERCISE 4 page 40

Time: 10–15 min

Answers: 1. have you been; **2.** Have you ever thought; **3.** 've taken; **4.** 've had to; **5.** has already improved; **6.** has always been; **7.** haven't always understood; **8.** have said; **9.** have usually been; **10.** 've had to; **11.** 've learned; **12.** 've even learned; **13.** 've gained; **14.** has gotten; **15.** 've already made; **16.** has involved

CONTEXT NOTE

Ask students about risk taking in their native countries. Point out that some risks are unique to certain countries (e.g., female pearl divers in Korea). Have students name examples of unique risks in their countries. Then draw students' attention to a universal type of risk taking (starting a business). Ask: *What risks do people take when they do this in your country?* Elicit examples from students and discuss the similarities and differences among countries with the class.

2.4 The Present Perfect— Overview of Uses, page 41

🕐 Time: 5–10 min

1. Have students cover grammar chart **2.4**. Write these sentences on the board: *Jeff has been a travel agent since 2010. He has traveled to Europe many times. Have you ever gone to Europe?* Ask students what they can tell about the use of the present perfect tense in each sentence. Tell students the present perfect is used to talk about experience. Remind students that it is used for actions that began in the past and continue to, or are still important in, the present.

2. Have students review the chart. Elicit or explain to students the differences in the three uses (continues: generally for facts, repeats: generally for actions, indefinite time: generally for actions and events still important).

3. Review the example sentences of each type of use. Tell students that they will study each use of the present perfect tense in detail in this lesson.

ADDITIONAL PRACTICE

After the review of example sentences, have students find examples of the present perfect in the reading. Elicit the type of continuing event or action for each sentence. (continues: being a photojournalist, photographing underwater animals; repeats: going to the Arctic, receiving awards; indefinite time: studying brain chemicals, doing something dangerous)

EXERCISE 5 page 41

🕐 Time: 5–10 min

Answers: 1. has been; **2.** 's become/has become; **3.** 's walked/has walked; **4.** 's never had/has never had

READING

Climbing Mount Everest, page 42

PRE-READING

🕐 Time: 10–15 min.

1. Have students look at the photo and read the caption. Ask: *Where are these two men?* (Mount Everest) *What are they doing?* (climbing the mountain)

2. Have students look quickly at the reading. Ask: *What is the reading about? What does it say about climbing Mount Everest? How do you know?* Have students use the title, the photo, and the words in bold to make predictions about the reading.

3. Pre-teach any vocabulary words your students may not know, such as *symbol, guide, inexperienced, dragged,* and *garbage.*

4. Activate students' prior knowledge about Mount Everest. Ask: *How high is Mount Everest?* (8,848 meters or 29,029 feet high) *What other mountain is higher?* (none) *What mountain range is it part of?* (the Himalayas) *What risks do climbers take?* (altitude sickness, avalanches, severe wind and weather) Have students discuss the questions in pairs.

5. Ask a few volunteers to share their answers with the class.

READING GLOSSARY

symbol: something that represents something else

guide: a person who shows the way and gives information

inexperienced: not experienced

to drag: to pull with difficulty

garbage: things you do not want anymore, trash

EXPANDING ON THE READING

The topic for this reading can be enhanced with the following items:

1. A map showing the location of Mount Everest
2. Photos of famous climbers
3. Facts about Sir George Mallory's failed climb
4. Pages from expedition journals
5. List of things to take on an expedition

READING 🎧 CD 1 TR 11

⏱ Time: 10–15 min

After students have read the article, go over the answers to the Comprehension Check on page 43: **1.** T; **2.** T; **3.** F

ADDITIONAL COMPREHENSION QUESTIONS

Who were the first climbers to reach the summit? (Edmund Hillary and Tenzing Norgay) *How many people have reached the top since 1953?* (about 4,000) *What is a result of the increased traffic on Everest?* (lots of garbage on the mountain)

PRACTICE IDEA: LISTENING

To practice listening skills, have students first listen to the audio alone. Ask a few comprehension questions such as: *Where is Mount Everest?* (between China and Nepal) *How many climbers now use expedition companies to climb Everest?* (90%) *How has technology helped Everest climbers?* (Weather conditions at the top can be predicted more accurately.) Repeat the audio if necessary. Then have students open their books and read along as they listen to the audio.

CONTEXT NOTE

As a symbol in Western culture, climbing Mount Everest has traditionally represented human endurance, nature's great challenges, and taking dangerous risks. Reaching the summit has symbolized a rare achievement: succeeding against all odds, and the determination to succeed. In Tibetan, the mountain's name is *Chomolangma* or "mother of the universe." Artists all over the world have made paintings of Mount Everest to represent these universal meanings. Today, artists are making art from garbage on Mount Everest, and reaching the summit is no longer a rare achievement. The meaning of Mount Everest as a symbol may be changing. Ask students if Mount Everest is a symbol in their culture and what it means. Elicit other natural symbols in students' cultures and their meanings. Have students say whether the meanings are changing, and why.

2.5 The Present Perfect with Indefinite Past Time— Overview, page 43

⏱ Time: 10–15 min

1. Have students look at the reading and underline the present perfect tense verbs. Ask: *Can you say exactly when the actions took place?* (No, the present perfect does not tell exactly when actions happen through time.)

2. Have students look at grammar chart **2.5**. Review the example sentences and explanations.

3. Have students look back at the reading and underline each instance of *ever, always,* and *recently.* Ask: *Is recently being used to show indefinite time?* (No, it is showing that more people have started climbing

since 1963.) Elicit the use of each adverb in its sentence (*ever:* to show indefinite time; *always:* to connect past to present; *recently:* to show recent past actions).

ADDITIONAL PRACTICE

Have students work in small groups. Have them write and then ask each other questions with *ever, always, recently,* and *yet.* When they are finished, have volunteers from each group share their questions with the class.

EXERCISE 6 page 44 CD 1 TR 12
🕐 Time: 10–15 min

Answers: 1. 've thought; **2.** 've heard; **3.** have died; **4.** Have you ever had; **5.** have just started; **6.** have never been; **7.** have just started; **8.** Have you ever heard; **9.** haven't; **10.** haven't finished; **11.** haven't had

EXERCISE 7 page 45
🕐 Time: 10–15 min

Answers: 1. 've just seen; **2.** Have you ever heard of; **3.** never have; **4.** 've already bought/have already bought; **5.** 've never been/have never been; **6.** haven't seen/have not seen

ADDITIONAL PRACTICE

After students complete Exercise 6, have them work in pairs. Have pairs model the conversation and then switch roles. Have each partner role-play Speaker A and Speaker B.

PRACTICE IDEA: SPEAKING

After students complete Exercise 6, have them work in pairs to invent a similar conversation of four or five lines. Students should use appropriate present perfect verbs and adverbs. Have pairs perform their conversations for the class.

2.6 The Present Perfect with Ever and Never, page 45

🕐 Time: 5–10 min

1. Have students cover grammar chart **2.6**. Write two example questions on the board with their answers: *Have you ever studied another language? / Yes, I have. / Has Sophie ever driven the new car? / Yes, she drove it yesterday.* Remind students that *ever* is used in present

perfect sentences to show indefinite time. Ask: *Are the answers in indefinite time?* (The first is, but the second is not.)

2. Have students review the grammar chart. Point out the use of *never* (for negative answers). Go over the examples and explanations.

ADDITIONAL PRACTICE

Have students work in small groups. Write answers in the present perfect and the simple past on the board and have students write questions for them with *ever* and *never.* When the groups are finished, have a few volunteers share their question and answer sets with the class.

EXERCISE 8 pages 46–47
🕐 Time: 10–15 min

Answers: 1. a. Have you ever done, **b.** have, **c.** went, **d.** 've never done; **2. a.** Have you ever flown, **b.** never have, **c.** haven't/have not; **3. a.** Have you ever played, **b.** have, **c.** ran, **d.** 've heard/have heard; **4. a.** Have you ever risked, **b.** have; **c.** started, **d.** 've lost/have lost/lost; **5. a.** Have you ever saved, **b.** haven't/have not, **c.** has, **d.** ran; **6. a.** Have you ever lent, **b.** Have, **c.** lent, **d.** paid; **7. a.** Have you ever climbed, **b.** never have, **c.** Have, **d.** climbed, **e.** 've never heard of/have never heard of; **8. a.** Have you ever made, **b.** have, **c.** 've made/have made; **9. a.** Have you ever had, **b.** went, **c.** fell, **d.** broke; **10. a.** Have you ever run, **b.** ran

EXERCISE 9 page 48
🕐 Time: 10–15 min
Answers will vary.

2.7 The Present Perfect with Yet and Already, page 48

🕐 Time: 5–10 min

1. Have students cover grammar chart **2.7**. Write on the board: *Have you gone bungee jumping? Have you gone bungee jumping yet? Have you gone bungee jumping already?* Ask: *How are these questions different?* (With *yet* and *already,* the questioner is expecting you to go bungee jumping. Without *yet* or *already,* the questioner is asking a general question about what you have done.)

2. Have students look at the grammar chart. Review the example sentences and explanations.

3. Draw students' attention to the Language Notes. Tell students that many people use the simple past with *yet* and *already* in informal conversations.

ADDITIONAL PRACTICE

1. Have students work in pairs to answer questions about *yet* and *already*.
2. Write these *True/False* questions on the board:
   a. *Yet* shows greater expectation of something happening than *already*. (F)
   b. "I have eaten already breakfast" is a correct sentence. (F)
   c. You cannot use the simple past to answer a question in present perfect. (F)
   d. You can use *not yet* as a short answer. (T)
   e. I've taken the test already = I took the test already. (T)
3. Assign 20 points for each correct answer. When students are finished, compare answers as a class. Have each pair report their scores. Discuss incorrect answers as a class.

EXERCISE 10 page 49
🕐 Time: 10–15 min
Answers: 1. a. Has, **b.** yet, **c.** came, **d.** hasn't had, **e.** yet; **2. a.** finished, **b.** yet, **c.** already; **3. a.** seen, **b.** yet/already, **c.** yet, **d.** already, **e.** made; **4. a.** thought, **b.** yet, **c.** already, **d.** went; **5. a.** 've/have, **b.** already

EXERCISE 11 page 50
🕐 Time: 10–15 min
Answers: 1. looked; **2.** yet; **3.** haven't; **4.** yet; **5.** already; **6.** Both are correct. **7.** I did; **8.** Both are correct. **9.** never have; **10.** Have you ever tried; **11.** haven't; **12.** Have; **13.** have; **14.** Have you; **15.** haven't; **16.** yet

2.8 The Present Perfect with *Lately, Recently,* and *Just,*
page 51

🕐 Time: 5–10 min

1. Write on the board: *lately, recently,* and *just.* Ask: *What kind of information do these words give?* (time) Have students skim the chart. Elicit predictions about the uses of *lately, recently,* and *just* with the present perfect. Ask: *Which word(s) indicates an action that happened very near the present?* (just) *Can all three*

words be placed at the end of a sentence? (No, only *lately* and *recently* can go at the end of a sentence.)
2. Review the example sentences and explanations.
3. Draw students' attention to the Language Notes. Stress that *lately* cannot be used with the simple present to refer to a single event; *recently* is used for this situation.

CONTEXT NOTE
After students have finished the examples and explanations on *just,* write on the board: *I just have $10; She just went to the store.* Elicit or say that in the first sentence *just* means *only.* For *just* to indicate recent past, the verb must show action. Point out that in the second sentence the meaning depends on the context. Ask: *What are two possible contexts?* (only: where she went. She didn't go many places; she went to one place: the store. Or, *recently*: when she went. She was here but left for the store a few minutes/hours ago.) Have students work in small groups to write two or three sentences with *just.* After they finish, have each group share a sentence with the class and have the class discuss the possible contexts.

PRACTICE IDEA: WRITING

Have students describe a recent change in a place they know. Brainstorm places and ways to approach the topic with the class and list ideas on the board (for example, a city, a favorite camping site, a beach; does it look better or worse, is it more crowded or lonelier and why, has weather affected it and how). Divide the class into pairs. Have each pair write a paragraph (5–7 sentences) and use *lately, recently,* and *just.* Give students a few minutes to think of places, then go around to each pair and offer help, if needed. Have pairs exchange papers and provide feedback.

EXERCISE 12 pages 51–52
🕐 Time: 10–15 min
Answers: 1. a. Have you read, **b.** haven't had/have not had, **c.** 've just finished/have just finished/just finished, **d.** have become; **2. a.** Have you taken, **b.** haven't/have not, **c.** 've been/have been, **d.** Have you done, **e.** haven't/have not, **f.** has, **g.** went; **3. a.** has had/has, **b.** have left, **c.** Have conditions improved, **d.** have, **e.** has started; **4. a.** 've just read/have just read; **5. a.** have been, **b.** have tried

EXERCISE 13 page 52

🕐 Time: 10–15 min

Answers will vary.

EXERCISE 14 page 53

🕐 Time: 10–15 min

Answers: 1. Have you seen it yet; **2.** saw; **3.** Have you ever dreamed; **4.** 've thought/have thought; **5.** Have you heard about the cost yet; **6.** yet; **7.** 've just changed/have just changed/just changed

2.9 The Present Perfect with No Time Mentioned, page 53

🕐 Time: 5–10 min

1. Have students look at grammar chart **2.9.** Review the example sentences and explanations in the chart.

2. Point out that this use of present perfect is similar to the use of the simple past to state facts but not completely the same. Ask: *How is it different?* (The present perfect connects the past with the present.)

3. Ask volunteers to give sentences about themselves using the present perfect tense with no time mentioned.

PRESENTATION IDEAS

1. Begin the review by writing on the board: *I've studied French* [or another subject], *but I still don't speak it well.*

2. Ask: *What is more important in this sentence: when I studied French, or the fact that I studied it?* (fact that I studied it)

3. Ask: *Why use the present perfect tense in this sentence?* (because when the action [studying] happened isn't that important, but the action [studying] is still important now [because I still don't speak French well])

PRACTICE IDEA: SPEAKING

Have students make up statements with no time mentioned about important decisions they have made or about people they admire. Have students work in small groups so that each person in the group can have the opportunity to speak. When groups are finished, have volunteers from each group share their information with the class. Provide feedback on use of the present perfect.

EXERCISE 15 page 53

🕐 Time: 10–15 min

Answers: 1. a. has photographed, **b.** 's received/ has received, **c.** hasn't been/has not been, **d.** 's given/ has given; **2. a.** have discovered; **3. a.** has walked, **b.** 's entertained/has entertained; **4. a.** has attracted, **b.** has saved

---

READING

Exploring the Ocean, page 54

PRE-READING

🕐 Time: 5–10 min

1. Have students look at the photo and read the caption. Ask: *Who is this woman?* (Sylvia Earle) *What is she doing?* (exploring the ocean floor)

2. Ask: *What is the reading about?* Have students use the title, photo, and caption to make predictions about the reading.

3. Have students skim the reading. Ask: *What will the story say about Sylvia Earle? How do you know?*

4. Pre-teach any vocabulary words your students may not know, such as *decades, marine, lecturer,* and *inspire.*

5. Activate students' prior knowledge about threats to Earth's oceans. Ask: *Has anything harmed the ocean recently?* (yes: drilling, overfishing, pollution) Have students discuss the question in pairs.

6. Ask a few volunteers to share their answers with the class.

READING GLOSSARY

decades: periods of ten years

marine: related to the ocean and ships

lecturer: a person who gives speeches or long serious talks to groups of people

to inspire: to cause to work hard or be creative

EXPANDING ON THE READING

The topic for this reading can be enhanced with the following items:

1. Photos of oil spills, crowds of trawlers, and trash in the ocean
2. List of less-known problems created by drilling, overfishing, and dumping
3. Video clip showing the effects of an oil spill on wildlife
4. Video clip showing the effects of plastic trash on the ocean and wildlife
5. A short biography of Sylvia Earle

READING CD 1 TR 13

🕐 Time: 10–15 min

After students have read the article, go over the answers to the Comprehension Check on page 55: **1.** T; **2.** T; **3.** T

ADDITIONAL COMPREHENSION QUESTIONS

What is Earle's occupation? (oceanographer) *Why is she a Hero for the Planet?* (She has spent her life trying to protect marine animals. She has lectured, written publications, and spent more than 7,000 hours underwater.)

PRACTICE IDEA: LISTENING

To practice listening skills, have students first listen to the audio alone. Have students write all the present perfect verbs they hear. Repeat the audio if necessary. Then have students open their books and read along as they listen to the audio.

ADDITIONAL PRACTICE

1. Have students skim the reading to find verbs used in descriptions of Earle's accomplishments. (paragraph 2: has taken, has spent, has led; paragraph 4: has won, has received, has been, has lectured, has written, has written)

2. Ask: *Why are the verbs in the present perfect and not in the simple past?* (The statements regard actions and events of a lifelong career that is nearing its end, or simple past facts, but ones that could repeat since Earle is still living.)

2.10 The Present Perfect with Repetition from Past to Present, page 55

🕐 Time: 10–15 min

1. Have students review the example sentences and explanations in the grammar chart.
2. Ask volunteers to make statements using the present perfect tense with repetition. Give one or two examples if necessary (e.g., *I have taught this class three times this week. / Sir Edmund Hillary has given many lectures on mountain climbing. / How much time have you spent playing video games?*).

PRESENTATION IDEAS

1. Draw a timeline on the board. Label it "Daniel's Mt. Everest Expeditions This Year." Make a vertical mark on the timeline and label it "Today's date" and write the date out in figures (e.g., 10/17). Make three vertical marks to the left and label them with earlier dates in this year (e.g., 4/2, 6/8, 8/14). Below each of those three dates, write *expedition*.

2. Ask: *When did Daniel go on his first expedition?* (on April 2); ask about the second and third expeditions.

3. Ask: *What can you say about Daniel's expeditions?* Elicit and write: *Daniel has gone on three expeditions this year.* Ask: *Is the year finished?* (no) *Is it possible for Daniel to go on more expeditions this year?* (yes) Say: *To talk about a repeating action that may happen again, use the present perfect tense.*

PRACTICE IDEA: WRITING

Have students review the example sentences and explanations in the chart. Then have students write statements about their lifetime accomplishments with repetition—one statement about actions they have done, one about people they have influenced or have been influenced by, and one about what they have learned.

EXERCISE 16 page 56

🕐 Time: 10–15 min

Answers: 1. has written; **2.** has done; **3.** 's led/has led; **4.** 's spent/has spent; **5.** have disappeared; **6.** have died; **7.** have reached; **8.** has gone; **9.** have appeared; **10.** 's experienced/has experienced; **11.** has, taken

EXERCISE 17 page 56

🕐 Time: 10–15 min

Answers: 1. won; **2.** has won; **3.** led; **4.** 've lost/have lost; **5.** 's written/has written; **6.** reached; **7.** have reached; **8.** has climbed; **9.** climbed; **10.** reached; **11.** was; **12.** has performed; **13.** crossed

EXERCISE 18 page 57

🕐 Time: 10–15 min

Answers: 1. Have you ever heard; **2.** 's directed/has directed; **3.** worked; **4.** was even; **5.** 's made/has made; **6.** had to; **7.** became; **8.** formed; **9.** 's led/has led; **10.** 's visited/has visited; **11.** 's worked/has worked

2.11 The Present Perfect with Continuation from Past to Present, page 58 ⭐

🕐 Time: 10–15 min

1. Have students cover grammar chart **2.11**. Tell students that this chart refers to the use of certain time words to show continuation. Ask: *Which two words are often used with present perfect tense?* (*since, for*) *How are these words different?* (*Since* is used with a specific time or event, e.g., 1998, Monday, she went on vacation; *for* is used with a period of time, e.g., 5 years, 10 minutes, or a long time.)

2. Have students review the grammar chart. Review the example sentences and explanations carefully. Check understanding. Ask: *What two time words can show duration?* (*for, all*) *Which word can show a starting point?* (*since*)

3. Direct students' attention to the Language Notes. Stress that *for* and *how long* are used with simple past for events that began and ended in the past. Ask: *Can* since *be used this way?* (No) Elicit or write on the board additional examples with *ever since*: *She got her first teddy bear when she was one. She has loved teddy bears ever since; He ran the marathon for the first time in 2001. He has run it every year ever since.*

4. Provide practice by making statements about yourself similar to those in the Language Notes. For example, to contrast the use of *for* with the present perfect and the simple past, say: *I have had this job for 2 years. I lived in California for 3 months.* Ask volunteers for sentences about themselves.

PRESENTATION IDEA

1. Before reviewing the chart with students, use a visual to model use of time words in the chart.

2. Draw a timeline on the board. Make a vertical mark at the right and label it for this year. Ask: *When did Daniel begin to climb mountains?* (1998)

3. Make a vertical mark in the center of the timeline; label it *1998*. Draw an arrow between the two marks. Say: *Daniel began climbing in 1998, and he's still climbing today. He has been climbing since 1998.*

4. Ask: *How long has Daniel loved to climb mountains?* (always) Draw an arrow from the far left of the timeline to this year's mark. Say: *Daniel has always loved to climb, and he still loves it today.*

PRACTICE IDEA: SPEAKING

1. Write this gapped profile on the board:

   My name is ___. I have ___ for ___. I have ___ since ___. I lived (or worked) there for ___, and I have been interested in ___ ever since ___.

2. Have students work in pairs to complete the sentences with information about their own lives, rearranging the sentences to present the information logically. Encourage them to refer to the grammar chart as needed. Then have partners take turns talking about themselves, using their sentences as notes.

3. When they are finished, ask volunteers to give the class a short profile of themselves. Discuss as a class any corrections that are needed and why.

PRACTICE IDEA: WRITING

1. Bring in news articles from a variety of sources and divide them among groups of students. Have students find five or six sentences with *for, since,* and *all* and analyze them. Have them write the sentences and decide how the words are being used. Review these examples with the class:

   Professor Jones has found numerous caches of treasure in the Marubi Caves since he started his explorations in 2003. Analysis of *since:* used to show the starting point of Jones's explorations (2003)

   The ship's engineer was trapped in the wreckage underwater for 3 weeks before he was rescued. Analysis of *for:* used to show how much time the engineer was under water

2. When groups have finished, have each group share a few sentences and analyses with the class.

EXERCISE 19 pages 58–59

🕐 Time: 5–10 min

Answers: 1. a. has worked, **b.** since; **2. a.** have been, **b.** for; **3. a.** has always had; **4. a.** Since, **b.** 's changed/has changed; **5. a.** have tried, **b.** since; **6. a.** In, **b.** climbed; **7. a.** since, **b.** 's led/has led; **8. a.** long, **b.** has Cameron been

EXERCISE 20 pages 59–60

🕐 Time: 10–15 min

Answers: 1. 've been; **2.** Ø; **3.** 've probably read/have probably read; **4.** 've taken/have taken; **5.** 've had/have had; **6.** been; **7.** since; **8.** Have; **9.** have; **10.** 've wanted/have wanted; **11.** since; **12.** 've never been/have never been; **13.** 've tried/have tried; **14.** Ø; **15.** started; **16.** 've become/have become

EXERCISE 21 page 60

🕐 Time: 5–10 min

Answers: 1. changed; **2.** started; **3.** learned; **4.** ever done; **5.** always wanted; **6.** ever had

EXERCISE 22 page 60

🕐 Time: 5–10 min

Answers will vary.

READING

Lonnie Thompson—Ice Investigator, page 61

PRE-READING

🕐 Time: 5–10 min

1. Tell students this article is about the work that a scientist has been doing. Have students use the title, photo, and caption to make predictions about the reading. Ask: *Who is the scientist?* (Lonnie Thompson) *What is he holding?* (ice from a glacier) *What kind of scientist is he?* (he studies glaciers, he is a glaciologist)

2. Have students skim the reading. Ask: *What will the reading say about Dr. Thompson's work with glaciers? How do you know?*

3. Pre-teach any vocabulary words your students may not know, such as *melting, lightning,* and *heart transplant.*

4. Activate students' prior knowledge about glaciers. Ask: *What are glaciers?* (mountains of ice) *Where can you find them?* (in polar areas like Antarctica, Greenland, and the Canadian Arctic) Have students share their ideas and discuss as a class.

READING GLOSSARY

to melt: to change from a solid to a liquid state

lightning: an electrical discharge in the sky, especially during a thunderstorm

heart transplant: to move the heart from one person to another person

READING 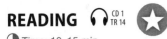 CD 1 TR 14

🕐 Time: 10–15 min

After students have read the article, go over the answers to the Comprehension Check on page 61: **1.** T; **2.** F; **3.** T

ADDITIONAL COMPREHENSION QUESTIONS

How long has Thompson spent above 18,000 feet (5.5 kilometers)? (over 1,100 days) *What dangers does Thompson face to study glaciers?* (lightning, avalanches, storms, and wind) *Has climbing made Thompson healthier?* (Yes, he thinks it has made him healthier.)

PRACTICE IDEA: LISTENING

To practice listening skills, have students first listen to the audio alone. Tell students to listen for the new form of present perfect that they are about to study. Have students write all the present perfect continuous verbs they hear. Repeat the audio if necessary. Then have students open their books and read along as they listen to the audio.

ADDITIONAL PRACTICE

Have students explore the comparison Thompson makes in the reading. Ask: *Why does Thompson compare his work to visiting a very sick person?* (The glaciers, like a cancer patient, have been dying because they are melting.) Have students skim or reread the story if needed and share their ideas with the class.

2.12 The Present Perfect Continuous, page 62

🕐 Time: 10–15 min

1. Have students find a few sentences from the reading that contain present perfect continuous tense verbs. Write them on the board. Have students close their books. Underline the present perfect continuous verb in each sentence. Ask: *What can you observe about the difference between this and the present perfect form you have learned so far?* (It uses *been* and the *-ing* form of the main verb.) *What kind of time does it show?* (action in progress) *What other tense is it like?* (the present continuous)

2. Have students skim the chart. Ask: *What kind of information does the chart provide?* (uses of the tense, time words used with it, verbs that can be used in either

present perfect or present perfect continuous with no change in meaning, warnings, and sentence patterns).

3. Review the example sentences and the explanations carefully.

4. Draw students' attention to the seven patterns at the bottom of the chart. Have students talk about themselves and ask questions using the examples as models. (*I have been studying . . . , I haven't been studying . . . ?*)

EXERCISE 23 page 63

🕐 Time: 5–10 min

Answers: 1. has been making, since; **2.** 's been exploring/ has been exploring, for; **3.** 's been working/has been working; **4.** has been studying, for; **5.** 's been learning/ has been learning; **6.** For, have been melting; **7.** has been performing, for; **8.** have been learning; **9.** has been studying, for; **10.** have been climbing, since

EXERCISE 24 pages 63–64

🕐 Time: 5–10 min

Answers: 1. a. have you been learning, **b.** For; **2. a.** has he been working, **b.** For; **3. a.** have you been thinking, **b.** Since; **4. a.** long has she been climbing, **b.** For; **5. a.** long has he been making, **b.** been, **c.** for, **d.** taking, **e.** 's been/ has been; **6. a.** been, **b.** have, **c.** 've been telling/have been telling, **d.** for; **7. a.** 've been reading/have been reading

EXERCISE 25 page 64

🕐 Time: 5–10 min

Answers will vary.

2.13 The Present Perfect, the Present Perfect Continuous, and the Simple Past, page 65

🕐 Time: 10–15 min

1. Have students cover chart **2.13**. On the board, write a set of sentences that contrasts the present perfect, the present perfect continuous, and the simple past tenses. For example, write:
   a. *Mina studied oceanography for 2 years.*
   b. *Mina has studied oceanography for 2 years.*
   c. *Mina has been studying oceanography for 2 years.*

2. Elicit or say the tense of each sentence and the function of the tense (a: simple past: referring to an event that started and ended in the past; b: present perfect: showing continuation and repetition past to present; can also be used for stating facts from past into present; c: present perfect continuous: showing ongoing action from past to present).

3. Have students look at the chart. Review the example sentences and explanations. Direct students' attention to the comparison of present perfect and present perfect continuous sentences. Ask: *Which sentences show that it is possible that the action is not happening now?* (the "a" sentences in present perfect) *Which show that the action is still in progress?* (the "b" sentences in present perfect continuous)

4. After you review each explanation and set of example sentences, elicit similar examples from the class to check understanding.

PRESENTATION IDEA

1. Bring in pictures that help to illustrate the perspective of each tense. Try the following: a traditional "still" portrait of someone sitting in a chair, someone standing before a camera reporting the news at the scene, someone accepting an award. Label them A, B, and C. Be sure the gender is the same in each picture.

2. Display the images. On the board, write: *1. He was a reporter. 2. He has been an excellent reporter. 3. He has been reporting for 10 years.*

3. Have students try to match the sentences with the pictures. (1. still portrait; 2. receiving award; 3. reporting live)

4. Ask for volunteers to explain their reasoning. If needed, elicit or say that the portrait is like the simple past because it conveys the sense of a single fact of a past moment; a reporter on the scene is like the present perfect continuous because the action that began before he arrived is live and ongoing; someone accepting an award is like the present perfect because it is action that began in the past and has continued into the present (receiving recognition for what you have done).

EXERCISE 26 pages 65–66
🕐 Time: 5–10 min

Answers: 1. is; **2.** 's been working/has been working; **3.** since; **4.** 's been exploring/has been exploring; **5.** for; **6.** arrived; **7.** went; **8.** have been going; **9.** went; **10.** were; **11.** has been improving; **12.** treated; **13.** has seen; **14.** takes; **15.** is; **16.** for; **17.** 's been helping/has been helping

EXERCISE 27 page 66
🕐 Time: 5–10 min

Answers: 1. has been climbing; **2.** 's done/has done; **3.** 's made/has made; **4.** began; **5.** went; **6.** 's increased/has increased/'s been increasing/has been increasing; **7.** used; **8.** made; **9.** did; **10.** 's appeared/has appeared; **11.** was

EXERCISE 28 page 67
🕐 Time: 5–10 min

Possible Answers: 1. has been climbing, 's climbed/has climbed; **2.** 's been preparing/has been preparing; **3.** 've seen/have seen, Have, seen; **4.** 've taken/have taken; **5.** has helped/has been helping; **6.** has been working; **7.** 've been working/have been talking

---

PRACTICE IDEA: SPEAKING

Have students work in pairs to brainstorm statements about the people they have read about in this lesson or other interesting people they know about. Have them use the simple past, present perfect, present perfect continuous, and a variety of time words including *for, since, lately, recently, never,* and *ever since.* Have each partner keep a list. After they have finished, combine pairs into small groups. Have each student tell the group about the people he has written about and try to avoid looking at his or her notes very often.

SUMMARY OF LESSON 2

🕐 Time: 20–30 min

PART A SIMPLE PRESENT AND PRESENT PERFECT

List a series of cues on the board and have students make complete sentences about a person using the simple present and present perfect (e.g., *is/has been, studies/has studied, explores/has explored, takes/has taken*). *(Sylvia*

Earle is an oceanographer. / She has been an oceanographer for 50 years.)

If necessary, have students review:

PRACTICE IDEA: WRITING

Write on the board phrases in the present perfect (*have lived, has traveled, has climbed, have melted, has discovered, has taken, has endured*, etc.). Have students write sentences about the explorers they have studied in this lesson (Paul Nicklen, Sylvia Earle, Lonnie Thompson). Write this vocabulary on the board and have students incorporate some of it into their sentences: *risks, dangers, extreme, glaciers, outstanding, drilling, summit, expedition, avalanches, wind, lightning, Gulf of Mexico, Arctic, Peru.* Have students share their information with the class.

PART B PRESENT CONTINUOUS AND PRESENT PERFECT CONTINUOUS

Provide a list of basic verbs and have students make general statements and related statements about themselves using the present continuous and the present perfect continuous tenses. Have them include *for, since,* and *lately* and use the words appropriately (e.g., *People all over the world are drinking lots of coffee. Lately, I have been drinking more coffee every day.*).

If necessary, have students review:

PART C SIMPLE PAST AND PRESENT PERFECT

Provide a list of prompts and have students talk about their own actions. Write these prompts on the board: *had an accident, took risks, helped others, taken photographs, have gone bungee jumping, started a new job.* (*I went bungee jumping last year and did not like it. / I have never gone bungee jumping again.*)

If necessary, have students review:

PRACTICE IDEA: WRITING

Write a list of base verbs on the board and have students write the simple past and past participle forms of each verb (e.g., *be, walk, climb, go, jump, do, dive, drive*). Have students share their answers with the class.

PART D PRESENT PERFECT AND PRESENT PERFECT CONTINUOUS WITH NO DIFFERENCE IN MEANING

Have students talk about their friends and families. Write these prompts on the board: *had scary accident, took dangerous risks, helped others, taken interesting photographs, gone skydiving, started career, has traveled a lot.* (*My sister has gone skydiving. / She has gone skydiving many times.*)

If necessary, have students review:

PART E PRESENT PERFECT AND PRESENT PERFECT CONTINUOUS WITH A DIFFERENCE IN MEANING

Provide an example pair of sentences and write them on the board. Have students write sentences and put an asterisk next to the sentence that could imply the action is not continuing in the present (e.g., *He has worked as a journalist.*/He has been working as a journalist.*).

If necessary, have students review:

2.4 The Present Perfect—Overview of Uses (page 41)

2.12 The Present Perfect Continuous (page 62)

2.13 The Present Perfect, the Present Perfect Continuous, and the Simple Past (page 65)

TEST/REVIEW

◷ Time: 15 min

Have students do the exercise on page 69. For additional practice, use the Assessment CD-ROM with Exam*View*® and the Online Workbook.

Answers: 1. haven't seen; **2.** in/for; **3.** have you been; **4.** 've had/have had; **5.** haven't had/have not had; **6.** 've been taking/have been taking; **7.** have you been doing; **8.** started; **9.** 've jumped/have jumped; **10.** 've never even thought/have never even thought; **11.** 've always wanted/have always wanted; **12.** since; **13.** talked; **14.** had; **15.** Have you ever had; **16.** 've had/have had; **17.** 've worked/have worked/'ve been working/have been working; **18.** For; **19.** 've been trying/have been trying; **20.** taught; **21.** was; **22.** 've been knitting/have been knitting; **23.** since; **24.** 've made/have made

WRITING

PART 1 EDITING ADVICE

◷ Time: 10–15 min

1. Have students close their books. Write the first few sentences without editing marks or corrections on the board. For example:

   Paul Nicklen has taking many pictures.

   Has he ever being to the South Pole?

2. Ask students to correct each sentence and provide a rule or an explanation for each correction. This activity can be done individually, in pairs, or as a class.

3. After students have corrected each sentence, tell them to turn to page 70. Say: *Now compare your work with the Editing Advice in the book.* Have students read through all the advice.

PART 2 EDITING PRACTICE

◷ Time: 10–15 min

1. Tell students they are going to put the Editing Advice into practice. Ask: *Do all the shaded words and phrases have mistakes?* (no) Go over the examples with the class. Then do #1 together.

2. Have students complete the practice individually. Then have them compare answers with a partner before checking answers as a class.

3. For the items students had difficulties with, have them go back and find the relevant grammar chart and review it. Monitor and give help as necessary.

Answers: 1. done; **2.** C; **3.** for; **4.** 's inspired/has inspired; **5.** 's taught/has taught; **6.** C; **7.** studied; **8.** have finished; **9.** C; **10.** been; **11.** were; **12.** C; **13.** 's always been/has always been; **14.** C; **15.** C; **16.** told; **17.** recently decided; **18.** C; **19.** learned; **20.** C; **21.** 's been studying/has been studying; **22.** C; **23.** C; **24.** C; **25.** C; **26.** 's never thought/has never thought; **27.** C

PART 3 WRITE ABOUT IT

◷ Time: 30–40 min

1. Review the present perfect tense and its uses to show actions and events that begin in the past and continue into, or are still important in, the present.

2. Have students read the two writing topics on page 71. Discuss them one at a time. For each topic, have the class brainstorm ideas. Write the ideas on the board. Brainstorm general ideas and types of details that could be included. For example, for topic 1: a living person who has done great things, the types of great things that people do, or that seem great to us, and details about where, when, how, and how long the person's actions occurred.

3. Tell students to choose one topic and tell a partner about it. Then have them write about their topics. If necessary, write an example introduction and conclusion on the board.

PART 4 EDIT YOUR WRITING

◷ Time: 15–20 min

Have students edit their writing by reviewing the Lesson Summary on page 68 and the Editing Advice on page 70. Collect for assessment and/or have students share their essays in small groups.

EXPANSION ACTIVITIES

1. Tell students that this activity is about their own experience. Ask: *What tense do you use to talk about experience?* (present perfect or present perfect continuous) Review question formation with the present perfect tense with students. Brainstorm topics and write them on the board (e.g., daily exercise, hours studying, vacations, sports, leisure activities). Have students divide into pairs and question each other about their experiences. If necessary, provide students with the option of writing their questions before asking their partner. When students have finished, have them report their results as a class. Ask: *Who has been exercising a lot lately?*

2. Have students role-play interviewing for a job as an explorer with National Geographic. Ask each pair to decide the type of job, place or area of work, and their accomplishments before they begin the interview. Have pairs switch roles and repeat the activity.

PRACTICE IDEA: SPEAKING

After pairs have finished their interviews, ask each interviewer whether he or she will hire the applicant. Have interviewers say why they made the decisions they did.

---

3 THE MOVIES

GRAMMAR CHARTS

LESSON OPENER

Have students look at the photo and read the caption. Ask: *What is happening in the photo? Do you know who Roger Ebert is? Do you agree with the quote?*

Background: The setting of the photograph is an old movie playing in a modern landscape. The scene indicates Americans' continuing love for classic movies and for Hollywood, the center for filmmaking in the United States. The motion picture industry began in Hollywood in the early twentieth century. Hundreds of feature films are produced in Hollywood every year (622 in 2013), including those that become well-loved classics such as *Casablanca* and *King Kong*.

Roger Ebert was a journalist and film critic. He was the first film critic to win a Pulitzer Prize. Along with Gene Siskel, he reviewed movies on the television program *Siskel and Ebert At the Movies*. He died in 2013.

CONTEXT

This unit is about movies. Students will read about Oscar night in Hollywood (when the Academy Awards are presented), the history of animation, and about the famous silent screen actor Charlie Chaplin.

1. Give students a few minutes to look through the lesson. Have them look at the photos and titles. How do they relate to the context?

2. Elicit the topics that will be discussed.

3. Have students discuss what they know about Hollywood and filmmaking in pairs or small groups.

GRAMMAR

Students will learn about passive and active voice, transitive and intransitive verbs, and participial adjectives.

1. To activate students' prior knowledge, ask what students know about passive and active voice.

2. Give several examples of sentences using the passive voice (e.g., *This film was made in Hollywood.*).

3. Have volunteers give examples. Write the examples on the board.

EXPANDING ON THE CONTEXT

The context for this lesson can be enhanced with the following items:

1. Entertainment section from a local newspaper or website showing movie listings

2. Reviews of recent movies

3. List of top 100 films of all time

4. Timelines showing the history of still photography and motion pictures

READING

Oscar Night in Hollywood, page 74

PRE-READING

⏱ Time: 10–20 min

1. Have students look at the photo on page 74. Ask: *Who do you see?* (Brad Pitt and Angelina Jolie) *Where are they?* (on the red carpet at the Oscars/Academy Awards)

2. Have students look briefly at the reading. Have students look at the title of the reading. Ask: *What is the reading about? How do you know?* Have students make predictions.

3. Pre-teach any essential vocabulary words your students may not know, such as *angle, gather, announced, presented, spectacular*.

4. Ask: *What happens at the Oscars?* Have students discuss in pairs.

5. Ask for a few volunteers to share their ideas with the class.

READING GLOSSARY

angle: viewpoint

to announce: to make public, declare

to gather: to meet, come together

to present: to give out, especially in front of other people in a ceremony

spectacular: wonderful, exciting

READING CD 1 TR 16

⏱ Time: 10–15 min

Go over the answers to the Comprehension Check on page 75: **1.** F; **2.** F; **3.** T

ADDITIONAL COMPREHENSION QUESTIONS

What are the Academy Awards? (awards given to actors and others in the movie business) *When are the Oscars held?* (in February or March) *How are the Oscars today different from the 1929 ceremony?* (No one knows the winners in advance; it's not open to everyone; the ceremony is broadcast all over the world.) *What happens as stars arrive?* (They get photographed and interviewed.) *Who makes predictions about winners?* (movie critics) *How many people attended the first ceremony?* (about 250) Repeat the audio if necessary. Then have students open their books and read along as they listen to the audio.

EXPANDING ON THE READING

The topic for this reading can be enhanced with the following items:

1. List of recent Oscar winners or an Oscar ballot

2. Photos of guests and/or award winners at an Academy Awards ceremony

3. Video clip of a recent Academy Awards ceremony

4. Discussion of other awards ceremonies (Nobel Prize, Pulitzer Prize), and other entertainment awards (Grammy Awards, Latin Grammys, Emmys, etc.)

3.1 Active and Passive Voice—Introduction, page 75

⏱ Time: 10–15 min

1. Have students cover grammar chart **3.1**. Write this example sentence from the chart on the board: *The children saw the movie*. Elicit or write the passive statement: *The movie was seen by the children*. Elicit the names of the parts of the sentences (*subject* and/ or *agent, verb, object*). Point out that the subject is the same as the agent in active sentences, but not in passive sentences.

2. Have students review the grammar chart. Ask: *Who was the movie seen by?* (the children) *Who will the next award be presented by?* (Brad Pitt) *In how many categories are the awards presented?* (twenty-four)

3. To help students understand the relationship between the passive and active voices, have them rewrite the sentences in the second box in the active voice.

4. Direct students to the Language Notes. Then have students review the second section of the grammar chart. If necessary, review the meaning of *pronoun* and *object pronoun*.

3.2 Comparison of Active and Passive Voice, page 76

⏱ Time: 5–10 min

1. Have students cover the right column of the first section of the grammar chart. Ask students to put the active sentences in the passive.

2. Have students uncover the examples in the first section. Have students identify the form of *be* and the past participle in each passive sentence. Ask: *Do we use the past participle in the passive with all the tenses?* (yes)

3. Ask students to say what they observe about the rules for forming the passive voice (e.g., the form of *be* changes to reflect the tense; all forms use the past participle).

4. Draw students' attention to the first example. Ask: *What is the agent?* (a committee) Tell students that they will study agents in later sections of the lesson.

EXERCISE 1 pages 76–77   CD 1 TR 17

Time: 10–15 min

Answers: 1. presented, A; **2.** was presented, P; **3.** is wearing, A; **4.** has been designed, P; **5.** designed, A; **6.** is being photographed, interviewed, P; **7.** live, A; **8.** Are, made, P; **9.** will be filmed, P; **10.** accept, give, A; **11.** was given, P; **12.** have been made, P; **13.** Have, seen, A; **14.** was, made, P; **15.** can be seen, P; **16.** was being repaired, P; **17.** was filmed, P; **18.** haven't gone, A

EXERCISE 2 pages 77–78

Time: 10–15 min

Answers: 1. wasn't based; **2.** was based; **3.** was the first film made; **4.** was produced; **5.** were called; **6.** were they called; **7.** Were snacks sold; **8.** wasn't sold/was not sold; **9.** were permitted; **10.** weren't permitted/were not permitted; **11.** was sold; **12.** was shown; **13.** was written; **14.** was usually played; **15.** was used; **16.** was sound added; **17.** was the first color movie made; **18.** were actually made; **19.** have been lost/were lost; **20.** were given

EXERCISE 3 page 78

Time: 5–10 min

Answers: 1. are shown; **2.** are told; **3.** are being dimmed; **4.** are used; **5.** are being shown; **6.** is limited; **7.** are presented; **8.** are asked; **9.** is a 7:30 movie shown

3.3 Active and Passive Voice—Use, page 79

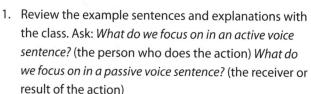

Time: 5–10 min

1. Review the example sentences and explanations with the class. Ask: *What do we focus on in an active voice sentence?* (the person who does the action) *What do we focus on in a passive voice sentence?* (the receiver or result of the action)

2. Ask: *In the examples in the second box, who is the agent?* (We don't know.) Write on the board: *In some passive voice sentences, the agent is not given.* Ask: *Who is the agent in this sentence?* (We don't know.)

ADDITIONAL PRACTICE

1. Provide additional examples of active and passive sentences with strong and weak agents (e.g., *The server served the food. / Did you know the actors? / People like the movies. / The award was presented by someone. / The award was presented by Brad Pitt.*). Have students identify the strong agents and weak subjects.

2. After students have reviewed the examples and explanations in the grammar chart, have them go back to the reading on page 74 to identify which explanation is appropriate for each of the passive voice verbs in the reading.

EXERCISE 4 page 80

Time: 10–15 min

Answers:

1. Beautiful dresses are designed for the actresses.
2. Anne Hathaway's dress was designed by Prada.
3. Music is composed to give the movie a mood.
4. The music for Star Wars was composed by John Williams.
5. Credits are shown at the end of the movie.
6. The first Hollywood movie was made in 1911.
7. Actors are nominated for the awards.
8. An award was presented by George Clooney.
9. Movie tickets can be bought online.
10. All the tickets have been sold out.
11. The popcorn machine was invented by Charles Cretors.
12. Popcorn is sold in movie theaters.
13. I was given free tickets for the movie.

PRACTICE IDEA: SPEAKING

1. Bring in the entertainment section of a local newspaper with movie listings. Have students review the listings and report on a movie they'd like to see, giving the movie title, theater information, and show times.

2. Have students work in groups to brainstorm vocabulary and phrases they know related to movies, theaters, and Hollywood. Have them include the vocabulary from the exercise and from the reading on page 74. If appropriate, set a time limit and have groups compete to make the longest list.

CONTEXT NOTE

Ask students about movies and theaters in their native countries. Ask: *Are food and drinks sold in movie theaters, or cinemas, in your country?* Discuss the various ways that students have seen American movies—in their countries, in a theater, on TV, at home on DVD, etc. Ask students if and how U.S. movies influence the impressions people in their countries have of life in the United States.

EXERCISE 5 page 81

⏱ Time: 5–10 min

Answers: 1. Do you like; **2.** smells; **3.** must be validated; **4.** often forget; **5.** arrive; **6.** are often sold out; **7.** can be bought; **8.** are taken; **9.** are created; **10.** prefer; **11.** can pay; **12.** can be borrowed; **13.** have; **14.** can be skipped; **15.** turn off; **16.** am not interrupted; **17.** invite; **18.** make; **19.** save

EXERCISE 6 pages 81–82

⏱ Time: 5–10 min

Answers: 1. is sold, P; **2.** can be bought, P; **3.** are shown, P; **4.** are, A; **5.** are shown, P; **6.** earn, A; **7.** are given, P; **8.** pay, A.

PRACTICE IDEA: WRITING

Have students write about the experience of going to a movie. They should write at least four sentences in the passive voice.

3.4 Verbs with Two Objects, page 82

⏱ Time: 5–10 min

1. Have students cover grammar chart **3.4**. Write an example sentence with a direct and an indirect object on the board, such as: *Someone gave these tickets to Rosa.* Ask students to identify the parts of the sentence (subject, verb, direct object, indirect object). Tell students that in this sentence, *tickets* is the direct object and *Rosa* is the indirect object (the person or thing to or for which the action in the sentence is done). Say: *We can write this sentence in the passive voice in two ways.* Write: *These tickets were given to Rosa. Rosa was given these tickets.*

2. Have students review the examples and explanations in the grammar chart.

3. Direct students' attention to the verb list in the Language Note. Explain any vocabulary students are unfamiliar with.

ADDITIONAL PRACTICE

After students have reviewed the examples in the grammar chart, have them work in groups. Have each group write sentences with three of the verbs in the Language Note. Have the groups exchange sentences and underline the direct and indirect objects in each other's sentences.

EXERCISE 7 page 82

⏱ Time: 10–15 min

Answers: 1. The actress was given an award. / An award was given to the actress. **2.** The actress was handed an Oscar. / An Oscar was handed to the actress. **3.** Alex will be given two free tickets. / Two free tickets will be given to Alex. **4.** I have been sent an invitation. / An invitation has been sent to me. **5.** We were shown the movie. / The movie was shown to us. **6.** The director has been lent money. / Money has been lent to the director.

READING

The History of Animation, page 83

PRE-READING

⏱ Time: 10–15 min

1. Have students look at the graphics on page 83. Ask: *What do you see?* (a cartoon of a dinosaur)

2. Have students look quickly at the reading. Ask: *What is the reading about? How do you know?* Have students use the title and the pictures to make predictions about the reading.

3. Pre-teach any vocabulary words your students may not know, such as *celluloid, transparent,* and *technique.*

4. Activate students' prior knowledge about animation. Ask: *What is animation?* (movies or films made with drawings, not with actors) *What is a cartoon?* (a humorous animated movie or short film) *Do you like animated films? Can you name a famous animated film or cartoon?* Have students discuss the questions in pairs.

5. Ask a few volunteers to share their answers with the class.

READING GLOSSARY

celluloid: photographic film

transparent: letting light pass through so that images can be seen

technique: a method or procedure of doing something

READING 🎧 CD 1 / TR 18

🕐 Time: 10–15 min

Go over the answers to the Comprehension Check on page 84: **1.** T; **2.** F; **3.** T

ADDITIONAL COMPREHENSION QUESTIONS

What happened in 1914? (The first animation was shown in theaters.) *How is movement created in a cartoon today?* (by illusion: by quickly replacing an image on a computer with similar images with small changes) *Who created the modern cartoon with sound and music?* (Walt Disney)

PRACTICE IDEA: LISTENING

To practice listening skills, have students first listen to the audio alone. Ask a few comprehension questions such as: *Who is the father of animation?* (Winsor McCay) *What was the first animated film?* (*Gertie the Dinosaur*) *Was Walt Disney an animator?* (No, he was a story editor.) *What was the first computer-animated film?* (*Toy Story*) Repeat the audio if necessary. Then have students open their books and read along as they listen to the audio.

CONTEXT NOTE

Movies often are categorized by their length: a full-length or feature film is usually 90 to 120 minutes long; a short feature or "short" can be 10 to 30 minutes long. Movie types include documentaries (nonfiction), docudramas (dramatic tellings of real stories), and biopics (biographical docudramas).

3.5 Transitive and Intransitive Verbs, pages 84–85

🕐 Time: 10–15 min

1. Have students close their books. On the board, write simple sentences with direct objects, such as: *Winsor McCay made the first cartoons. / Walt Disney employed many artists.* Ask: *What is the direct object in each of these sentences?* (the first cartoons; many artists) Have volunteers write passive voice sentences for each example (*The first cartoons were made by Winsor McCay. / Many artists were employed by Walt Disney.*). Say: *The verbs* make *and* employ *are transitive verbs; they take a direct object.*

2. Have students look at the first two sections of grammar chart **3.5**, defining transitive/intransitive on page 84. Review the example sentences and explanations.

3. Draw students' attention to the rest of the chart on pages 84–85. Review the explanations on transitive and intransitive verbs. Ask: *Which verbs can be active or passive?* (transitive) *Which can only be active?* (intransitive)

4. Provide several additional examples with verbs from the chart, such as: *We walked to the theater / It rained for two days.* Ask: *Can these sentences be rewritten in the passive voice?* (no)

PRESENTATION IDEA

Have students go back to the reading on pages 83–84. Have students say whether each bold-faced verb is in the active or passive voice. For sentences in the passive voice, have students change the sentence to the active voice.

EXERCISE 8 pages 85–86

🕐 Time: 10–15 min

Answers: 1. made, The first animated film was made by Winsor McCay. **2.** became, no change; **3.** worked, no change; **4.** offered, He was offered a job as a newspaper artist. **5.** left, no change; **6.** moved, no change; **7.** considered, The *Herald Tribune* was considered to have the highest quality color. **8.** happened, no change; **9.** see, Can it be seen today? **10.** preserve, Was it preserved? **11.** find, It can be found online. **12.** seems, no change; **13.** changed, no change; **14.** create, Today most animation is created on computers. **15.** left, A good article about McCay was left on the table.

EXERCISE 9 page 87

⏱ Time: 10–15 min

Answers: 1. was born; **2.** began; **3.** was given; **4.** worked; **5.** became; **6.** moved; **7.** started; **8.** recognize; **9.** was first created; **10.** looked; **11.** was named; **12.** changed; **13.** was introduced; **14.** created; **15.** were added; **16.** was produced; **17.** won; **18.** earned; **19.** won; **20.** built; **21.** was being built; **22.** died; **23.** have been built

EXERCISE 10 page 88

⏱ Time: 10–15 min

Answers: 1. was elected; **2.** became; **3.** worked; **4.** appeared; **5.** wasn't considered/was not considered; **6.** won; **7.** was scheduled; **8.** happened; **9.** was shot; **10.** didn't die/did not die; **11.** was also wounded; **12.** was postponed; **13.** recovered; **14.** finished; **15.** died

CONTEXT NOTE

After students have finished Exercise 10, ask: *What happened to the Academy Awards ceremony after Reagan was shot?* (It was postponed.) Public events in the United States are frequently postponed or canceled after a disaster or tragic event, including severe weather and earthquakes. Ask students what disasters or tragic events have recently affected public events in their countries.

3.6 The Passive Voice with *Get,*
page 88

⏱ Time: 5–10 min

1. Have students cover the grammar chart. Write one or two examples using the passive with *get* on the board, such as: *I get paid every 2 weeks / My backpack got stolen last year.* Ask: *Are these sentences in the passive voice?* (yes) *Do you think these are formal written sentences or informal spoken sentences?* (informal spoken) *Can you use a form of* be *instead of* get *in these sentences?* (yes)

2. Have students review the grammar chart. Then ask them to convert each example with *get* to a passive voice sentence with a form of *be.*

EXERCISE 11 page 89

⏱ Time: 5–10 min

Answers: 1. Ronald Reagan got shot on the day of the Oscars. **2.** One of his aides got shot too. **3.** Reagan didn't get killed by the shooter. **4.** Did the aide get killed? **5.** Did the shooter get caught? **6.** Movie stars get paid a lot of money. **7.** Who will get picked for the starring role of the movie? **8.** I didn't get invited to the Academy Awards.

READING

Charlie Chaplin, page 90

PRE-READING

⏱ Time: 5–10 min

1. Have students look at the photo. Ask: *Who is the man?* (Charlie Chaplin) *What was his occupation?* (He was an actor.) *What time period do you think his films are from?* (early twentieth century)

2. Have students look quickly at the reading. Ask: *What is the reading about? How do you know?* Have students use the title and photo to make predictions about the reading.

3. Pre-teach any vocabulary words your students may not know, such as *tramp, abandoned, version, declining,* and *views.*

4. Activate students' prior knowledge about early movies. Ask: *What were the first movies like?* (silent, black and white) Have students discuss the question in pairs. Try to pair students of different cultures together.

5. Ask a few volunteers to share their answers with the class.

READING GLOSSARY

tramp: homeless person
to abandon: to leave behind
version: an account of something
to decline: to move downward; become less
views: opinions

EXPANDING ON THE READING

The topic for this reading can be enhanced with the following items:

1. Photos of tramps from the early 1900s in the United States

2. A short biography of Charlie Chaplin from a website, film history, or encyclopedia

3. Video of a Chaplin movie

CONTEXT NOTE

Charlie Chaplin's poverty-stricken tramp character was typical of the times he lived in. Although not in use in conversational English in the United States, the term *tramp* was common before and especially during the Great Depression in the 1930s. After a stock market crash, people all over the country lost their money, jobs, and homes, creating large numbers of homeless people who were referred to at the time as tramps or hobos.

READING CD 1 TR 19

🕐 Time: 10–15 min

Go over the answers to the Comprehension Check on page 91: **1.** F; **2.** F; **3.** T

ADDITIONAL COMPREHENSION QUESTIONS

Where was Charlie Chaplin from? (London, England) *What else did Charlie Chaplin do besides act?* (He also produced, directed, and wrote his movies.)

PRACTICE IDEA: LISTENING

To practice listening skills, have students first listen to the audio alone. Have students write all the adjectives they hear. Repeat the audio if necessary. Then have students open their books and read along as they listen to the audio.

3.7 Participles Used as Adjectives, page 91

🕐 Time: 10–15 min

1. On the board, write: *This is an interesting movie. Are you interested in watching it with me?* Ask: *What kind of word is* interesting? (present participle) *What kind of word is* interested? (past participle) Explain that although present and past participles are usually used to form verb tenses, they can also be used as adjectives.

2. On the board, rewrite the sentences from grammar chart **3.7** with gaps: *Chaplin's movies are ___. We are ___ in his movies.* Write *interesting* and *interested* on the board. Ask: *Which one goes in which sentence?* Review the difference between present and past participles.

3. Review the grammar chart with students. Draw students' attention to the explanation of present versus past participles used as adjectives, as well as the causes and recipients of feelings.

4. Provide pairs of students with cues for practice. Ask students to make simple sentences with both forms, e.g., *frightened* (I am frightened by thunder.) and *frightening* (The cost of college is frightening.).

5. Direct students to the Language Note. Review the list of paired participles with the class. Check that students are comfortable with the meaning of each pair.

EXERCISE 12 page 92

🕐 Time: 10–15 min

Answers: 1. The movie was entertaining. / We were entertained. **2.** Violent movies are frightening. / The children are frightened. **3.** Chaplin was amusing. / The audience was amused. **4.** The adventure movie was exciting. / The audience was excited. **5.** The TV show was boring. / I was bored. **6.** The end of the movie was surprising. / We were surprised. **7.** The movie was confusing. / She was confused. **8.** The movie was terrifying. / They were terrified.

EXERCISE 13 page 93

🕐 Time: 5–10 min

Answers: 1. interesting; **2.** surprising; **3.** surprised; **4.** confused; **5.** convinced; **6.** excited; **7.** declining; **8.** depressed; **9.** surprised; **10.** interested; **11.** boring

EXERCISE 14 page 93

🕐 Time: 5–10 min

Answers: 1. boring; **2.** exciting; **3.** convincing; **4.** disappointed; **5.** amazing; **6.** interesting; **7.** annoyed; **8.** disappointing; **9.** satisfying

3.8 Other Past Participles Used as Adjectives, page 94

🕐 Time: 10–15 min

1. On the board, write: *My DVD player is broken.* Ask: *What is* broken *in this sentence?* (an adjective and a past participle) Say: *I don't know who broke it or when, but it's not really important now.* Explain that in this sentence, what is important is the result—the DVD player is broken and doesn't work.

2. Have students review the grammar chart. In the first section, review each example and its explanation together.

3. Provide additional practice by having students complete sentences such as: *The _____ looks _____. / I am done with _____.*

ADDITIONAL PRACTICE

Have pairs work to complete these sentences with the correct adverb. Some adverbs can be used more than once.

well   **badly**   **over**   **under**   **newly**   **little**

1. Steve and Dinah are a _____ married couple. They got married last month.
2. *To Kill a Mockingbird* was written by Harper Lee, a _____-known author from the South.
3. My English professor was a _____-educated man from Connecticut.
4. Bibi will be upset. Her toy is _____ broken.
5. I am afraid of having accidents, so I am ____-insured.
6. Some CEOs are really _____-paid. They make too much money!
7. If you don't study, you'll be _____-prepared when you come to class.
8. He was _____ wounded in the war.

Answers: 1. newly; **2.** little; **3.** well; **4.** badly; **5.** over; **6.** over; **7.** under; **8.** badly

EXERCISE 15 page 94
🕐 Time: 5–10 min
Answers: 1. paid; **2.** born; **3.** educated; **4.** interested; **5.** located; **6.** married; **7.** known; **8.** closed; **9.** worried; **10.** taken; **11.** finished

3.9 *Get vs. Be* with Past Participles and Other Adjectives, page 95

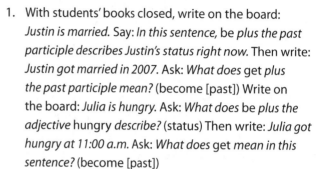

🕐 Time: 10–15 min

1. With students' books closed, write on the board: *Justin is married.* Say: *In this sentence,* be *plus the past participle describes Justin's status right now.* Then write: *Justin got married in 2007.* Ask: *What does* get *plus the past participle mean?* (become [past]) Write on the board: *Julia is hungry.* Ask: *What does* be *plus the adjective* hungry *describe?* (status) Then write: *Julia got hungry at 11:00 a.m.* Ask: *What does* get *mean in this sentence?* (become [past])

2. Have students look at grammar chart **3.9**. Review the example sentences and explanations.

3. Direct students' attention to the Language Note. Review the examples. Then ask volunteers to talk about themselves using the examples as models (*I am married. I married ..., I got married ...,* etc.).

4. Direct students' attention to the lists of past participles with *get* and adjectives with *get* in the chart. Explain any vocabulary students are unfamiliar with.

EXERCISE 16 page 95
🕐 Time: 10–15 min
Answers: 1. got; **2.** got married; **3.** is; **4.** is; **5.** is; **6.** get; **7.** be; **8.** be **9.** got

SUMMARY OF LESSON 3

🕐 Time: 20–30 min

PART A PASSIVE VOICE

Provide a series of cues and have students make complete sentences using the passive voice (*got lost, was written, was made, have been told, is shown,* etc.).

If necessary, have students review:

3.1 Active and Passive Voice—Introduction (page 75)

3.2 Comparison of Active and Passive Voice (page 76)

3.3 Active and Passive Voice—Use (page 79)

3.4 Verbs with Two Objects (page 82)

3.5 Transitive and Intransitive Verbs (pages 84–85)

3.6 The Passive Voice with *Get* (page 88)

PRACTICE IDEA: WRITING

Write on the board phrases used in passive voice sentences (*was built, is known for, are made, is located*, etc.). Have students write sentences about the history of, places in, or facts about their native countries. Have students share their information with the class.

PART B PARTICIPLES AND OTHER ADJECTIVES

Have students make statements about life in the United States, using pairs of words from the list of participles in the Language Note on page 91 (e.g., *Some traffic laws in the United States. are confusing. / I'm confused about what* yield *means on traffic signs*.).

If necessary, have students review:

3.7 Participles Used as Adjectives (page 91)

3.8 Other Past Participles Used as Adjectives (page 94)

3.9 *Get* vs. *Be* with Past Participles and Other Adjectives (page 95)

PRACTICE IDEA: SPEAKING

Write a list of participles used as adjectives on the board (e.g., *upset, pleased, thrilled, tired*, and *amused*). Have students talk about themselves using the adjectives.

TEST/REVIEW

🕐 Time: 15 min

Have students do the exercise on page 97. For additional practice, use the Assessment CD-ROM with Exam*View*® and the Online Workbook.

Answers: 1. was made; **2.** saw; **3.** see; **4.** don't remember; **5.** decides; **6.** comes; **7.** sinks; **8.** survives; **9.** die; **10.** interesting; **11.** was shown; **12.** remember; **13.** arrive;

14. disappears; **15.** is rescued; **16.** disappointing; **17.** got saved; **18.** lived; **19.** frightening; **20.** were done; **21.** amazed; **22.** advanced; **23.** happens; **24.** Was; **25.** made; **26.** be done; **27.** read; **28.** knew; **29.** amazed; **30.** was directed; **31.** Was; **32.** nominated; **33.** was; **34.** ends; **35.** interests

---

WRITING

PART 1 EDITING ADVICE

🕐 Time: 10–15 min

1. Have students close their books. Write the first few sentences without editing marks or corrections on the board. For example:
   The movie didn't made in Hollywood.
   The main character was died at the end of the movie.

2. Ask students to correct each sentence and provide a rule or an explanation for each correction. This activity can be done individually, in pairs, or as a class.

3. After students have corrected each sentence, tell them to turn to page 98. Say: *Now compare your work with the Editing Advice in the book.* Have students read through all the advice.

PART 2 EDITING PRACTICE

🕐 Time: 10–15 min

1. Tell students they are going to put the Editing Advice into practice. Ask: *Do all the shaded words and phrases have mistakes?* (no) Go over the examples with the class. Then do #1 together.

2. Have students complete the practice individually. Then have them compare answers with a partner before checking answers as a class.

3. For the items students had difficulty with, have them go back and find the relevant grammar chart and review it. Monitor and give help as necessary.

Answers: 1. C; **2.** should see; **3.** C; **4.** C; **5.** was shown; **6.** exhausted; **7.** fell; **8.** ended; **9.** C; **10.** was surprised; **11.** Did; **12.** die; **13.** did; **14.** rescued; **15.** happened; **16.** agreed; **17.** C; **18.** C; **19.** was kidnapped; **20.** C; **21.** remained; **22.** C; **23.** can be found; **24.** was directed; **25.** him; **26.** C; **27.** C; **28.** C; **29.** was written; **30.** nominated; **31.** C; **32.** wasn't; **33.** disappointed; **34.** Are; **35.** seen

PART 3 WRITE ABOUT IT

⏱ Time: 30–40 min

1. Review the topics with students before they choose one to write about. Ask: *Which tenses will you most likely use? Why?* Advise students to tell a partner about the topic they have chosen before they write. For the first topic, have students brainstorm American movies and movies made in their native countries. Encourage students to organize their thoughts and make notes before they begin to write. Tell them to brainstorm general ideas and specific details. If necessary, write model topic sentences and conclusions on the board first.

2. Repeat the procedure for the second topic. Have students brainstorm movies they have seen or heard about over the years and the ways they have changed. Elicit or say to consider technology, subjects or themes, costumes, actors, types (adult, children's), etc. Then have them write their compositions. If necessary, write model topic sentences and conclusions on the board first.

PART 4 EDIT YOUR WRITING

⏱ Time: 15–20 min

Have students edit their writing by reviewing the Lesson Summary on page 96 and the Editing Advice on page 98. Collect for assessment and/or have students share their essays in small groups or with a partner.

EXPANSION ACTIVITIES

Tell students to watch the movie *Titanic* (1997), *A Night to Remember* (1957), or two of Charlie Chaplin's short movies such as *City Lights* (1931) and *Modern Times* (1936). Have them write a summary of the movie(s) they choose. Have students share their summaries in groups. If some students are unable to rent and view the movies at home, consider bringing one of the movies to class, if possible, to view a few scenes together.

4 TRAVEL BY LAND, SEA, AND AIR

GRAMMAR CHARTS

LESSON OPENER

Have students look at the photo and read the caption. Ask: *What is happening in the photo? Where are these people?* Have students read the quotation. Ask: *Do you agree with the quote? How can having new eyes help you discover new things or give you a new perspective?*

Background: Americans are a species of travelers. In the early nineteenth century, the discovery of the Northwest Passage opened an entire continent for exploration. Early Americans often had to go on foot over narrow trails to reach the Pacific. By 1868 they were taking trains. A century later, the introduction of cruise ships and passenger air travel brought such faraway places as California much closer, and made traveling more comfortable and convenient. Today in the United States, two billion domestic trips are made on average every year, and travel for both business and pleasure is a common part of American life.

Marcel Proust was a French author and intellectual. His famous novel, *In Search of Lost Time*, 1871, is about time and how we see the world. In the novel, characters live but let the world pass by because they do not really see it. Consisting of seven volumes, the novel is believed to be one of the greatest works of literary art in the world.

CONTEXT

This unit is about travel. Students will read about the Lewis and Clark expedition that discovered the passage across the United States to the Pacific Ocean, the luxury ship *Titanic* that sank in the Atlantic Ocean, and the DC-3 airplane that initiated modern passenger air travel.

1. Give students a few minutes to look through the lesson. Have them look at the photos and titles. How do they relate to the context?

2. Elicit the topics that will be discussed.

3. Have students discuss what they know about the different types of travel by land, sea, and air in pairs or small groups.

GRAMMAR

Students will learn about past continuous, past perfect, and past perfect continuous tenses.

1. To activate students' prior knowledge, ask what students know about continuous and perfect tenses.

2. Give several examples of sentences using the three tenses (e.g., *That summer, we were taking a bus trip. / We had taken a train to St. Louis, but we flew from there to Chicago. / Mr. Douglas had been working on a design for several years*).

3. Have volunteers give examples and write them on the board.

`READING`

Travel by Land: The Lewis and Clark Expedition, page 102

PRE-READING

🕑 Time: 10–20 min

1. Have students look at the illustration and read the caption. Ask: *What is in the illustration?* (a fish, a salmon trout) *Who drew it?* (Clark)
2. Have students read the title and then skim the reading. Ask: *What is the reading about? How do you know?* Have students make predictions.
3. Pre-teach any essential vocabulary words your students may not know, such as *continent, passage,* and *aide.*
4. Ask: *Where did Lewis and Clark go? Why did they go there?* Have students discuss in small groups and share their answers with class.

READING GLOSSARY

continent: one of the seven great land masses in the world
passage: a way between two places
aide: a helper; assistant

READING CD 1 TR 20

🕑 Time: 10–15 min

Go over the answers to the Comprehension Check on page 103: **1.** F; **2.** T; **3.** F

CONTEXT NOTE

Lewis and Clark encountered American Indian tribes of three major culture areas during their expedition: the nomadic Plains Indians who lived in teepees, the Plateau Indians who lived in permanent villages, and the Northwest Coast tribes who lived in big houses. One important role of the Lewis and Clark expedition was to introduce the American Indian tribes to American settlers. Previously, these tribes had not met white people or had only met French, British, or Spanish explorers. When they encountered American Indians, the expedition captains met with them peacefully and gave them presents from President Jefferson.

ADDITIONAL COMPREHENSION QUESTIONS

What was the main goal of the expedition? (to find a land passage to the Pacific Ocean) *How many people went on the expedition?* (thirty-three men) *Who became their guide?* (Sacagawea, a Shoshone Indian) *Where did the expedition start and end?* (St. Louis, Missouri) *What tasks did Lewis do?* (Lewis studied plants and animals on land.) *What did Clark do?* (Clark stayed on the boat, drew maps, and planned their course.) *How long did the expedition take?* (almost 2½ years) *Did Lewis and Clark succeed?* (yes)

EXPANDING ON THE READING

The topic for this reading can be enhanced with the following items:

1. An online search offering descriptions of the American Indians Lewis and Clark encountered
2. Biography of Sacagawea
3. An online search giving more details of the expedition

PRACTICE IDEA: WRITING AND SPEAKING

Distribute copies of a simple map labeled with key locations of the expedition. Have students work in pairs and reread the article, taking notes of key events. Have partners then retell the path of the expedition by pointing to locations on the map and using complete sentences.

4.1 The Past Continuous— Form, page 103

⏲ Time: 10–15 min

1. Have students cover grammar chart **4.1**. Give examples about yourself using the present and past continuous. (*Today I'm teaching. Yesterday, I was teaching.*) Ask: *How are these sentences alike?* (both use *be* + present participle) *How are they different?* (*am* versus *was:* present versus past) Elicit the names of the two tenses. (present continuous, past continuous) Write the sentences on the board, and underline the auxiliary and main verbs in each sentence. Say: *Today you're studying English. What were you doing yesterday?* Have several volunteers answer.

2. Have students review Part A of the grammar chart. Ask volunteers to say what they observe about the rules for forming the past continuous. (past form of *be* + present participle of the main verb)

3. Direct students' attention to Part B of the chart. Review the examples of statements, *Yes/No* questions and short answers, and *Wh-* questions in past continuous. Ask: *How do you form the passive in past continuous?* (past form of *be* + *being* + past participle)

EXERCISE 1 page 104

⏲ Time: 10–15 min

Answers: 1. a. were most Americans living, **b.** were living; **2. a.** was working, **b.** Was Clark working, **c.** wasn't; **3. a.** they were crossing, **b.** were traveling; **4. a.** weren't they traveling; **5. a.** they were crossing, **b.** were sleeping; **6. a.** was helping, **b.** was she helping; **7. a.** were waiting, **b.** were waiting

---

4.2 The Past Continuous— Use, pages 104–105

⏲ Time: 5–10 min

1. Tell students that the past continuous has two key uses. Demonstrate them by giving examples from your own life [e.g., *a) In July 2010, I was traveling in California. b) As I was eating in a restaurant, there was an earthquake.*]. Elicit or explain how the continuous is used in each sentence. (to show action in progress at a certain time; to connect an action in progress to a simple past time, act, or event)

2. Review the examples, timelines, and explanations in the chart with students. To help them connect simple past times/acts to continuous actions, write one or two pairs of time/action + event on the board (e.g., 1930/Charlie Chaplin making *City Lights*; Lewis and Clark searching passage, met Sacagawea). Elicit sentences from students and ask volunteers to write them on the board. (*In 1930, Charlie Chaplin was making* City Lights. *Lewis and Clark were searching for a passage through the Rocky Mountains when they met Sacagawea.*) Ask: *Do these sentences connect a progressive action/event with a simple time/event?* (yes)

3. Draw students' attention to the Punctuation Note. Make sure that students understand the meanings of *clause* and *comma*, noting the reversed order of information.

PRESENTATION IDEAS

1. Have students work in groups. Assign each group to review one of the three sections of the grammar chart (including the Punctuation Note). Have groups review the examples and explanations in their section and then have each group present its section to the class.

2. Have students look back at the reading on page 102 and try to match each of the past continuous verbs with the correct explanation of use in the grammar chart.

EXERCISE 2 page 105
Time: 10–15 min
Answers: 1. L; **2.** S; **3.** L; **4.** L; **5.** S; **6.** L; **7.** S; **8.** S; **9.** L; **10.** S; **11.** S; **12.** S; **13.** L

EXERCISE 3 page 105
Time: 5–10 min
Answers will vary.

4.3 The Past Continuous vs. the Simple Past, page 106

Time: 5–10 min

1. Have students look at the first section of the grammar chart. Review the examples. Say: *There are three actions in these two pairs of sentences. What are the actions?* (heard the news, eating breakfast, called my friend) Ask: *Which happened first?* (heard the news) *Second?* (called my friend) *At the same time?* (eating breakfast)

2. Have students review the second section of the chart. Ask them to identify events that were happening when the main event occurred. (*When the* Columbia *broke up….*)

PRESENTATION IDEA

Have students look back at the reading on page 102. Ask students to identify actions in the reading that were in progress after the expedition left St. Louis in 1804. Then review the examples and explanations in the chart.

ADDITIONAL PRACTICE

Have students work in small groups. Bring in news articles and distribute them among the groups. Have students skim the articles to identify the main event and events leading up to it. Have each group report their findings to the class.

EXERCISE 4 pages 106–107
Time: 5–10 min
Answers: 1. a. was living, **b.** were you doing, **c.** was getting, **d.** was eating, **e.** listening, **f.** heard, **g.** did you do, **h.** ran, **i.** did you do, **j.** called; **2. a.** was the *Columbia* going, **b.** happened, **c.** was traveling, **d.** were you doing, **e.** was getting, **f.** told, **g.** turned, **h.** showed, **i.** started; **3. a.** was reading, **b.** found, **c.** did you do, **d.** put

EXERCISE 5 pages 107–108
Time: 5–10 min
Answers: 1. a. was looking, **b.** found, **c.** did you do, **d.** took; **2. a.** were crossing, **b.** died, **c.** did they do, **d.** buried; **3. a.** was explaining, **b.** fell, **c.** was the teacher talking about, **d.** was talking, **e.** was sleeping, **f.** woke, **g.** tried, **4. a.** was visiting, **b.** did you do, **c.** went; **5. a.** were you doing, **b.** was watching, **c.** were you doing, **d.** was sleeping, **e.** turned

PRACTICE IDEA: SPEAKING

Have students work in pairs and retell conversations in the exercise. Tell partners to switch roles. After they have finished, have a few pairs perform the conversations for the class.

PRACTICE IDEA: WRITING

Have students write a brief paragraph about what they were doing when a disaster happened in their country. Have them use sentences with continuous action related to time (e.g., 2010) and related to a single event (e.g., when the tsunami hit).

CONTEXT NOTE

Take time to find out how familiar your students are with sea disasters (or other disasters) that might make them uncomfortable with the context of the next reading or this lesson as a whole. If you have students whose families or friends have been lost or missing in a disaster, be sensitive to this during discussions and activities.

Travel by Sea: The First and Last Voyage of the *Titanic*,

page 109

PRE-READING

🕐 Time: 10–15 min

1. Have students look at the photo and read the caption. Ask: *Where is the ship?* (on the ocean floor) *What's happening?* (its anchor is being explored)

2. Have students skim the reading. Ask: *What does the reading say about the* Titanic? *What is the main idea?* Have students use the title and the photo to make predictions about the reading.

3. Pre-teach any vocabulary words your students may not know, such as *voyage, elevators, emigrants, warnings, mild,* and *lifeboat.*

4. Activate students' prior knowledge about sinking ships. Ask: *What happens when a ship sinks?* (It goes underwater.) *What do passengers and the crew do?* (use lifeboats to get off the ship) Discuss the questions as a class.

READING GLOSSARY

voyage: a long journey

elevators: box-like cars used to carry people and objects between floors in a building

emigrants: people who leave their country to live somewhere else

warnings: statements that something bad might happen

mild: not cold or hot

lifeboat: a small boat used in emergencies

EXPANDING ON THE READING

The topic for this reading can be enhanced with the following items:

1. Photos of the luxury interior of the *Titanic*
2. Descriptions of amenities offered by the *Titanic*
3. The movie *Titanic*
4. Photos of the wreckage
5. Descriptions of the expedition that discovered the wreckage (French-American scientific team led by Jean-Louis Michel and Bob Ballard)

READING 🎧 CD 1 TR 22 ⭐

🕐 10–15 min

Go over the answers to the Comprehension Check on page 110: **1.** T; **2.** F; **3.** F

ADDITIONAL COMPREHENSION QUESTIONS

Had the car been invented by the time the Titanic *took its voyage?* (yes) *What kind of passengers were traveling on the ship?* (all kinds, the very rich and poor emigrants) *How many voyages had the ship taken before?* (none, this was the first) *What caused the ship to sink?* (It hit an iceberg.) *Why didn't all the passengers leave on lifeboats?* (There weren't enough lifeboats.) *How many passengers survived?* (less than one-third)

CONTEXT NOTES

1. Captain Edward Smith of the *Titanic* was last seen on the bridge as the ship was going down. Smith did not try to save himself. The idiom "to go down with the ship" is taken from the tradition that a sea captain holds final responsibility for the safety of his passengers, crew, and ship and that he will die trying to save them.

2. The phrase "women and children first" is commonly believed to have come from a tradition of putting women and children into lifeboats first when a ship was in danger of sinking.

3. In the transportation and hotel or leisure industries in the United States, seating and accommodations are divided into *classes* according to features offered. First-class accommodation on a cruise ship is the most expensive but gives the greatest space, comfort, and service.

PRACTICE IDEA: LISTENING

To practice listening skills, have students first listen to the audio alone. Have them write all the key verb phrases they hear. Repeat the audio if necessary. Then have students open their books and read along as they listen to the audio.

4.4 The Past Perfect— Form, page 110

⏱ Time: 5–10 min

1. Have students review the example sentences and explanations in Part A of the grammar chart. Ask: *How do you form the past perfect?* (had [*not*] + past participle)

2. Review the Language Notes. Write additional examples on the board such as: *He'd wanted to* and *He'd like to.* Ask students what each *'d* means. (had, would) Elicit or point out the location of adverbs. (between the auxiliary *had* and the past participle) Have students briefly look at the list of irregular past tenses and past participles in Appendix H, if needed.

3. Draw students' attention to Part B of the chart. Review the example statements, questions, and short answers. Write on the board an additional example: *By 2014, I had had ten cars.* Explain that in sentences in which *had* appears twice, the first is the auxiliary and the second is the main verb/past participle of *had*.

ADDITIONAL PRACTICE

1. After students have reviewed the chart, have them chart five past perfect sentences from the reading. Divide the class into groups. Have each group draw a four-column chart, labeled as follows: Subject, *Had* (+ *not*), Past Participle, Complement. Have them locate past perfect sentences and write their parts in the correct column. Students can use the list of verbs from the Listening practice to help them, if available. Tell them to chart only the main subject, verb, and complement, and not to include introductory modifying phrases, such as "Cold and afraid."

2. As students are working, go around the room and offer help as needed.

3. Have each group report their findings to the class, including how many of their sentences used adverbs.

EXERCISE 6 page 111

⏱ Time: 10–15 min

Answers: 1. had just said; **2.** had happened; **3.** had met; **4.** had already left; **5.** had jumped; **6.** had survived; **7.** had died; **8.** had taken; **9.** had been; **10.** had died

4.5 The Past Perfect— Use (Part 1), page 112

⏱ Time: 10–15 min

1. Have students close their books. Ask review questions about the reading. Ask: *Did a rescue ship arrive?* (yes) *Did it arrive before or after the* Titanic *went down?* (after) Draw a timeline on the board similar to the one in the chart. Say: *Use the past perfect to show the connection between past times, events, and actions. The past perfect can show which came first.* Elicit students' help to write the sentence: *When the rescue ship arrived, the* Titanic *had already gone down.* Point out that the adverb *already* emphasizes the time relationship.

2. Review each section of the chart. Have students study the timelines. Check understanding by asking questions such as: *What happened first: the ship hit an iceberg or the ship was at sea for five days?* (The ship was at sea for five days.)

3. Elicit the devices or words that indicate time in the examples. (by…, *by the time, already, never, until, when, yet, for…, before*). Ask: *Where do we use these time phrases: with the simple action (main clause) or with the time clause?* (with both) Ask: *What job do* never, before, *and* yet *do if they are in the main clause?* (They emphasize the earlier time.)

4. Ask students to make statements about themselves using the examples in the chart as models.

PRESENTATION IDEA

Write four or five past perfect sentences on the board like the ones in grammar chart **4.5**. Use *before, yet, when*, etc. Have students diagram the sentences as shown in the chart to show the relationship between events. Ask volunteers to draw their diagrams on the board. When they are finished, say: *Let's see if we're correct* and begin the review of the chart.

EXERCISE 7 pages 112–113

🕐 Time: 10–15 min

Answers: 1. had already been invented; **2. a.** left, **b.** had been removed; **3.** had broken; **4. a.** had received, **b.** hit; **5. a.** had been, **b.** realized; **6. a.** felt, **b.** had already gone; **7. a.** jumped, **b.** 'd gotten/had gotten; **8. a.** 'd spent/had spent, **b.** was rescued; **9. a.** arrived, **b.** had already died; **10. a.** was found, **b.** had been

EXERCISE 8 page 113

🕐 Time: 10–15 min

Answers:

1. When the Lewis and Clark expedition traveled to the ²
   west, no one had done it before. ¹

2. They finally entered a territory that no white man had ²
   ever entered before. ¹

3. It was 1803. For almost 20 years, President Jefferson had ²
   thought about sending an expedition to the West. ¹

4. The expedition had traveled more than 600 miles by ¹
   the end of July. ²

5. Up to this time, most of the trip had been done by ² ¹
   boat.

6. Lewis and Clark were the first white Americans to go ²
   west of the Rocky Mountains. But these lands had ¹
   been occupied by native people for a long time.

7. Many American Indians had never seen a white man ¹
   before they met Lewis and Clark. ²

8. Only one man had died by the end of the expedition. ¹ ²

9. He had died long before the expedition ended. ¹ ²

10. They returned to St. Louis, almost two and one-half ²
    years after they had left. ¹

4.6 *When* with the Simple Past or the Past Perfect, page 114

🕐 Time: 5–10 min

1. Review the examples and explanations in grammar chart **4.6**. Write on the board: *When I got home, I heard the news. When I was driving home, I'd already heard the news.* Ask: *What does* when *mean: before or after I heard the news?* (first sentence: after; second sentence: before)

2. Ask volunteers to give examples about themselves using the simple past or past perfect, beginning with *When I came home ….*

ADDITIONAL PRACTICE

Provide a list of several additional sentences using *when* with the simple past and past perfect. Have students identify main clauses and determine the meaning of *when* for each sentence. Discuss the answers as a class.

EXERCISE 9 page 114

🕐 Time: 5–10 min

Answers: 1. had never seen; **2.** were; **3.** had been removed; **4.** started; **5.** had received; **6.** went; **7.** ran; **8.** came; **9.** 'd had/had had; **10.** had not yet been published; **11.** learned; **12.** told; **13.** 'd never heard/had never heard

4.7 The Past Perfect—Use (Part 2), page 115

⏱ Time: 5–10 min

1. Review the examples and explanations in grammar chart **4.7**. Elicit the four uses (with *because*, noun clauses, superlative forms, and adjective clauses).

2. Confirm comprehension of the use of *because* with past perfect. Write on the board: *Result / Cause*. Underneath, write: *We succeeded because we had worked so hard.* Say: Because *indicates the reason something happened, or the cause that created a result. This is why* because *indicates an earlier time.* Have students identify what happened (we succeeded) and why (because we'd worked so hard). Ask volunteers to identify causes and results in the example *because* sentences.

3. To help clarify the use of past perfect in noun clauses, explain that the noun clause is acting as the object of the verb (the past action). Ask: *Why can the past perfect be used in a time clause?* (because it explains what had been thought, known, or realized before the time of speaking)

4. Complete the review of the chart. Note that superlatives and *ever* are often avoided in academic English since the use tends to overstate or exaggerate. Point out that students will learn more about adjective clauses in Lesson 7 and more about noun clauses in Lesson 10.

PRACTICE IDEA: SPEAKING

Have students work in pairs and make statements about the sinking of the *Titanic* or another disaster. Have them use the past perfect with *because;* in noun clauses; with the superlative and past tense main verbs; and in adjective clauses.

EXERCISE 10 page 115

⏱ Time: 10–15 min

Answers: 1. a. went, **b.** had felt; **2. a.** had gotten, **b.** jumped; **3. a.** reported, **b.** had heard; **4. a.** was, **b.** had ever happened; **5. a.** became, **b.** had died; **6. a.** didn't know, **b.** hadn't published; **7. a.** knew, **b.** had given; **8. a.** had written, **b.** wasn't

EXERCISE 11 page 116

⏱ Time: 10–15 min

Answers: 1. a. entered, **b.** had ever entered; **2. a.** was, **b.** had ever done; **3. a.** kept, **b.** had seen; **4. a.** repaired, **b.** had become; **5. a.** entered, **b.** had warned, **c.** was, **d.** 'd ever seen/had ever seen; **6. a.** thought, **b.** 'd reached/had reached; **7. a.** were, **b.** had already been occupied

EXERCISE 12 page 116

⏱ Time: 5–10 min
Answers will vary.

4.8 The Past Perfect Continuous—Form, page 117

⏱ Time: 5–10 min

1. Have students review the example sentences and explanations in Part A of the grammar chart. Ask: *How do you form the past perfect continuous?* (had [not] + been + present participle)

2. Review the Language Note on the placement of adverbs. Elicit additional example sentences with *often, usually, already,* and *sometimes.* Note that longer time word adverbials such as the phrase *once in a while* are more often placed at the end, or possibly the beginning, of the sentence.

3. Draw students' attention to Part B of the chart. Review the example statements, questions, and short answers. Write on the board an additional example with *how long,* such as *How long had you been working for the corporation?* Elicit other examples from the class.

EXERCISE 13 page 117

⏱ Time: 5–10 min

Answers: 1. had been traveling; **2.** had been running; **3.** had died; **4.** hadn't spoken; **5.** had learned; **6.** had been living

4.9 The Past Perfect Continuous—Use, page 118

🕐 Time: 10–15 min

1. On the board, write: *The captain had been commanding ships for 25 years when he died on the* Titanic. Ask: *What had been happening before the captain died?* (past experience: 25 years' commanding ships) Ask: *What does* for *indicate in the sentence?* (how long the action or event lasted; duration)

2. Direct students' attention to the second section of the chart. Make incorrect sentences in past perfect continuous such as: *The captain had been knowing that there was an iceberg nearby. / She had been being in the lifeboat when the rescue ship found the survivors.* Ask: *Are these sentences correct?* (no) *What is the problem?* (*know* and *be* are nonaction verbs that cannot be used in past perfect continuous)

PRESENTATION IDEA

Put students in groups. Ask students to write true or false statements about themselves at age 15, using the past perfect continuous and a time phrase with *for* (e.g., *for 4 years, for 3 months*). The other students guess if the statements are true or false. Model an example. Say: *By the time I was 15, I had been cooking dinner every night for 5 years. True or false?* Elicit the answer. After the class has finished, begin the review of the chart.

ADDITIONAL PRACTICE

Write a mix of action and nonaction verbs on the board such as: *sound, walk, talk, seem, taste, like, own,* and *get.* Have students work in pairs and write sentences for the verbs. Then have pairs exchange papers for feedback.

EXERCISE 14 page 118

🕐 Time: 10–15 min

Answers: 1. a. died, **b.** had been living; **2. a.** had been working, **b.** chose; **3. a.** had been traveling, **b.** met; **4. a.** saw, **b.** 'd been crossing/had been crossing; **5. a.** wrote, **b.** 'd been thinking/had been thinking; **6. a.** was rescued, **b.** 'd been holding on/had been holding on; **7. a.** was found, **b.** had been resting; **8. a.** exploded, **b.** had been traveling

EXERCISE 15 page 119

🕐 Time: 10–15 min

Answers: 1. a. came, **b.** had been studying; **2. a.** 'd been waiting/had been waiting, **b.** got; **3. a.** 'd been living/had been living, **b.** left; **4. a.** felt, **b.** 'd been working/had been working; **5. a.** 'd been studying/had been studying, **b.** broke out; **6. a.** left, **b.** had been going on; **7. a.** had been waiting, **b.** got; **8. a.** got, **b.** 'd been traveling/had been traveling

4.10 The Past Perfect (Continuous) vs. the Present Perfect (Continuous), page 120

🕐 Time: 10–15 min

1. Tell students this chart is about the difference in perspective of past perfect and present perfect. Have them close their books. Say: *I am thinking about a book I am reading. I started it 3 weeks ago.* Ask: *What tense would I use to describe time taken in reading the book?* (present perfect) *Why?* (because it relates events in the past to the present) Ask a volunteer to write on the board a sentence in present perfect continuous describing the time. (*I have been reading this book for 3 weeks.*)

2. Say: *I am thinking about when I learned to drive. It took me 2 months of practicing and studying my driver's manual before I could take the driver's test.* Ask: *What tense would I use to connect these two events: practicing/studying and taking the test?* (past perfect)

Why? (because it connects two past events) Ask a volunteer to write on the board a sentence in past perfect continuous describing this experience. *(By the time I took my driving test, I had been studying my manual and practicing driving for 2 months.)*

3. Elicit examples from students' own experiences and then review the examples and explanation of uses in the chart.

EXERCISE 16 page 121
🕐 Time: 10–15 min

Answers: 1. have you been; **2.** 've always been/have always been; **3.** 'd never been/had never been; **4.** 'd always wanted/had always wanted; **5.** had been studying; **6.** 've become/have become; **7.** Have you ever seen; **8.** 've never heard/have never heard; **9.** 's made/has made; **10.** 've seen/have seen; **11.** haven't been/have not been; **12.** 've been watching/have been watching; **13.** had ever been made; **14.** had been traveling

---

PRACTICE IDEA: SPEAKING

Have students work in pairs and make up a conversation similar to the one in the exercise. When they are finished, have a volunteer pair perform their conversation for the class.

`READING`

Travel by Air: The DC-3, page 122

PRE-READING
🕐 Time: 5–10 min

1. Have students look at the photo and read the caption. Ask: *What do you see?* (an airplane exhibit at a museum) *What kind of airplane is it?* (a DC-3)

2. Have students skim the reading. Ask: *What is the reading about? How do you know?* Have students use the title and photo to make predictions about the reading.

3. Pre-teach any vocabulary words your students may not know, such as *aviation, military, equivalent, alternative*, and *preferred.*

4. Activate students' prior knowledge about the airline industry. Ask: *Do you think you would like flying in a DC-3? How is flying different now?* Have students discuss the questions in pairs. Try to pair students of the same culture. Have a few pairs share their answers with the class.

READING GLOSSARY

aviation: the manufacture and use of aircraft, especially airplanes

military: a group of armed forces of a nation

equivalent: equal; the same

alternative: another choice

preferred: liked better

EXPANDING ON THE READING

The topic for this reading can be enhanced with the following items:

1. Photos of passenger airplanes from different eras

2. Articles about innovations in passenger airplanes (e.g., Thomson Airways' family booths and kids' club)

3. Predictions about the future of aviation

READING CD 1 TR 24
🕐 Time: 10–15 min

Go over the answers to the Comprehension Check on page 123: **1.** F; **2.** T; **3.** T

ADDITIONAL COMPREHENSION QUESTIONS

What was the goal of early airlines? (to attract passengers away from train travel) *Why did passengers not enjoy the Boeing flights?* (dizziness, fainting, fear for safety) *What did airlines have to do to attract passengers?* (become faster, safer, and more comfortable) *Did airlines win their competition with trains?* (yes)

PRACTICE IDEA: LISTENING

To practice listening skills, have students first listen to the audio alone. Have students write all of the past tense verbs they hear. Repeat the audio if necessary. Then have students open their books and read along as they listen to the audio.

ADDITIONAL PRACTICE

Have students scan the reading for the answers to these questions:

1. How long did the DC-3 flight from Newark to California take? (18 hours and 40 minutes)

2. How long had a flight from New York to Los Angeles taken before? (25 hours)

3. How many times did that flight have to stop? (fifteen)

4. Which airline company bought sixty Boeing passenger planes? (United)

5. Which improvement made airplanes go faster? (they got lighter)

6. When did the airlines begin improving air travel? (1930s)

7. What happened in 1931? (a famous football player died in a plane crash)

8. Where did the crash occur? (Kansas)

9. What helps air traffic controllers today separate air traffic? (advanced radar systems)

10. Where can you see the original DC-3? (Smithsonian National Air and Space Museum)

PRACTICE IDEA: SPEAKING

Ask students to describe to a partner a terrible airplane flight they experienced and then a very good flight they experienced.

4.11 Comparison of Past Tenses, page 123

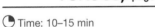

🕐 Time: 10–15 min

1. Have students cover the Explanation column of grammar chart **4.11**. Review each set of examples with the class. Ask: *Which tense is used in these examples? How do you know?* Elicit the explanation for each set of examples from the class. Then have students look at each explanation as you finish its section.

2. Direct students' attention to the Language Notes. Review the examples and explanations.

PRESENTATION IDEA

Have students close their books. Divide students into teams. At random, choose example sentences from the left side of the grammar chart to read aloud. Give a point to the first team to correctly identify the tense in the sentence you have read. The team with the most points is the winner. Then review the chart with the class.

🕐 Time: 10–15 min

Answers: 1. were living; **2.** didn't go; **3.** traveled; **4.** had already been built; **5.** was; **6.** used; **7.** invented; **8.** started; **9.** had already been; **10.** was called; **11.** was starting; **12.** were making; **13.** had developed; **14.** was; **15.** raised; **16.** fell; **17.** rose; **18.** was disappearing

---

PRESENTATION IDEAS: READING

1. Have students scan the article about Henry Ford before they listen to the audio. Ask a few comprehension questions, such as: *When did Ford invent an assembly line for manufacturing cars?* (by 1913) *How did Ford keep his workers happy?* (raised their salaries) *When did the term* passenger car *replace the term* pleasure car? (during the 1920s)

2. Bring in facts and photos about automobile firsts, such as previous inventions of steam, electric, and gasoline automobiles in France, Scotland, and Germany. Display the photos and review the facts with the class.

EXERCISE 18 pages 124–127

🕐 Time: 15–20 min

Answers: 1. a. Have you ever heard, **b.** invented, **c.** produced, **d.** didn't know/did not know, **e.** 've driven/have driven/'ve been driving/have been driving, **f.** has always been, **g.** 've never had/have never had, **h.** 've always preferred/have always preferred; **2. a.** gave, **b.** 'd been driving/had been driving/'d driven/had driven, **c.** decided, **d.** bought, **e.** 's been riding/has been riding, **f.** started, **g.** has improved/has been improving, **h.** has been helping; **3. a.** Have space missions always been, **b.** had been, **c.** occurred, **d.** was; **4. a.** learned, **b.** was working, **c.** was learning, **d.** became; **5. a.** were they called, **b.** had, **c.** were used; **6. a.** was studying, **b.** realized, **c.** did he do, **d.** realized, **e.** developed; **7. a.** read, **b.** had ever crossed, **c.** had died; **8. a.** 've been thinking/have been thinking, **b.** Have you ever bought, **c.** Have you looked, **d.** Have you thought; **9. a.** had ever been built, **b.** was traveling/had been traveling, **c.** hit, **d.** started, **e.** had already left

---

EXERCISE 19 page 127

🕐 Time: 5–10 min

Answers will vary.

SUMMARY OF LESSON 4

🕐 Time: 20–30 min

PART A PRESENT PERFECT

Have students talk about school, sports and leisure activities, possessions, work, and where they live. If needed, provide a general stem such as: *Have you …?* (e.g., *I've played baseball. / My wife and I have lived in the United States since 2012.*).

If necessary, have students review:

4.10 The Past Perfect (Continuous) vs. the Present Perfect (Continuous) (page 120)

4.11 Comparison of Past Tenses (page 123)

PRACTICE IDEA: WRITING

Write these situations on the board: looking back from the present, looking back from the past. Have students choose which situation describes present perfect and provide an example sentence with a timeline illustrating the relationship of events.

PART B PRESENT PERFECT CONTINUOUS

Have students say what they have been learning in this course, using a variety of related verbs, such as *learn, study, practice, read, find out about, discover, listen, work on,* and *write*. Have them include some *for* phrases to show duration (e.g., *I've been learning about travel in the United States. / We've been practicing the present perfect for 2 weeks.*).

If necessary, have students review:

4.10 The Past Perfect (Continuous) vs. the Present Perfect (Continuous) (page 120)

4.11 Comparison of Past Tenses (page 123)

PRACTICE IDEA: SPEAKING

In groups have students talk about recent extracurricular activities and thoughts, basing statements on some of their ideas from Part A if they wish (e.g., *I've been working at a restaurant for about 6 months. / I've been thinking about my apartment. It's noisy and I need to move.*).

PART C SIMPLE PAST

Provide cues from the article on the Lewis and Clark expedition, such as: *St. Louis, 1804, Thomas Jefferson, American Indians, boat/land, Northwest Passage*. Have students make simple past statements about short, long, and repeated actions (e.g., *They left from St. Louis. / It took two and a half years. / They met several American Indian tribes.*).

If necessary, have students review:

4.11 Comparison of Past Tenses (page 123)

PART D PAST CONTINUOUS

Have students describe the sinking of the *Titanic*, relating an act in progress or connecting an act in progress to a single act/event (e.g., *The lifeboats were leaving half-empty. / Survivors heard singing when the ship was going down.*).

If necessary, have students review:

4.1 The Past Continuous—Form (page 103)

4.2 The Past Continuous—Use (pages 104–105)

4.3 The Past Continuous vs. the Simple Past (page 106)

4.11 Comparison of Past Tenses (page 123)

PRESENTATION IDEA: WRITING

Have students skim the reading on page 109 and take notes. Advise them to note ideas only and to avoid copying sentences word for word. Then have them describe the sinking of the *Titanic*.

PART E   PAST PERFECT

Ask students to make statements connecting two past events in the development of passenger airplanes (e.g., *By 1940, airlines had built more comfortable planes. / They didn't like to fly because the air in the planes had made them dizzy. / The DC-3 was the most comfortable plane ever built at that time.*).

If necessary, have students review:

4.4   The Past Perfect—Form (page 110)

4.5   The Past Perfect—Use (Part 1) (page 112)

4.6   *When* with the Simple Past or the Past Perfect (page 114)

4.7   The Past Perfect—Use (Part 2) (page 115)

4.10 The Past Perfect (Continuous) vs. the Present Perfect (Continuous) (page 120)

4.11 Comparison of Past Tenses (page 123)

PRESENTATION IDEA: SPEAKING

Have groups brainstorm events in the reading before students begin speaking.

PART F   PAST PERFECT CONTINUOUS

Have students write about events in the development of air passenger travel, connecting an ongoing event to a simple act/fact/time (e.g., *The airlines had not been serving food. / Before 1938, people had been refusing to fly because they were afraid.*). Have them use information from Part E if they wish.

If necessary, have students review:

4.8   The Past Perfect Continuous—Form (page 117)

4.9   The Past Perfect Continuous—Use (page 118)

4.10 The Past Perfect (Continuous) vs. the Present Perfect (Continuous) (page 120)

4.11 Comparison of Past Tenses (page 123)

TEST/REVIEW

🕐 Time: 15 min

Have students do the exercise on page 129. For additional practice, use the Assessment CD-ROM with *ExamView*® and the Online Workbook.

Answers: 1. 've never; **2.** departed; **3.** 's been flying/has been flying; **4.** Has she arrived; **5.** arrived; **6.** changed; **7.** have you used; **8.** have used; **9.** was traveling; **10.**

used; **11.** went; **12.** had; **13.** missed; **14.** put; **15.** got; **16.** 'd been traveling/had been traveling; **17.** had gotten; **18.** did you do; **19.** told; **20.** did they find; **21.** found; **22.** 'd already been/had already been; **23.** was visiting; **24.** gave; **25.** has just arrived/just arrived; **26.** touched; **27.** 've already downloaded/have already downloaded/already downloaded; **28.** did; **29.** were showing

---

WRITING

PART 1   EDITING ADVICE

🕐 Time: 10–15 min

1. Have students close their books. Write the first few sentences without editing marks or corrections on the board. For example:
    > The plane was arrived at 6:44 a.m.
    > The *Titanic crossing the Atlantic when it hit an iceberg.*

2. Ask students to correct each sentence and provide a rule or an explanation for each correction. This activity can be done individually, in pairs, or as a class.

3. After students have corrected each sentence, tell them to turn to page 130. Say: *Now compare your work with the Editing Advice in the book.* Have students read through all the advice.

PART 2   EDITING PRACTICE

🕐 Time: 10–15 min

1. Tell students they are going to put the Editing Advice into practice. Ask: *Do all the shaded words and phrases have mistakes?* (no) Go over the examples with the class. Then do #1 together.

2. Have students complete the practice individually. Then have them compare answers with a partner before checking answers as a class.

3. For the items students had difficulties with, have them go back and find the relevant grammar chart and review it. Monitor and give help as necessary.

Answers: 1. saw; **2.** C; **3.** 've been/have been; **4.** C; **5.** saw; **6.** had originally planned; **7.** C; **8.** were getting; **9.** 'd never even seen/had never even seen; **10.** had ever been built; **11.** C; **12.** heard; **13.** C; **14.** took; **15.** put; **16.** C; **17.** saw; **18.** C; **19.** became; **20.** had gone; **21.** decided; **22.** died; **23.** was traveling; **24.** C; **25.** C; **26.** When; **27.** C; **28.** waited; **29.** C; **30.** died; **31.** didn't remember/did not remember; **32.** 've been reading/have been reading

PART 3 WRITE ABOUT IT

Time: 30–40 min

1. Review the topics with students before they choose one. Ask: *Which tenses will you most likely use? Why?* Advise students to tell a partner about the topic they have chosen before they write. For the first topic, have students think about the two articles on exploration or transportation they found. Tell them they are going to summarize the articles. Encourage students to organize their thoughts and make notes before they begin to write. Have them brainstorm general and specific information about the key people, events, and times in the articles and how events connect. Remind them to include any useful and relevant vocabulary from this lesson on land, air, or sea travel, and to use their own words. If necessary, write model topic sentences and conclusions on the board first. When students have finished, have them attach the articles to the summary.

2. Repeat the procedure for the second topic. Have students brainstorm a problematic trip they took, thinking of general and specific information on the type of travel, traveling time, accommodations, and connections between events. Then have them write their compositions. If necessary, write model topic sentences and conclusions on the board first.

PART 4 EDIT YOUR WRITING

Time: 15–20 min

Have students edit their writing by reviewing the Lesson Summary on page 128 and the Editing Advice on page 130. Collect for assessment and/or have students share their essays in small groups.

EXPANSION ACTIVITIES

1. Tell students to find articles about the Lewis and Clark expedition. Have them write a summary of one of the articles. Have students share their summaries in groups.

2. Tell students to choose one of the other two readings in this lesson. Have them interview a friend or family member about events, summarize their results, and report them to the class using such stems as *She* or *he said/believed/knew/realized/thought that* ….

5 TECHNOLOGY

GRAMMAR CHARTS

LESSON OPENER

Have students look at the photo and read the caption. Ask: *Where are the men? What are they doing?* Have students read the quotation. Ask: *Do you agree? What might happen if we think like computers?*

Background: During the twentieth century, technology advanced faster than at any other time in history. However, while technology is convenient and necessary, it is also frustrating, invasive, and even addicting. Today about 1.4 billion smartphones are in use, and 600 billion text messages are being sent each month. Nearly 2 billion people are playing video games, and 2 billion are using social media. Psychologists are now recognizing a new computer-related disorder: Internet addiction, which causes impulsiveness, distraction, feeling distant from real people, and the inability to interact face-to-face.

Sydney J. Harris was a journalist for Chicago newspapers for five decades. As a young man, he studied philosophy at the University of Chicago and became friends with Saul Bellow, the Nobel Prize–winning novelist. A newspaper columnist, critic, and essayist, Harris remained concerned throughout his life with questions of morality, ethics, and humanness. He died in 1986.

CONTEXT

This unit is about technology. Students will read about frustrations with technology, the need to balance our use of technology, and one use of technology that has proven to be a nuisance to many people: video surveillance of drivers.

1. Give students a few minutes to look through the lesson. Have them look at the photos and titles. How do they relate to the context?

2. Elicit the topics that will be discussed.

3. Have students discuss what they know about recent technological advances and overdependence on the Internet in pairs or small groups.

GRAMMAR

Students will learn about modals and related expressions.

1. To activate students' prior knowledge, ask what students know about modals and expressions connected to modals.

2. Give several examples of sentences using modals and related expressions (e.g., *I can't change a tire. / Should we go to the party? / May I leave the room, please? / You must not drive over the speed limit.*).

3. Have volunteers give examples. Write the examples on the board.

EXPANDING ON THE CONTEXT

The context for this lesson can be enhanced with the following items:

1. Photos of early telephones and the first computers

2. Timeline showing the speed of recent technological advances

3. Statistics on computer/Internet usage

4. Articles on computer/Internet frustrations from magazines and websites

5. Information about the effects of excessive Internet use on school work and/or social life

Passwords, Passwords, Passwords, page 134

PRE-READING

⏱ Time: 10–20 min

1. Have students look at the photo and read the caption. Ask: *What do you see?* (a lock on a computer) *What does it mean?* (The user cannot access the computer.)
2. Have students read the title, noting the increasing size of the letters. Have students look briefly at the reading. Ask: *What will the reading say about passwords?* Have students make predictions.
3. Pre-teach any essential vocabulary words your students may not know, such as *passwords, frustrating, overwhelmed,* and *bank account.*
4. Ask: *Are passwords frustrating? Why?* Have students discuss in pairs and share their answers with class.

READING GLOSSARY

passwords: secret words used to get into a protected system
frustrating: preventing someone from doing something
overwhelmed: upset too much
bank account: amount of money in a bank that a person adds to or subtracts from

> ### PRESENTATION IDEA
> Before pairs begin their discussions, elicit and write on the board the numerous things they need passwords for, such as websites, apps, and TV service, and examples of security questions they have to answer.

READING

⏱ Time: 10–15 min

After students have read the article, go over the answers to the Comprehension Check on page 135: **1.** T; **2.** F; **3.** F

CONTEXT NOTE

Ask students how they get into password-controlled websites. Ask: *What happens if you forget your password?* Write on the board related vocabulary, such as: *user name, sign in/log in, e-mail address, reset* (password), *codes, CAPTCHA, authentication,* and *password masking* (using asterisks to hide the password as it is typed in).

ADDITIONAL COMPREHENSION QUESTIONS

How can you prevent identity theft? (by changing your password at least once a month) *Why do you click "forgot password"?* (to get a new password) *Can security questions have more than one answer?* (yes)

> ### EXPANDING ON THE READING
> The topic for this reading can be enhanced with the following items:
>
> 1. Troubleshooting list of password problems for PCs or Macs
> 2. Magazine or Web articles on the problems with passwords (e.g., *Forbes, Consumer Reports*)

> ### PRACTICE IDEA: WRITING
> Have students work in pairs to explain in writing how to change a password, including choices of security questions and instructions for what to do if you forget your password. When they are finished, have pairs exchange papers for feedback. Ask a few pairs to share their work with the class. To save time, have students work in groups; split the assignment up and assign different parts to each group.

5.1 Modals—An Overview, page 135

⏱ Time: 10–15 min

1. Have students look at grammar chart **5.1**. Review the examples and explanations in the first section. Check understanding. Ask: *Can modals be singular or plural?* (no) *Do their endings change?* (no) *What are the two rules for modals?* (the base form follows a modal; modals never have an *-s* ending)
2. Review the other three sections of the chart and the sentence patterns. Have students close their books. Write on the board: *I won't change. / I can't change. / I shouldn't change. / I must not change. / It must not be changed.* Direct students' attention to the statement at the top of the chart. Ask: *How do modals change the meaning of the verbs that follow them?* Explain that modals show the ability, possibility, advisability,

necessity, permissibility, or probability of an action (the verb) happening. Ask volunteers to explain the meanings of *change* with the different modals.

PRESENTATION IDEA

Elicit the seven modals at the top of the grammar chart from students; provide any modals that students do not provide. Write the modals on the board. Point to one at random and ask a volunteer to provide a sentence about himself or herself using the modal. Ask students what they can observe or know about the rule for the modal. Assess students' answers, noting areas of difficulty to address later in the lesson. Then review the grammar chart as a class.

EXERCISE 1 pages 135–136 CD 1 TR 27

🕐 Time: 10–15 min

Answers: 1. can't remember; **2.** 'm not able to remember; **3.** have to write; **4.** might forget; **5.** can never remember; **6.** shouldn't write; **7.** can get; **8.** have to pick; **9.** must choose; **10.** 've got to think; **11.** have to log in; **12.** was supposed to make; **13.** may simplify

PRACTICE IDEA: LISTENING

Have students close their books and listen to the audio again. Ask comprehension questions, such as: *What is the first speaker trying to do?* (get into a credit card account) *What is the problem?* (She can't remember the password.) *What's one problem with using the "forgot your password" link?* (have to create completely new password or one not used in the past year) *What's a frustration with online banking?* (website times out) *What happens when a website times out?* (you lose all your information and have to put it back in) Repeat the audio as needed.

PRACTICE IDEA: SPEAKING

Have students act out the conversation in Exercise 1. Encourage actors to imagine the feelings of each character (e.g., annoyance, frustration, disgust) and act them out as they role-play the conversation.

5.2 Possibility: *May, Might, Could,* page 136

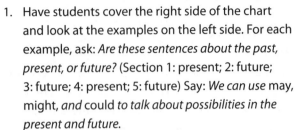

🕐 Time: 10–15 min

1. Have students cover the right side of the chart and look at the examples on the left side. For each example, ask: *Are these sentences about the past, present, or future?* (Section 1: present; 2: future; 3: future; 4: present; 5: future) Say: *We can use* may, might, *and* could *to talk about possibilities in the present and future.*

2. Review the explanations in the chart with students and the Language Note. Ask: *What is the difference in meaning between these two sentences: Maybe my account is locked. / My account may be locked.* (The meaning is basically the same, but *may be* is more formal and the word order changes.)

PRACTICE IDEA: SPEAKING

1. After reviewing the chart, write these questions on the board: *Is the school's name Central High School? / Is your first grade teacher's name Mrs. Jones? / Is Tom's house on Third Street? / Is the car repair expensive? / Is your e-mail account safe?*

2. Say: *These questions have two or three possible answers.* Model a longer answer with three possibilities:
   A: *Is the company legitimate?*
   B: *It might be legitimate, or it might not be legitimate, or it could be legitimate. I don't know.*

3. Have students work in pairs to ask the questions and answer them with two to three possibilities.

ADDITIONAL PRACTICE

Provide several examples of sentences with *maybe* for students to convert to sentences with *may be*, such as: *Maybe it's a scam. / Maybe it isn't true.* (It may be a scam. It may not be true.)

EXERCISE 2 pages 136–137

🕐 Time: 10–15 min

Answers: 1. I might buy; **2.** You may think; **3.** You may want; **4.** You may have; **5.** It might be; **6.** You could be; **7.** I may not remember; **8.** you might steal

5.3 Necessity/Obligation: *Must, Have To, Have Got To,* page 137

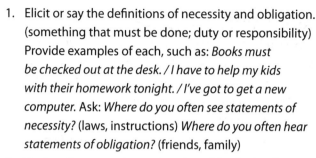

⏱ Time: 5–10 min

1. Elicit or say the definitions of necessity and obligation. (something that must be done; duty or responsibility) Provide examples of each, such as: *Books must be checked out at the desk. / I have to help my kids with their homework tonight. / I've got to get a new computer.* Ask: *Where do you often see statements of necessity?* (laws, instructions) *Where do you often hear statements of obligation?* (friends, family)

2. Review the examples and explanations in the chart with students.

3. Draw students' attention to the Language and Pronunciation Notes and review the examples. Point out that in polite or formal speech, *have to* is pronounced /hæv to/ and *has to* as /hæz to/. As a reminder, elicit situations in which it is important to use polite or formal speech.

4. Have students pronounce the sentences in the chart with both formal and informal pronunciation.

PRACTICE IDEA: SPEAKING

Write on the board these two situations: *1) Job interview for a position with your dream employer for a salary of $250,000 a year; 2) Conversation with your parent/spouse/roommate about household chores.* Have students brainstorm obligations and necessities that the employer or parent/spouse/roommate might bring up. Have students develop and practice a short conversation for each situation. Ask a few pairs to perform their conversations for the class.

EXERCISE 3 page 138

⏱ Time: 10–15 min

Answers: 1. 've got to leave; **2.** have to log on; **3.** have to click; **4.** have to fill out; **5.** 's got to match; **6.** must use; **7.** must have; **8.** 've got to include; **9.** have to remember; **10.** have to do; **11.** 've got to copy; **12.** must be copied; **13.** had to learn; **14.** 've got to meet

EXERCISE 4 page 139

⏱ Time: 5–10 min

Answers will vary.

5.4 Expectation: *Be Supposed To,* page 139

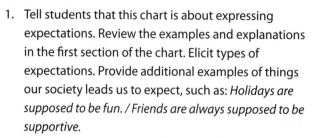

⏱ Time: 5–10 min

1. Tell students that this chart is about expressing expectations. Review the examples and explanations in the first section of the chart. Elicit types of expectations. Provide additional examples of things our society leads us to expect, such as: *Holidays are supposed to be fun. / Friends are always supposed to be supportive.*

2. Review the second section of the chart with students. Elicit additional examples from students of rules they habitually break.

3. Review the fourth section of the chart and elicit from students promises they broke or obligations they did not meet. Stress that *be supposed to* in the past means expectations were not met.

4. Direct students' attention to the Pronunciation Note. Point out that formal pronunciation includes the *d* and pronounces the *-ed* ending as /zd/.

PRESENTATION IDEA

Introduce *be supposed to* by telling students three things students or staff at your school are supposed to do (e.g., *Students are supposed to keep their phones turned off.*). Say: *Be supposed to is used to express expectations.* Elicit or say that expectations are what we think people should do. Ask: *Do students always keep their phones off in school?* (no) *We use* be supposed to *to show that our expectations may not be met or were not met.*

ADDITIONAL PRACTICE

1. Brainstorm and write examples on the board of things that have rules and instructions to follow, such as: *putting furniture together, installing a printer, eating or packaging foods, taking medicine.* After students have reviewed the chart, have them identify rules and guidelines for things that they sometimes break.

2. Write these sentences on the board and have students identify the use of *be supposed to* in each sentence:

   a. *I was supposed to clean house yesterday.* (obligation not met)

   b. *Love is supposed to make you happy.* (something we are told to expect)

c. *Dogs are supposed to obey their masters.* (something we are told to expect)

d. *You're supposed to open a letter with a salutation such as "Dear Mr. Smith," not with "Hello!"* (requirement)

e. *Jenny is supposed to do dishes this evening.* (personal obligation)

EXERCISE 5 pages 139–140

🕐 Time: 5–10 min

Answers: 1. 're supposed to read; **2.** is supposed to make; **3.** 're supposed to copy; **4.** 're supposed to pay; **5.** 'm supposed to memorize; **6.** aren't supposed to text; **7.** is supposed to send; **8.** was supposed to use; **9.** aren't supposed to open; **10.** 'm supposed to help; **11.** were supposed to meet

---

PRACTICE IDEAS: SPEAKING

1. Have students discuss in small groups obligations they have now at work or school. Remind students to use *must* for rules that cannot be broken without punishment.

EXERCISE 6 page 140

🕐 Time: 10–15 min

Answers will vary.

EXERCISE 7 page 140

🕐 Time: 5–10 min

Answers will vary.

5.5 Advice: *Should, Ought To, Had Better,* page 141

🕐 Time: 10–15 min

1. Have students close their books. Ask review questions about the reading. Ask: *What do experts say to do to prevent identity theft?* (change our password at least once a month) *What modal did experts use to give us their advice?* (should) Provide other examples of advice (e.g., *You should lock your doors at night. / People shouldn't give out their Social Security numbers.*). Elicit additional examples from students and write them on the board. Elicit or present *ought to* and *had better.* Say: *If something is a good idea, we can say that it's advisable. When we suggest rules to follow or things*

other people should, ought to, or had better do, that's advice.

2. Review each section of the chart with the class and the Language Note. Point out that the contraction *'d* in *had better* is only omitted in speech, not in writing.

ADDITIONAL PRACTICE

Have students close their books. Write these sentences on the board and have students work in pairs to correct them. For sentences that are correct, have them write a *C*.

1. *We ought had to leave the library now.* (ought to)

2. *You shouldn't talk so loudly in class.* (C)

3. *You better not stay up too late.* (C in speech; *had better* or *'d better* in writing)

4. *Really, you ought be more careful!* (ought to)

EXERCISE 8 page 141 ⭐

🕐 Time: 10–15 min

Answers will vary.

EXERCISE 9 pages 142–143

🕐 Time: 10–15 min

Answers: 1. a. Should I buy, **b.** I should give, **c.** he shouldn't play, **d.** He ought to play; **2. a.** You ought to protect, **b.** You shouldn't make, **c.** You'd better be, **d.** I'd better do, **e.** You'd better not use; **3. a.** should I do, **b.** You ought to set up, **c.** You should choose, **d.** 'd better choose

---

PRACTICE IDEAS: SPEAKING

1. Have students work in pairs and practice the conversations from Exercise 9. When students are finished, have several pairs perform their conversations for the class.

EXERCISE 10 page 143

🕐 Time: 10–15 min

Answers: 1. 'd better not; **2.** 've got to; **3.** 're supposed to; **4.** do I have to; **5.** have to; **6.** should; **7.** ought to/should; **8.** had to; **9.** must; **10.** should; **11. a.** is supposed to, **b.** is supposed to; **12.** 've got to

EXERCISE 11 page 144

🕐 Time: 5–10 min

Answers will vary.

5.6 Suggestion: *Can/Could,*
page 144

⏱ Time: 10–15 min

1. Tell students that *can* and *could* are mild modals. Review the explanations and examples in the chart. To help students understand the use of *can/could* to give suggestions, make additional comparisons with *should*. Say: Should *can be strong. It can even be impolite.* Could *is milder. It does not tell someone what to do.*

2. Write these pairs of sentences on the board: *You should be here on time. / You could be here on time. / You should act like an adult. / You could act like an adult.* Elicit the differences in meaning between *should* and *could.* (strong advice versus suggestion)

3. Ask students to make suggestions using the examples in the chart as models.

PRACTICE IDEA: SPEAKING

Divide the class into small groups. Have each group brainstorm a conversation using suggestions and advice for a grandparent on how to open up an account on a website. When they are finished, have each group perform their conversation for the class. Have other groups provide feedback.

EXERCISE 12 page 144

⏱ Time: 10–15 min
Answers will vary.

READING

Taking a Break From Technology, page 145

PRE-READING

⏱ Time: 10–15 min

1. Have students look at the photo and read the caption. Ask: *Where is the young woman?* (by a lake, in the mountains) *What is she doing?* (yoga)

2. Have students read the title and skim the reading. Ask: *What is the reading about? What is the main idea?* Have students make predictions.

3. Pre-teach any vocabulary words your students may not know, such as *grounded, devices, unplug, control,* and *balance.*

4. Activate students' prior knowledge about getting away from technology. Ask: *Do you ever need to get away from your phone and computer? What do you do?* Have students discuss the questions in pairs and share their answers with the class.

READING GLOSSARY

grounded: sensible; having a good grasp on reality
devices: electrical machines, such as smartphones or tablets
to unplug: to disconnect from technology
control: power to (not) do or say something
balance: equal strength or weight

EXPANDING ON THE READING

The topic for this reading can be enhanced with the following items:

1. Video clips on texting addiction
2. Online articles on Internet and gaming addiction

READING 🎧 CD 1 TR 28

⏱ Time: 10–15 min
After students have read the article, go over the answers to the Comprehension Check on page 146: **1.** F; **2.** F; **3.** T

ADDITIONAL COMPREHENSION QUESTIONS

Who is Levi Felix? (founder of Camp Grounded) *Where is Camp Grounded?* (California) *What is the purpose of the summer camp?* (to unplug from technology) *What kind of activities do people do at the camp?* (swim, hike, take yoga classes, enjoy nature) *Why do people go to Camp Grounded?* (because they can't stop using technology)

PRACTICE IDEA: LISTENING

After students listen to the audio, have them listen to the audio again. With books closed, have students write all the modal phrases they hear. Then have them answer these questions: *What is it campers must not do? Are not able to do? May not do? Are not permitted to do? Can't control?* Repeat the audio if necessary.

5.7 Negative Modals, page 146

🕐 Time: 5–10 min

1. Review the examples and explanations in grammar chart **5.7** carefully and then review them again. On the second review, ask volunteers to provide a sentence for each section (e.g., *Small children must not ride in the front seat of a car.*)

2. Draw students' attention to the Language Notes. Point out the difference in meaning between *don't have to* and *must not* and between *shouldn't* and *don't have to*. Provide additional examples (e.g., *You must not eat on the subway. / We don't have to take the subway; we can walk. / You shouldn't leave your computer in the classroom during breaks. / You don't have to bring a computer to class.*).

PRESENTATION IDEA

Have students cover grammar chart **5.7**. Write the negative modals (*must not, be not supposed to, cannot, may not, should not, do not have to*) on the board. Read the meanings in grammar chart **5.7** in random order. Ask students to match each meaning with a modal, e.g., *Which one means it's a bad idea, or is not advisable?* (should not) When the class is finished, begin the review of the chart.

EXERCISE 13 pages 146–147

🕐 Time: 5–10 min

Answers: 1. may not; **2.** cannot; **3.** shouldn't; **4.** are not allowed to; **5.** aren't supposed to; **6.** must not/may not; **7.** don't have to; **8.** don't have to; **9.** may not

---

PRACTICE IDEA: SPEAKING

Have students work in pairs to discuss their own ability to unplug from technology, and the rules and regulations about technology that they are supposed to abide by at home, at school, at work, or another place.

EXERCISE 14 page 147

🕐 Time: 10–15 min

Answers: 1. shouldn't; **2.** can; **3.** can't; **4.** may not/might not; **5.** shouldn't; **6.** should; **7.** could/can; **8.** don't have to; **9.** don't have to; **10.** shouldn't; **11.** can't; **12.** have to; **13.** can't; **14.** have to/'ve got to

---

EXERCISE 15 page 147

🕐 Time: 5–10 min

Answers will vary.

READING

Using Technology to Enforce the Law

PRE-READING

🕐 Time: 5–10 min

1. Have students look at the photo and read the caption. Ask: *What do you see?* (a red light with a photo camera) *What is happening?* (A camera is watching traffic.)

2. Have students look briefly at the reading. Ask: *What is the reading about? How do you know?* Have students use the title and photo to make predictions.

3. Pre-teach any vocabulary words your students may not know, such as *enforce, intersection, officials,* and *collisions.*

4. Activate students' prior knowledge about technology in law enforcement. Ask: *Have you ever noticed cameras at traffic lights? What other kinds of technology does law enforcement use?* Have students discuss the questions in pairs. Try to pair students of the same culture. Have a few pairs share their answers with the class.

READING GLOSSARY

to enforce: to make people obey

intersection: crossing of roads

officials: people who work for the government or other organizations

collision: a crash

EXPANDING ON THE READING

The topic for this reading can be enhanced with the following items:

1. Lists of technology used in law enforcement (e.g., voice response translators, video surveillance)
2. Articles on technology in law enforcement and pros and cons
3. News stories on backlash against traffic cameras (e.g., at www.npr.org)

READING CD 1 TR 29

🕙 Time: 10–15 min

After students have read the article, go over the answers to the Comprehension Check on page 149: **1.** F; **2.** T; **3.** F

ADDITIONAL COMPREHENSION QUESTIONS

Where are photo-enforced red lights put? (busy intersections) *How do cities decide where to put a camera?* (They study intersections with the most serious accidents.) *What are three reasons some people do not like this technology?* (It's a nuisance; it's just a way for the government to make money; the government shouldn't have so much information about us.)

PRACTICE IDEA: LISTENING AND SPEAKING

Have students listen to the audio alone and then retell the main points of the article to a partner. Repeat the audio if necessary. Have students open their books, read along as they listen to the audio, and check their versions of the article.

PRACTICE IDEA: SPEAKING

Have students describe their experiences with traffic cameras or other types of technology used in law enforcement in the United States or other countries. Have them discuss the issue in small groups. When groups are finished, ask a few volunteers to share their experiences with the class.

5.8 Ability/Possibility: *Can, Be Able To,* page 149 ⭐

🕙 Time: 5–10 min

1. Tell students this chart is about modals of ability or possibility. Have students review the example sentences and explanations in the chart.

2. To help students understand the uses of *could,* contrast the uses that have been presented. Write on the board: *a) I couldn't go to Paris last month. b) You could get a speeding ticket. c) He could lift 100 pounds when he was a teenager.* Say: *Which sentences are about ability?* (a and c) *Why?* (because they express what somebody wasn't able to do and used to be able to do)

3. Direct students' attention to the use of *be able to* in the past for affirmative past statements about a single action. Provide additional examples and have students choose the sentences that are correct; e.g., *a) Siri was able to get her car this morning. b) We could go after the show was over. c) He can't stop, and we ran through a red light.)* Say: *The modals* can/could/be able to *express ability, but in some of these sentences they are used incorrectly. Why?* (b is incorrect because for a past single action you must use *be able to*; c is incorrect because *can* is in the present tense.)

4. Review the Pronunciation Note. Give additional examples to help students discriminate *can* and *can't* in sentences (e.g., *You can take that book. / She can't go to the movies.*). Have students write the word they hear.

PRACTICE IDEA: SPEAKING

1. Have students close their books. Write on the board several verb phrases with *can, could,* and *be able to,* mixing present/past and negative/affirmative (e.g., *couldn't watch, was able to go through, can't hear, were able to speak to, couldn't drive, am able to run, could see*).

2. Have students make a pair of sentences for each phrase. The pair should include the modal sentence, a context sentence, and a time phrase to clearly show past or present time (e.g., *I couldn't watch TV last night; the power went out. I was able to go through the intersection this morning; the light was green.*). Have students share their work in small groups for feedback.

3. When groups are finished, ask each student to share a pair of *could/be able* to sentences with the class.

EXERCISE 16 pages 149–150

🕐 Time: 5–10 min

Answers: 1. can do; **2.** Are you able to keep; **3.** are able to read; **4.** can change; **5.** can eat; **6.** are able to reach; **7.** can talk; **8.** can look at; **9.** couldn't answer

5.9 Logical Conclusion: *Must,* page 150

🕐 Time: 10–15 min

1. On the board, write a few sentence pairs with *must*: *It is 6:00; Dad must be coming home. / I hear thunder; it must be raining. / The phone died; the battery must be dead.*

2. Ask: *How is* must *used in these sentences? Does it mean* have to? (No, it shows something we decide is probably true.) Say: *The modal* must *is also used to express logical conclusions.* Elicit or explain what a logical conclusion is. (an opinion or judgment based on reasoning) Have students identify the conclusion and reasoning in each pair of sentences.

3. Review the examples and explanations in the grammar chart with the class. Ask volunteers to give example sentences for each use of *must* to make a conclusion based on observation and to make an estimate.

🕐 Time: 10–15 min

Possible answers: 1. a. feel; **2. a.** get; **3. a.** know; **4. a.** send, **b.** like; **5. a.** have, **b.** be; **6. a.** know; **7. a.** love/like; **8. a.** be, **b.** have; **9. a.** know

5.10 Probability vs. Possibility: *Must* vs. *May, Might, Could,* page 152

🕐 Time: 10–15 min

On the board, write situations that contrast *could* (possibility) and *must* (probability). For example, write:

1. *A: Where's Ana?*
   B: I don't know. She could be at work.

2. *A: Where's Ana?*
   B: It's only 4:00. She must be at work.

Say: *Which one shows that Ana is probably at work?* (2) *Which one shows that it's possible that Ana is at work?* (1) *How do you know?* (Because probability means very likely; i.e., Ana is always at work at 4:00. It's 4:00 now, therefore it's very likely she is at work. Possibility means maybe and expresses uncertainty; i.e., If you don't know where Ana is, you are not sure.)

1. Have students look at the grammar chart. Review the example sentences and explanations.

2. Elicit examples of *must* versus *may, might, could* sentences from the class and give feedback.

PRACTICE IDEA: WRITING

Bring in magazine pictures showing people whose situation or emotions students can conclude from the picture. Be sure that the images only include the person and exclude text. Have students work in groups to write statements about the people and their conclusions (e.g., *She is holding her stomach. She must have a stomachache.*).

EXERCISE 18 pages 152–153

🕐 Time: 10–15 min

Answers will vary.

CONTEXT NOTE

Ask students if drivers have vanity plates in their countries and if so, what kinds. Ask: *What are the topics of the vanity plates?* Have students discuss in small groups and share their answers with the class.

EXERCISE 19 pages 153–154

🕐 Time: 10–15 min

Answers: 1. a. couldn't, **b.** do you have to, **c.** must; **2. a.** couldn't, **b.** had to, **c.** 've got to, **d.** 're supposed to; **3. a.** is supposed to, **b.** can't, **c.** must, **d.** should, **e.** must, **f.** is able to, **g.** might; **4. a.** were supposed to; **5. a.** can't, **b.** must; **6. a.** don't have to, **b.** could, **c.** can, **d.** must; **7. a.** 'm supposed to; **8. a.** 'd better, **b.** should; **9. a.** might, **b.** don't have to

5.11 Continuous Modals,
page 154

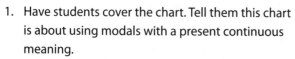

🕐 Time: 5–10 min

1. Have students cover the chart. Tell them this chart is about using modals with a present continuous meaning.

2. Activate students' prior knowledge of continuous tense forms. Ask: *How do you predict modals are formed in a continuous tense?* (modal + *be* + present participle) Tell them to write their answers on a piece of paper.

3. Say: *We can use modals to express what is happening now.* Review the examples and explanation in the chart with students. Give one or two additional examples, such as: *You shouldn't be looking at your book right now. You should be looking at the board.* Have them check their predictions and report the results.

> **PRACTICE IDEA: SPEAKING**
>
> Ask: *What do you think your husband/child/ roommate is doing right now? What is he or she supposed to be doing right now?* Have students work in pairs and tell partners their conclusions.

EXERCISE 20 page 155

🕐 Time: 10–15 min

Answers: 1. a. might be taking, **b.** could be charging; **2. a.** must be making, **b.** might be preventing; **3. a.** shouldn't be texting; **4. a.** should be slowing down; **5. a.** must be talking; **6. a.** shouldn't be using; **7. a.** should be reading

🕐 Time: 20–30 min

PART A NECESSITY/OBLIGATION AND EXPECTATION

Before looking at the first three rows of the summary chart, have students make statements about necessity/ obligation and expectation based on information from the readings (e.g., *You must not go through red lights. / I've got to be careful when I drive through intersections. / At Camp Grounded, you're supposed to leave your devices at home.*).

If necessary, have students review:

5.1 Modals—An Overview (page 135)

5.3 Necessity/Obligation: *Must, Have To, Have Got To* (page 137)

5.4 Expectation: *Be Supposed To* (page 139)

> **PRACTICE IDEA: WRITING**
>
> Have students list necessary duties, obligations, and tasks they are expected to fulfill, as well as societal or cultural expectations (e.g., *I have to study every night. / People are supposed to marry in their early twenties.*).

PART B ADVISABILITY AND WARNING

To review the fourth and fifth rows of the chart, ask students to give advice and warnings about using the Internet, opening online accounts, and using passwords (e.g., *You ought to include numbers and capital letters in your password. / You shouldn't write your passwords down; someone will see them.*).

If necessary, have students review:

5.1 Modals—An Overview (page 135)

5.5 Advice: *Should, Ought to, Had Better* (page 141)

> **PRACTICE IDEA: SPEAKING**
>
> Have students discuss in small groups advice and warnings their family and friends gave them when they came to the United States.

PART C PERMISSION

Ask students to discuss what is and isn't permitted to do at camps that help people disconnect from their devices (e.g., *You're not allowed to use your devices. / You can do yoga. / Campers aren't permitted to give their real names.*).

If necessary, have students review:

5.1 Modals—An Overview (page 135)

5.7 Negative Modals (page 146)

PRACTICE IDEA: WRITING AND SPEAKING

Divide students into pairs. Have students write what is/isn't allowed in their neighborhoods and/or country (e.g., *You're not allowed to throw trash on the ground in the parks. / We can't drive over 40 kilometers an hour.*). Have them tell their partners about these things, trying not to look at their list. When they are finished, have partners exchange papers for feedback on their grammar.

PART D ABILITY/INABILITY AND POSSIBILITY

Gather examples of sentences of ability/inability and possibility from the readings and charts in the lesson. Read sentences at random; for example, say: *You might be asked your mother's maiden name.* Ask students to say what the modal in each sentence means. (possibility)

If necessary, have students review:

5.2 Possibility: *May, Might, Could* (page 136)

5.8 Ability/Possibility: *Can, Be Able To* (page 149)

5.10 Probability vs. Possibility: *Must* vs. *May, Might, Could* (page 152)

PRACTICE IDEA: SPEAKING

Write situations such as the following on the board with the degree of probability in parentheses next to them: *pass the driving test (don't know); make good grades (very likely), like pizza (very likely); use social media (not sure); think the light was green (possible but no evidence); text every day (very likely).* Have students work in pairs and make statements about each situation, including a context statement (e.g., *You must like pizza; you get it every night. / You might think the light was green, but it was red.*).

PART E SUGGESTIONS

Provide cues to have students develop short conversations that include a suggestion, such as *pass test, have headache, miss my mom's dog, have too much work, want to relax, love sports.* Model a conversation, such as *A: My father may not pass his driving test. B: You could help him practice driving.*

If necessary, have students review:

5.6 Suggestion: *Can/Could* (page 144)

PART F LOGICAL CONCLUSION ABOUT THE PRESENT

To review the last row of the chart, distribute a variety of photos from magazines and have students draw conclusions about the content (e.g., *This must be in a northern area. Look at the snow!*). If needed, narrow the topic content to encourage students to draw more logical conclusions.

If necessary, have students review:

5.9 Logical Conclusion: *Must* (page 150)

TEST/REVIEW

⏱ Time: 15 min

Have students do the exercise on page 157. For additional practice, use the Assessment CD-ROM with Exam*View*® and the Online Workbook.

Answers: 1. a. can, **b.** could; **2. a.** can't; **3. a.** have/'ve got, **b.** am I supposed to; **4. a.** don't have to, **b.** can; **5. a.** can; **6. a.** don't have to; **7. a.** ought to/should; **8.** 'm supposed to; **9. a.** can; **10. a.** can; **11. a.** must, **b.** was supposed to; **12.** a. should; **13. a.** must/have to, **b.** can't

---

WRITING

PART 1 EDITING ADVICE

⏱ Time: 10–15 min

1. Have students close their books. Write the first few sentences without editing marks or corrections on the board. For example:

   You should to drive more carefully.
   You are suppose to stop at a red light.

2. Ask students to correct each sentence and provide a rule or an explanation for each correction. This activity can be done individually, in pairs, or as a class.

3. After students have corrected each sentence, tell them to turn to page 158. Say: *Now compare your work with the Editing Advice in the book.* Have students read through all the advice.

PART 2 EDITING PRACTICE

🕐 Time: 10–15 min

1. Tell students they are going to put the Editing Advice into practice. Ask: *Do all the shaded words and phrases have mistakes?* (no) Go over the examples with the class. Then do #1 together.

2. Have students complete the practice individually. Then have them compare answers with a partner before checking answers as a class.

3. For the items students had difficulties with, have them go back and find the relevant grammar chart and review it. Monitor and give help as necessary.

Answers: 1. should play; **2.** C; **3.** must spend; **4.** C; **5.** 'd better/had better; **6.** can we do; **7.** are supposed to; **8.** be able to; **9.** C; **10.** 's not permitted to/isn't permitted to/is not permitted to; **11.** 's got to/has got to/has to; **12.** allowed; **13.** C; **14.** can't I; **15.** C; **16.** 've got to/have got to/have to

PART 3 WRITE ABOUT IT

🕐 Time: 30–40 min

1. Review the topic with students before they choose a device. Ask: *Which modals will you most likely use? Why?* Brainstorm everyday technology. Have students say the advantages and disadvantages of each device. List all examples and ideas on the board. Have students choose one device and help you begin writing a paragraph on the board, describing its advantages and disadvantages. Have students choose a device to write about. Encourage students to organize their thoughts and make notes before they begin to write.

2. Ask students to think about the time they or others they know spend on social media, texting, or other computer- or Internet-related activities. Tell them to analyze the effects, deciding how good or bad they are, and things they should and shouldn't do. Tell students to take a position (yes or no) and write their compositions, stating their position clearly and the reasons for it.

PART 4 EDIT YOUR WRITING

🕐 Time: 15–20 min

Have students edit their writing by reviewing the Lesson Summary on page 156 and the Editing Advice on page 158. Collect for assessment and/or have students share their essays in small groups.

EXPANSION ACTIVITIES

1. Tell students to check the costs of hi-tech TVs in stores to find out how much one costs to own and use. Have students report the information they get to the class. Ask: *Do you have a hi-tech TV? Do you think everyone should have one?*

2. Tell students to think of a product they bought. Have them report to the class what it was supposed to do, what you expected it to do, and what it actually did. Ask: *Would you buy it again? Why or why not?*

3. Tell students to make a copy of their apartment lease, if they have one, and circle all the modals. Have students bring the copies to class and work in groups to compare the modals they find in their leases. Pair students who have leases with those who don't.

6 U.S. PRESIDENTS AND ELECTIONS

GRAMMAR CHARTS

6.1 Modals in the Past—Form (page 165)

6.2 Past Regrets or Mistakes—*Should Have* (page 164)

6.3 Past Possibility—*May/Might/Could + Have* (page 165)

6.4 Logical Conclusion about the Past—*Must Have* (page 167)

6.5 Past Direction Not Taken—*Could Have* (page 170)

6.6. *Must Have* + Past Participle vs. *Had to* + Base Form (page 173)

6.7 Ability and Possibility in the Past (page 174)

6.8 Modals in the Past: Continuous Forms (page 175)

LESSON OPENER

Have students look at the photo and read the caption. Ask: *What do you see in the photo? Where is the carving?* Have students read the quotation. Ask: *Do you agree with the quote?*

Background: The Mount Rushmore National Memorial was a tourism project conceived by a North Dakota historian. The monument covers about 2 square acres and features 60-foot (18- meter) carved busts of 4 of the most influential U.S. presidents: George Washington, Thomas Jefferson, Abraham Lincoln, and Theodore Roosevelt. It was carved by Danish-American Gutzon Borglum and his son Lincoln between 1927 and 1941. The project was a success. More than two million people visited Mount Rushmore in 2014. The memorial has become an American icon and a symbol of presidential leadership and strength.

Abraham Lincoln was the sixteenth president of the United States (1861–1865). Lincoln served during a time of a violent civil war that left 620,000 dead and tore the country apart. Lincoln is loved and respected by Americans, who admire him for holding the country together and for his firm belief in equality for all that changed the path of the nation.

CONTEXT

This unit is about U.S. presidents and elections. Students will read about the Gettysburg Address, the Cuban missile crisis, and the influence of media in presidential elections in the 1960s and today.

1. Give students a few minutes to look through the lesson. Have them look at the photos and titles. How do they relate to the context?
2. Elicit the topics that will be discussed.
3. Have students discuss what they know about U.S. presidents and the media and elections.

GRAMMAR

Students will learn about modals in the past.

1. To activate students' prior knowledge, have students identify modals they have learned. Elicit their ideas or predictions about modals in the past.
2. Give several examples of sentences with modals in the past (e.g., *She should have won the election. / The war shouldn't have lasted so long. / The city could have been destroyed by the storm. / It must have been impossible to stay warm.*).
3. Have volunteers give additional examples. Write the examples on the board.

EXPANDING ON THE CONTEXT

The context for this lesson can be enhanced with the following items:

1. Video mini-biographies of Roosevelt, Jefferson, and Washington
2. Milestones in media and politics
3. Lists of ways media is used in modern U.S. elections
4. Articles on the global use of social media for elections
5. Letters to a newspaper or online advice column with answers using *should have (been), could have (been),* etc.

Lincoln and the Gettysburg Address, page 162

PRE-READING

 Time: 10–20 min

1. Have students look at the illustration and read the caption. Ask: *Who is the man?* (Abraham Lincoln) *What's he doing?* (giving a speech)

2. Have students read the title and look briefly at the reading. Ask: *What is the reading about?* Have students make predictions.

3. Pre-teach any essential vocabulary words your students may not know, such as *slaves, doubts, opponents,* and *dedicated.*

4. Ask: *What is a civil war?* (a war between people within a nation) Elicit students' ideas. Discuss as a class what students know about the American Civil War.

READING GLOSSARY

slaves: people owned by someone who makes them work for no money

doubts: uncertainty, lack of sureness

opponents: people who take the opposite side in a fight, game, contest, etc.

dedicated: given completely

READING CD 1 TR 30

Time: 10–15 min

After students have read the article, go over the answers to the Comprehension Check on page 163: **1.** T; **2.** T; **3.** F

CONTEXT NOTES

1. The Battle of Gettysburg shocked the country and people around the world. The death toll rose to 51,000, the highest in the war which, by today's standards, cost a total of 6 million lives. Some historians believe that the high numbers were caused by new technology combined with outdated war strategy.

2. Students may come across the beginning of the Gettysburg Address in numerous contexts in U.S. culture. These opening words are famous and frequently alluded to: *Four score and seven years ago [our fathers brought forth on this continent a new nation conceived in Liberty, and dedicated to the proposition that all men are created equal ….]*

3. Lincoln had not been feeling well before he gave the Gettysburg Address and looked very ill after he gave it. He was soon diagnosed with smallpox.

ADDITIONAL COMPREHENSION QUESTIONS

Why did southern farmers want to keep slaves? (They needed them to be prosperous.) *Who doubted Lincoln's abilities before the election?* (many people) *How long had Lincoln attended school?* (18 months) *Who also gave a speech at Gettysburg?* (Edward Everett) *How long did Lincoln's speech last?* (2 minutes)

EXPANDING ON THE READING

The topic for this reading can be enhanced with the following items:

1. Video mini-biography of Abraham Lincoln
2. Maps showing the division of states across the Union
3. Interactive maps showing battles of the Civil War
4. Photo of the president of the Confederacy, Jefferson Davis

PRACTICE IDEA: LISTENING

Have students first listen to the audio alone. Ask a few comprehension questions (e.g., *What year did Lincoln win the election?* (1860) *What happened after the election?* (The Civil War began.) *When did the Civil War end?* (April 9, 1865) Repeat the audio if necessary. Then have students open their books and read along as they listen to the audio.

6.1 Modals in the Past— Form, page 163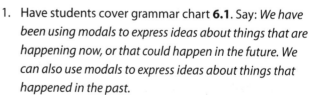

Time: 10–15 min

1. Have students cover grammar chart **6.1**. Say: *We have been using modals to express ideas about things that are happening now, or that could happen in the future. We can also use modals to express ideas about things that happened in the past.*

2. Have students review the example sentences in the chart. Ask students to say what they observe about the rules for using modals in the past. If needed, say:

To use modals in the past, we add have *for the active voice and* have been *for the passive voice plus the past participle.*

EXERCISE 1 pages 163–164
🕐 Time: 10–15 min

Answers: 1. a. should have read, **b.** must have learned; **2. a.** could have lasted, **b.** shouldn't have used, **c.** couldn't have gotten; **3. a.** must have been, **b.** must not have paid, **c.** should have paid; **4. a.** must have written, **b.** might have been; **5. a.** could have used, **b.** should have asked

---

PRACTICE IDEA: SPEAKING

Have students model a conversation from Exercise 1. For example, ask: *Why do you think Lincoln's speech was only 2 minutes?* Have students discuss in small pairs using Conversation 4 as a model. Have a few students share their conversations with the class.

6.2 Past Regrets or Mistakes— *Should Have*, page 164

🕐 Time: 5–10 min

1. Tell students that *should have* is used to express regret. Ask: What is *regret*? (sadness at a mistake or event, a feeling that you wish you had done something differently) Elicit from students things we regret (e.g., a bad mistake, a fight or argument, not doing something, an accident, saying something inappropriate or incorrectly). Say: *These are situations in which you might use* should have.

2. Review the examples and explanations in the chart. Ask: *What did Lincoln regret?* (the brevity of his speech)

CONTEXT NOTES

1. The phrase *second guessing* is used to refer to the criticism of someone else's actions after the fact (e.g., *I knew this would happen. You should have bought more pizza.*). Saying *I told you so* after someone makes a mistake is also second guessing. Second guessing is usually not socially appropriate unless the people involved know each other well or are not taking the conversation too seriously.

2. Note to students that *should have* is also used as a polite way of thanking someone for a gift or act of kindness, especially for something which may not always require formal thanks. Model this conversation: *A: You helped me pass this course; you were a lifesaver. Here's something just to show my appreciation. B: You shouldn't have [done that]. That's very thoughtful.*

EXERCISE 2 pages 164–165
🕐 Time: 10–15 min

Answers: 1. a. have seen, **b.** have told, **c.** have written; **2. a.** have watched, **b.** have paid; **3. a.** have voted, **b.** have given; **4. a.** have shortened, **b.** have helped; **5. a.** have used, **b.** have paid

---

PRACTICE IDEA: SPEAKING AND WRITING

Have students work in groups. Assign one of the conversations from Exercise 2 to each group. Ask groups to brainstorm ideas about the people in the conversation and their relationship, based on the way they address one another and the way they comment on one another's past mistakes. Ask groups to write a short description of the people and their relationship. Collect and redistribute the descriptions. Have each group guess which conversation matches the description they have been given.

6.3 Past Possibility—*May/ Might/Could + Have*, page 165

🕐 Time: 5–10 min

1. Have students close their books. Elicit modals they know that express possibility (*may, might could*) and write them on the board. Ask: *What is the difference in meaning between these modals?* (not much) Ask students for example sentences for each one. Elicit students' ideas of how these modals could be used in the past. (modal [+ *not*] + *have* + past participle)

2. Review the examples and explanations in the chart. Point out that *could not have* is not used to express past possibility but instead expresses past impossibility or disbelief (e.g., *He couldn't have seen her because she was at home that day.*).

ADDITIONAL PRACTICE

Write a list of base verbs on the board (e.g., *go, tell, fly, travel, elect, give, drive, sign on, change,* and *know*). Have students work alone and write forms of the verbs to show past possibility. Have students exchange lists with a partner for feedback. Review the correct forms as a class and write them on the board.

PRACTICE IDEA: SPEAKING

Ask students to recall a historical event from the distant past and speculate on possibilities: what people might have thought, what their expectations might have been, how they could have felt, etc. Brainstorm a few ideas with students and write them on the board. Have students retell the event to a partner. Ask volunteers to share their events with the class.

EXERCISE 3 page 166

⏲ Time: 5–10 min

Answers: 1. have learned; **2.** not have heard; **3.** not have been; **4.** have been; **5.** not have planned/not have been planning; **6.** have written; **7.** have written; **8.** have stabbed; **9.** have been

6.4 Logical Conclusion about the Past —*Must Have,*
page 167

⏲ Time: 5–10 min

1. Have students close their books. Elicit from the class the modal that expresses high probability. (*must*) Have students predict the form of *must* in past sentences. (*must + have +* past participle)

2. Ask: *How would I express this situation: I saw a woman on the subway. I'm almost certain it was my college roommate.* (It must have been my college roommate. OR, The woman on the subway must have been my college roommate.)

3. Have students review the example sentences and explanations in the chart.

ADDITIONAL PRACTICE

Bring in several photos from magazines of famous celebrities and public figures. Hold each one up and display it for just a few seconds; then put it face down on your desk. Ask: *Who was that?* Have students speculate using *could/might/must have been.*

EXERCISE 4 pages 167–168

⏲ Time: 5–10 min

Possible answers: 1. a. have been, **b.** have liked; **2. a.** have entered, **b.** have planned/have been planning, **c.** have had; **3. a.** have felt, **b.** have felt; **4. a.** have had, **b.** have been; **5. a.** have heard, **b.** have been, **c.** have been, **d.** have been; **6. a.** have been; **7. a.** have come; **b.** have fallen

---

READING

The Cuban Missile Crisis, page 169

PRE-READING

⏲ Time: 10–15 min

1. Have students look at the photo and read the caption. Ask: *Who is in the photo?* (President Kennedy) *What is he doing?* (signing an important order/paper)

2. Have students look at the title and skim the reading. Ask: *What does the reading say about the Cuban missile crisis? What is the main idea?* Have students make predictions.

3. Pre-teach any vocabulary words your students may not know, such as *crisis, nuclear, missiles,* and *weapons.*

4. Activate students' prior knowledge about border threats. Ask: *Why are countries concerned with their borders?* (They fear invasion or attack.) Have students discuss the question in pairs. Try to pair students from the same cultural background. Ask a few students to share their ideas with the class.

READING GLOSSARY

crisis: an emergency
nuclear: related to the production of atomic energy
missiles: cigar-shaped rockets with explosives
weapons: tools used to harm or kill

EXPANDING ON THE READING

The topic for this reading can be enhanced with the following items:

1. Mini-biography video of President John Kennedy
2. Map showing Cuba and its proximity to Florida
3. Photo of Fidel Castro
4. Timeline of the Cuban Missile Crisis
5. News footage video of President Kennedy's announcement of the end of the crisis

READING CD 1 TR 32

🕐 Time: 10–15 min

After students have read the article, go over the answers to the Comprehension Check on page 170: **1.** T; **2.** F; **3.** T

ADDITIONAL COMPREHENSION QUESTIONS

When did the crisis begin? (October 1962) *What country sent ships with nuclear missiles to Cuba?* (the Soviet Union) *Why did President Kennedy send the Navy to meet the ships?* (to block them from delivering the weapons) *What solved the crisis?* (diplomacy)

6.5 Past Direction Not Taken— *Could Have,* page 170

🕐 Time: 10–15 min

1. Provide an example of a past goal and a path not taken, such as: *When I was 18, I had a scholarship to an art school. I could have gone to art school, but I decided to teach instead.* Write on the board: *I could have gone to art school.* Ask: *What does this statement express?*

(a past possibility not taken) *How does it express a possible past choice?* (could have)

2. Have students look at the chart. Review the examples, explanations, and Language Notes.

3. Ask students to make statements about paths they did not take.

PRESENTATION IDEA

When reviewing the Language Notes, note that people in the United States sometimes say, "I was so happy I could have cried." Ask students what they think this means. Ask students to share similar exaggerated expressions from their own cultures.

EXERCISE 5 page 170

🕐 Time: 5–10 min

Answers: 1. have started; **2.** have ended; **3.** have been killed; **4.** have made; **5.** have continued; **6.** have sent; **7.** have bombed; **8.** have tried

EXERCISE 6 page 171

🕐 Time: 5–10 min

Answers: 1. have dressed; **2.** have been; **3.** have married; **4.** have broken; **5.** have given; **6.** have killed

EXERCISE 7 page 171

🕐 Time: 5–10 min

Answers will vary.

EXERCISE 8 page 171

🕐 Time: 10–15 min

Answers will vary.

The Media and Presidential Elections, page 172

PRE-READING

🕐 Time: 5–10 min

1. Have students look at the photo and read the caption. Ask: *What is happening?* (Kennedy and Nixon are in a televised debate.)

2. Have students skim the reading. Ask: *What will the reading say about the media and presidential elections?* Have students make predictions.

3. Pre-teach any vocabulary words your students may not know, such as *media, influence, race, candidate,* and *blog.*

4. Activate students' prior knowledge about the media and elections. Ask: *How do people become rulers in your country? Is the media important to them?* Have students discuss the questions in pairs. Try to pair students of the same culture. Have a few pairs share their answers with the class.

READING GLOSSARY

media: the combination of TV, radio, news magazines, large circulation papers

to influence: to have an effect on

race: a contest

candidate: person running for a political office

blog: one's thought expressed on a website

EXPANDING ON THE READING

The topic for this reading can be enhanced with the following items:

1. Videos of the Kennedy-Nixon debate showing both candidates

2. Lists of changes in social media since the 2008 election

3. Predictions on the use of social media in future elections

---

READING
CD 1
TR 33

🕐 Time: 10–15 min

After students have read the article, go over the answers to the Comprehension Check on page 173: **1.** T; **2.** F; **3.** T

ADDITIONAL COMPREHENSION QUESTIONS

What was the first televised debate? (Kennedy-Nixon, 1960) *Did people agree who won the debate?* (no) *How did Kennedy do on television?* (well) *How did Nixon do?* (not well; he sweated and seemed uncomfortable) *Who first used social media in a presidential election?* (Barack Obama) *How did Internet skills help Obama win the 2012 election?* (His team was able to collect data online and use it more effectively.)

PRACTICE IDEA: LISTENING

Have students first listen to the audio alone. Ask additional comprehension questions, such as: *Who thought Nixon won the debate?* (people who heard it on the radio) *Did John McCain use Internet skills during the 2008 election?* (no) *During the 2012 election what percent of people said friends and family on social media urged them to vote?* (30%) Repeat the audio if necessary. Then have students open their books and read along as they listen to the audio.

PRACTICE IDEA: SPEAKING

Elicit from students ways the media reports political events and write them on the board. (e.g., using cameras/recording, interviewing candidates/leaders, talking to ordinary people for their feelings/opinions, analyzing the exchange, interviewing experts on the issues). Ask: *How do politicians use the media in your country?* Have students describe a debate or public exchange between two leaders or candidates for office in their country and how the media was involved. Have students tell what happened in small groups.

6.6 *Must Have* + Past Participle vs. *Had to* + Base Form,
page 173

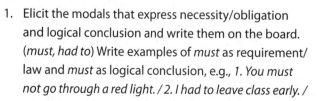

🕐 Time: 10–15 min

1. Elicit the modals that express necessity/obligation and logical conclusion and write them on the board. (*must, had to*) Write examples of *must* as requirement/law and *must* as logical conclusion, e.g., *1. You must not go through a red light. / 2. I had to leave class early. /*

3. That must be the journalist who did the interview.
Elicit the use of *must /had to* in each sentence. (1. law, 2. obligation, 3. conclusion)

2. Ask: *How do these sentences show past tense?* Ask volunteers to come to the board to underline the correct words (modal/verb phrases) in the sentences.

3. Review the example sentences and explanations in the chart.

4. Ask students to provide examples of their own.

EXERCISE 9 pages 173–174

🕐 Time: 10–15 min

Answers: 1. had to count; **2.** must have been; **3.** had to wait; **4.** must have been; **5.** had to be made; **6.** must have voted; **7.** must have been; **8.** had to work

6.7 Ability and Possibility in the Past, page 174

🕐 Time: 5–10 min

1. Have students cover the right side of grammar chart **6.7** and read the example sentences in the first section. Elicit the use of each modal. (ability) Ask: *How long did Lincoln have these abilities?* (a long time) Say: Could *and* be able to *can express people's general abilities: things they're able to do over a long period of time.*

2. Review the examples and explanations in the remaining sections of the chart. To help students distinguish *couldn't have* as impossibility and as disbelief, write these sentences on the board: *Thank you for helping me carry in the books this morning. I couldn't have done it alone. / Luz says she was here on November 6. She couldn't have been here! It was Election Day, and the school was closed.* Elicit from the class which example expresses past impossibility (first one) and which expresses disbelief (second one). Have

students provide other examples and discuss them as a class.

ADDITIONAL PRACTICE

Have students identify the correct explanation for each of these sentences.

a. *She was able to debate the candidate on television in June.* (single action)

b. *That salesman could convince you to buy anything.* (ability over a period of time)

c. *Obama couldn't have won the election without social media.* (impossibility)

d. *I couldn't understand what happened in the movie. Were you able to?* (interchangeable use for negative statements and questions)

e. *A: Neal got a speeding ticket. B: Neal? He couldn't have gotten a ticket; he never speeds.* (disbelief)

EXERCISE 10 pages 174–175

🕐 Time: 10–15 min

Answers: 1. couldn't use; **2.** couldn't understand; **3.** couldn't have listened; **4.** Were you able to/Could you; **5.** could have voted; **6.** were able to use/could have used; **7.** couldn't have happened; **8.** couldn't/wasn't able to; **9.** couldn't/wasn't able to; **10.** couldn't use; **11.** could have been; **12.** couldn't read; **13.** was able to teach

6.8 Modals in the Past: Continuous Forms, page 175

🕐 Time: 5–10 min

1. Have students review the example in the grammar chart. Ask: *How is this use of a modal in the past different from what we have covered so far?* (It's in continuous tense.)

2. Give one or two examples of your own (e.g., *I shouldn't have been talking on a cell phone while I was driving. / My*

mom sounded tired. I think she might have been sleeping when I called.). Elicit additional examples from students using the different modals. Write them on the board.

EXERCISE 11 page 175

⏱ Time: 5–10 min

Answers: 1. have been using; **2.** have been thinking; **3.** have been having; **4.** have been preparing; **5.** have been protecting; **6.** have been planning

---

PRACTICE IDEA: WRITING AND SPEAKING

Have students work in pairs. Have pairs use the sentences in Exercise 11 to create short conversations. Model one and write it on the board (e.g., *A: Famers shouldn't have been using slaves. B: I agree. They shouldn't have used slaves. / A: That's right. They should have been using paid workers.*). Have them write the conversations and then practice saying them. Have pairs perform their conversations for the class.

SUMMARY OF LESSON 6

🌓 Time: 20-30 min

PART A *SHOULD HAVE*

Have students talk about their regrets about a family member's or friend's decisions and choices (e.g., *My brother shouldn't have bought a used car; it's always breaking down.*).

If necessary, have students review:

6.1 Modals in the Past—Form (page 163)
6.1 Past Regrets or Mistakes—*Should Have* (page 164)

PRACTICE IDEA: SPEAKING

Ask students to think about a mildly embarrassing personal situation. Have them discuss their regrets about it in small groups. Ask a few students to share their stories with the class.

PART B *MAY/MIGHT/COULD HAVE*

List the modals from this section on the board. Have students make statements about themselves or someone else using the modals from the list (e.g., *Alfredo didn't call me; he could have forgotten. / I may have done the homework incorrectly.*).

If necessary, have students review:

6.1 Modals in the Past—Form (page 163)
6.3 Past Possibility—*May/Might/Could + Have* (page 165)

PART C *MUST HAVE*

Provide cues related to the reading on the Gettysburg Address and write them on the board (e.g., *Lincoln only in school 18 months, Lincoln ill, audience quiet*). Have students draw conclusions based on the cues and the reading (e.g., *He only went to school for 18 months, so people must have thought he was stupid.*).

If necessary, have students review:

6.4 Logical Conclusion about the Past—*Must Have* (page 167)

PART D *COULD HAVE*

Have students describe events that could have happened during the Cuban missile crisis (e.g., *The Soviet ships could have attacked the U.S. ships. World War III could have started.*).

If necessary, have students review:

6.5 Past Direction Not Taken—*Could Have* (page 170)

PRACTICE IDEA: WRITING AND SPEAKING

Have students describe events that could have happened during a crisis in their countries. Have them work alone to make complete sentences, exchange their writing with a partner for feedback, and then tell their story to a small group.

PART E *COULDN'T HAVE*

Provide a list of false statements and have students react with disbelief or attempt to disprove them (e.g., *John Kennedy often texted his wife. / George Washington used social media in his presidential campaign. / I saw five presidents carved into Mount Rushmore. / In January 1804, Thomas Jefferson flew to Europe.*).

If necessary, have students review:

6.7 Ability and Possibility in the Past (page 174)

PART F *COULD/BE ABLE TO*

Divide students into groups and have them describe their past abilities (e.g., *When I was ten, I was able to drink four milkshakes and not get sick. / I could stay up all night and go to class the next morning.*).

If necessary, have students review:

6.7 Ability and Possibility in the Past (page 174)

PART G *HAD TO*

Ask students to make statements of past necessity/obligation on topics they have read about in this course so far. Write prompts on the board if needed, such as: *Lincoln's education; Lincoln's belief about government of the people, by the people, for the people; Kennedy and Nixon's debate questions; Lewis and Clark's job; airlines' goal in 1930s* (e.g., *Lincoln had to teach himself. Lewis and Clark had to find the Northwest Passage.*).

If necessary, have students review:

6.6 *Must Have* + Past Participle vs. *Had to* + Base Form (page 173)

PART H CONTINUOUS PAST MODALS

Write several modals and verbs on the board (e.g., *might, may, could, must; plan, talk, write, study, think*). Ask students to describe the past plans of a classmate or someone they know (e.g., *He finally went to Europe to study. He must have been thinking about it for a long time.*).

If necessary, have students review:

6.8 Modals in the Past: Continuous Forms (page 175)

TEST/REVIEW

🕐 Time: 15 min

Have students do the exercise on page 177. For additional practice, use the Assessment CD-ROM with Exam*View®* and the Online Workbook.

Answers: 1. a. had to rely, **b.** must; **2. a.** couldn't read, **b.** was able to, **c.** wasn't able to/couldn't; **3. a.** could, **b.** was able to end; **4. a.** shouldn't, **b.** might not; **5. a.** must have thought; **6. a.** had to take; **7. a.** weren't able to agree, **b.** may/might, **c.** could/may; **8. a.** could have happened, **b.** must; **9. a.** may/might; **b.** could, **c.** should

WRITING

PART 1 EDITING ADVICE

🕐 Time: 10–15 min

1. Have students close their books. Write the first few sentences without editing marks or corrections on the board. For example:
   Lincoln should has had more protection.
   The bodyguard shouldn't left the theater.

2. Ask students to correct each sentence and provide a rule or an explanation for each correction. This activity can be done individually, in pairs, or as a class.

3. After students have corrected each sentence, tell them to turn to page 178. Say: *Now compare your work with the Editing Advice in the book.* Have students read through all the advice.

PART 2 EDITING PRACTICE

🕐 Time: 10–15 min

1. Tell students they are going to put the Editing Advice into practice. Ask: *Do all the shaded words and phrases have mistakes?* (no) Go over the examples with the class. Then do #1 together.

2. Have students complete the practice individually. Then have them compare answers with a partner before checking answers as a class.

3. For the items students had difficulties with, have them go back and find the relevant grammar chart and review it. Monitor and give help as necessary.

Answers: 1. couldn't remember; **2.** C; **3.** must have remembered; **4.** could have been; **5.** C; **6.** must have been; **7.** C; **8.** couldn't get/could not get; **9.** couldn't understand; **10.** must have known; **11.** must have crashed; **12.** C; **13.** should have flown; **14.** C; **15.** may not have been able to; **16.** could have been; **17.** could have used; **18.** C

PART 3 WRITE ABOUT IT

🕐 Time: 30–40 min

1. Review the two topics with students before they choose one and the modals they would use. Elicit and write on the board the modals students will use to show regret for mistakes (*should have*); conclusions (*must have*); path not taken (*could have*); possibility, ability, and necessity (*could, was able to, had to, must*); advisability (*should, must*). Brainstorm ideas for both topics with students and write them on the board. Have students choose one and research it. Remind students they must include a list of sources. Tell them they are going to write a complete essay with five paragraphs: introduction, three body paragraphs, and conclusion.

2. Write on the board *Abraham Lincoln, John Kennedy,* and *John Kennedy Jr.* Elicit from students who they were, how they died, and how their deaths might have been prevented. Write students' ideas on the board. Elicit other tragic deaths of famous persons. Have students choose one and research their topic. Tell them to answer the questions: *What happened? Why? Could it have been prevented? How?* Point out to students that they must include a list of sources. Tell them they are going to write a complete essay with five paragraphs: introduction, three body paragraphs, and conclusion.

PART 4 EDIT YOUR WRITING

◷ Time: 15–20 min

Have students edit their writing by reviewing the Lesson Summary on page 176 and the Editing Advice on page 178. Collect for assessment and/or have students share their essays in small groups.

EXPANSION ACTIVITIES

1. Tell students that this activity is about giving advice. Have students work in pairs to brainstorm a list of imaginary personal problems from people in the past based on the readings in the lesson. Have them give advice for each problem (e.g., *problem: person in audience couldn't hear what Lincoln said at Gettysburg Address; advice: He shouldn't have been standing so far away. He should have moved closer.*).

2. Have students bring in an application (e.g., credit card, job, library card) and complete it with many mistakes. Then have students work in pairs to find and comment on the mistakes. Have pairs switch roles and review each other's application.

7 ONLINE INTERACTIONS

GRAMMAR CHARTS

LESSON OPENER

Have students look at the photo and read the caption. Ask: *What is Patrick Meier looking at?* (social media websites and satellite imagery*) Why?* (to help with global relief efforts) Have students read the quotation. Ask: *Do you agree? Should people all over the world be able to communicate over the Internet?*

Background: Interactions over the Internet have been growing steadily since the invention of the World Wide Web. In fact, between 2000 and 2014, global use of the Internet grew by 741%. Since their invention, the Internet and Web have transformed daily life, changing everything from the way we shop to the way scientists experiment. Today, more than three billion people across the world use the Internet to find a job, get a home, bank, shop, get the news, fund and staff projects, and chat with friends, family, and others. The Internet has become a vast meeting space, an international marketplace, and a powerful source of information, providing data, statistics, practical information, and resources for research into just about any subject.

Tim Berners-Lee is the British inventor of the World Wide Web. Lee, who has never made money from his invention, originally devised the Web only as a means of sharing information. Lee has been named by *Time Magazine* as one of the 100 Most Important People of the 20th Century, by the United Kingdom as one of the 100 Greatest Britons, and has won countless awards and

honorary degrees. Today Lee is involved in several areas of computer science, including artificial and collective intelligence. He was born in 1955.

CONTEXT

This unit is about online interactions. Students will read about founders of two types of successful websites, Pierre Omidyar of eBay and Deron Beal of Freecycle, and the founder and inventor of the Web, Tim Berners-Lee.

1. Give students a few minutes to look through the lesson. Have them look at the photos and titles. How do they relate to the context?

2. Elicit the topics that will be discussed.

3. Have students discuss what they know about online interactions and the World Wide Web in pairs or small groups.

GRAMMAR

Students will learn about adjective clauses and descriptive phrases.

1. To activate students' prior knowledge, ask what students know about adjectives, clauses, and describing.

2. Give several examples of sentences with adjective clauses and descriptive phrases (e.g., *Lincoln, who died in 1865, was the first U.S. president to be assassinated. The camera that I bought on the Internet didn't work. We started a website, which cost about $1,400.*).

3. Have volunteers give their own examples and write them on the board.

READING

Pierre Omidyar and eBay, page 182

PRE-READING

🕐 Time: 10–20 min

1. Have students look at the photo and read the title. Ask: *Who is this man?* (Pierre Omidyar) *What did he do?* (started eBay)
2. Have students look briefly at the reading. Ask: *What will the reading say about Omidyar and eBay?* Have students make predictions.
3. Pre-teach any essential vocabulary words your students may not know, such as *garage sales, hobby, upgraded,* and *fired.*
4. Ask: *How do people sell household goods in your country? How did they do it before the Internet?* Have students discuss in pairs or small groups and share their answers with class.

READING GLOSSARY

garage sales: sales of used household items inside or near a person's garage

hobby: an activity done for pleasure

to upgrade: to improve

to fire: to dismiss from employment

READING

🕐 Time: 10–15 min

After students have read the article, go over the answers to the Comprehension Check on page 183: **1.** T; **2.** F; **3.** T

How did people in the United States use to sell their old things? (newspapers, garage sales, and local flea markets) *What did Omidyar do before he began eBay?* (He was a computer programmer.) *What happened in 1998?* (Omidyar hired a business expert.) *Why did Omidyar hire Meg Whitman?* (eBay had become very big.)

> ### PRACTICE IDEA: WRITING
>
> Have students work in groups to write a description of an item to sell on eBay. Have each group choose an item and describe it. Brainstorm types of information to include (e.g., size, shape, color, age, use, price). Have each group share their ad with the class. Have them describe the item and have the class guess what it is.

7.1 Adjective Clauses— Introduction, page 183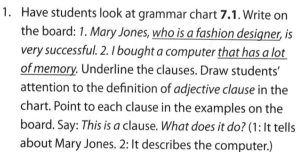

🕐 Time: 10–15 min

1. Have students look at grammar chart **7.1**. Write on the board: *1. Mary Jones, <u>who is a fashion designer</u>, is very successful. 2. I bought a computer <u>that has a lot of memory</u>.* Underline the clauses. Draw students' attention to the definition of *adjective clause* in the chart. Point to each clause in the examples on the board. Say: *This is a* clause. *What does it do?* (1: It tells about Mary Jones. 2: It describes the computer.)
2. Review the examples and explanations in the chart. Ask volunteers to identify the adjective clauses in the sentences and who or what they modify. (*present, sellers, business account*)

3. Elicit additional sentences with adjective clauses from students and write them on the board. Have other students identify the clauses in each.

4. Review the Language Notes. Have students close their books. Ask: *Which words can begin adjective clauses?* (*who, whom, that, which, whose, where, when*)

ADDITIONAL PRACTICE

Write sentences on the board with misplaced adjective clauses such as the following. Elicit the correct sentences from volunteers and provide feedback.

a. *The company grew, which was started in 2003, to be very successful.*

b. *We got wedding we didn't like gifts and returned them.*

c. *The project, whom most people had never met, had to begin with the manager.*

d. *Mr. Smith started the writers camp, who wrote the first really successful detective novel.*

e. *Berners-Lee, which has been very successful, invented the World Wide Web.*

f. *Then the taxi driver got lost, who had never driven in New York.*

EXERCISE 1 pages 183–184
🕐 Time: 10–15 min

Answers: 1. who; **2.** which; **3.** that; **4.** that, that; **5.** whose; **6.** that; **7.** whose; **8.** that; **9.** who; **10.** when; **11.** where; **12.** that

EXERCISE 2 page 184
🕐 Time: 5–10 min
Answers:

1. Amazon was founded in 1994 by Jeff Bezos, <u>who predicted that the Internet offered an opportunity to make money.</u>

2. Amazon, <u>which is now the largest online retailer,</u> began by selling books.

3. First he made a list of about twenty products <u>that could be sold online.</u> He eventually decided on selling books.

4. Bezos wanted a name <u>that began with "A."</u> He decided on Amazon, because it is a place <u>that is "exotic and different."</u>

5. But a good company name is not enough. He needed to hire people <u>whose talents would improve the company.</u>

6. Since many big Internet companies started in a garage, he decided to buy a house <u>that had a garage.</u>

7. He needed money to start his company. He went to his parents, <u>whose first response was "What's the Internet?"</u>

8. Some people thought that his parents would lose all the money <u>that they invested.</u>

9. The 1990s was a time <u>when people were just beginning to use the Internet.</u>

10. Bezos created a place <u>where customers could make recommendations to other users.</u>

11. He and his parents were never unhappy about the decision <u>that he made in 1994.</u>

PRACTICE IDEA: SPEAKING

Have students work in groups and briefly tell the story of a successful Internet or other entrepreneur from their country. Have them describe the entrepreneur's experience, using Exercise 2 as a model. When students are finished, have someone from each group share a story with the class.

7.2 Relative Pronoun as Subject, page 185

🕐 Time: 10–15 min

1. Review relative pronouns. Ask students to name as many as they can (*who, which, that, whom, whose*). Write on the board: *Mary Jones opened a shop that sells stationery. / The man who bought the computer is happy with it.*

2. Have students look at the example diagrams in the chart. Clarify how *who, that,* and *which* can act as subjects of an adjective clause. Say: *In the first example,* that/which *represent* toy *and act as the subject of* is. Elicit the referent for *who/that* in the second example and the verb for which they are the subject (*person, bought*). Direct students' attention to the examples on the board. Ask: What do *that* and *who* represent? (*shop, man*) *What are the subjects of* sells *and* bought? (that/shop, who/man)

3. Draw students' attention to the Language Notes. Ask: *Which relative pronouns are used with people?* (*who, that*) *Which are used with things?* (*that, which*) Elicit the agreement rule. (a present tense verb in an adjective clause must agree with its subject)

ADDITIONAL PRACTICE

1. Have students make a game of combining sentences. Work as a class. Ask a student to make a simple sentence (e.g., *I have a dog.*). Elicit a second sentence about the first (e.g., *He likes ice cream.*). Ask a volunteer to combine the sentences (e.g., *I have a dog who/that likes ice cream.*). Go around the room in a chain, with the first student making the first sentence, the next making the second sentence, and the third combining the sentences with an adjective clause.

2. Have students survey classmates to describe changes they would like at school (e.g., when the computer lab is open, where the bookstore is located). Have a student or group of students take responsibility for each item. Have students or groups move around the room and survey other students or groups on their preferences. When they are finished, have students or groups report the results of their survey (e.g., *Most students would like to have a computer lab that is open before 8:00 a.m.*).

EXERCISE 3 pages 185–186

⏱ Time: 10–15 min

Answers: 1. who buys; **2.** who buy/that buy; **3.** who reads/that reads; **4.** that lost; **5.** who have created/that have created; **6.** who understood/that understood; **7.** who believed/that believed; **8.** that became; **9.** who bought/that bought; **10.** that are; **11.** that help

EXERCISE 4 page 186

⏱ Time: 5–10 min

Answers will vary.

7.3 Relative Pronoun as Object, page 187

⏱ Time: 10–15 min

1. Review direct objects. Write on the board: *I read a funny joke.* Ask students to identify the object in the sentence. (*a funny joke*) Say: *Remember: A direct object answers the question* what *of a main verb: You read what? A funny joke.*

2. Have students look at the example diagrams in the chart. Elicit the verb in the second sentence of each example. Ask: *What was it the aunt* gave? (the lamp) *Who/Whom have you never* met? (the seller) Elicit or present the use of a relative pronoun to represent a direct object. Write an additional example on the board, such as *I saw the e-mail. You sent the e-mail.* With the class, write a sentence combining the two with an adjective clause. (*I saw the e-mail that you sent.*) Ask a volunteer to explain how and what was combined. Make sure that students are familiar with the null symbol that means *nothing*.

3. Draw students' attention to the Language Notes. Ask: *Which is formal:* who *or* whom? (*whom*) To help students understand when relative pronouns can be omitted in this type of adjective clause, clarify that the subject of the clause has to be stated (~~that~~ the <u>children</u> love).

CONTEXT NOTE

There are many differences in English, as in most languages, between formal language—often used in writing, in speeches, or to show respect—and informal language, which is usually used in conversations between friends and family members and in relaxed settings. Students may be interested in giving some examples from their own languages and cultures of differences between formal and informal usages regarding speakers (e.g., *who* versus *whom* or *who/whom* versus *that*).

ADDITIONAL PRACTICE

1. Have students work in pairs to practice identifying relative pronouns that can be left out. Write a list on the board with sentences such as the following:

    a. *I have a car that I really like.*

    b. *My brother lives in a city that has a lot of noise and traffic.*

    c. *Darcie is a good worker who does her job efficiently.*

    d. *My professor is a person whom I really admire.*

    e. *I advertised a table on eBay that sold very quickly.*

2. Have students circle relative pronouns that can be omitted (*a* and *d*) and exchange answers with other pairs for feedback.

3. Have pairs make up sentences of their own and share with the class some that can/can't leave out the relative pronoun.

EXERCISE 5 pages 187–189

🕐 Time: 10–15 min

Answers: 1. (that) I bought; **2. a.** (that) I get, **b.** (that) I don't know, **c.** (that) I use, **d.** (that) I buy/(that) I bought, **e.** (that) you use, **f.** (that) I prefer, **g.** (that) I need;
3. a. (who) you had/(whom) you had/(that) you had, **b.** (that) I have, **c.** (that) you give/(that) you've given/(that) you have given/(that) you're giving/(that) you are giving;
4. a. (that) you've got/(that) you have got, **b.** (that) I've got/(that) I have got, **c.** (that) you had, **d.** (that) she gave;
5. a. (that) you see, **b.** (that) I rented, **c.** (that) I'm going to rent/(that) I am going to rent, **d.** (that) I got/(that) I've gotten, **e.** (who) we find/(whom) we find/(that) we find

---

PRACTICE IDEA: SPEAKING

Have students work in pairs and retell the conversations in Exercise 5. Tell partners to switch roles. After they have finished, have a few pairs perform the conversations for the class.

7.4 Relative Pronoun as Object of Preposition, page 190

🕐 Time: 10–15 min

1. Review prepositions. Have students cover the grammar chart. Ask students to name as many prepositions as they can. Write the list on the board. Elicit from students examples of prepositional phrases and have them identify the prepositions and objects (e.g., *to* my <u>house</u>, *about* a new <u>book</u>, *of* my <u>nephew</u>, *with* the <u>group</u>).

2. Have students look at the example diagrams in the chart. Elicit which word in a prepositional phrase a relative pronoun will refer to. (the object) Write an additional example sentence on the board, such as *Bezos borrowed money from some people.* With the class, rewrite the sentence with a relative pronoun. (*The people from whom Bezos borrowed money were his parents.*) Ask a volunteer to explain the combination. Elicit or point out that the sentence with the relative pronoun reverses the order of the prepositional phrase. Note that the sentence does not repeat every word in the prepositional phrase (e.g., *from* ~~some~~ *people* > *The people from whom; to* ~~a~~ *person* > *The person who/that I… to*).

3. Draw students' attention to the Language Notes. Review the example sentences and the differences between formal and informal placement of prepositions. Write on the board: *The person to that I loaned my notebook hasn't returned it.* Ask: *Is this correct?* (no) *Why?* (You can't use *that* directly after a preposition; you must use *whom* for people.)

CONTEXT NOTE

Students may be interested in additional examples of the differences between formal and informal English and when each is used. If possible, bring in samples of written material showing the use and omission of the relative pronouns (especially *whom*) with prepositions, such as in academic writing, junk mail, and newspaper articles.

ADDITIONAL PRACTICE

Provide students with a list of prepositional phrases. Have students work in pairs to convert the phrases to formal and informal English for adjective clauses. Use phrases such as *to French class, with my co-workers, at the swimming pool, over the river, on the bookshelf, etc.* Write an example on the board (e.g., *the French class that … to* [informal] OR *the French class to which ….* [formal]). Go around the room offering help if needed and monitoring students' progress. Ask a few pairs to share their work with the class.

EXERCISE 6 pages 190–191

🕐 Time: 10–15 min

Answers:

1. There are several travel websites I'm interested in.

2. There is a new website everyone is talking about.

3. The link you click on will take you to that site.

4. The information you are looking for can be found on that site.

5. Vacation Rentals is not a website I'm familiar with.

6. Finding a vacation home online is not a method I'm accustomed to.

7. The house we decided on is in the mountains.

8. The owner I spoke to was very helpful.

9. There's one thing I'm sure about: renting a vacation home is a good deal.

EXERCISE 7 page 191

🕐 Time: 5–10 min

Answers: 1. has vacation rentals (which/that) I'm interested in, has vacation rentals in which I'm interested; **2.** (which/that) I'm interested in has three bedrooms, in which I'm interested has three bedrooms; **3.** (who/whom/that) I'm taking a vacation with want to rent a house, with whom I'm taking a vacation want to rent a house; **4.** (who/whom/that) I spoke to, to whom I spoke; **5.** we are responsible for is cleaning the house, for which we are responsible is cleaning the house

READING

The Freecycle Network,™ page 192

PRE-READING

🕐 Time: 10–15 min

1. Have students look at the photo and read the caption. Ask: *What is the man doing?* (making art) *What is the art made of?* (discarded books)

2. Have students read the title and skim the reading. Ask: *What is the reading about? How do you know?* Have students make predictions.

3. Pre-teach any vocabulary words your students may not know, such as *discarded, generate, tons,* and *pick (it) up.*

4. Activate students' prior knowledge about organizations like Freecycle. Ask: *Are there other organizations that accept used household goods? Do you think they are like Freecycle?* Have students discuss the questions and make predictions in small groups. Have groups share their predictions with the class.

READING GLOSSARY

to discard: to throw away

to generate: to produce, create

ton: a unit of weight (U.S.: 2,000 pounds, U.K.: 2,240 pounds); plural: tons

to pick up: go and get something or someone

READING 🎧 CD 2 TR 4

🕐 Time: 10–15 min

After students have read the article, go over the answers to the Comprehension Check on page 193: **1.** F; **2.** T; **3.** F

ADDITIONAL COMPREHENSION QUESTIONS

Can people buy and sell goods on Freecycle? (no) *Where is Freecycle located?* (online) *What is a landfill?* (a place where garbage is buried) *If you want an item on Freecycle, how do you get it?* (The giver/owner tells you where to pick it up.) *Do the giver and receiver meet?* (sometimes)

PRACTICE IDEA: LISTENING

Have students close their books and listen to the audio. Tell them to write all the phrases with *whose/where/when* that they hear. Ask additional comprehension questions such as: *Why did Deron Beal create Freecycle: what was his idea?* (to protect the environment) *Where is Deron Beal from?* (Tucson, Arizona) Repeat the audio if necessary.

ADDITIONAL PRACTICE

Ask students how garbage is dealt with in their countries. Have a brief discussion about recycling and its importance if appropriate.

EXPANDING ON THE READING

The topic for this reading can be enhanced with the following items:

1. Articles on the beginning of www.Freecycle.org

2. Deron Beal's profile or biography

3. Information on gifting programs versus gifting scams

4. A page of ads from a local neighborhood on Freecycle

7.5 Place and Time in Adjective Clauses, page 193

🕐 Time: 10–15 min

1. Have students go back to the reading on page 192 and underline all the phrases that show place and time. Ask: *Which words do you observe that begin phrases about place and time?* (*where, when*) Write example sentences from the reading on the board, such as *You join in the area where you live. The giver will specify a time when the receiver can pick up the item.* Ask: *What does* where *refer to?* (a place: where you live) *What does* when *refer to?* (a time: when you can pick something up)

2. Review each section of the chart with the class. Remind students that *where/in which/that/when/ during which* are the beginnings adjective clauses. Ask: *What kind of information do adjective (clauses) give?* (which, what kind of, and how many)

3. Point out that *where* and *when* are related to adverbs but in adjective clauses they act as adjectives and answer the question *which (one)*: *Which city? the city where I live; Which place? the place where I leave packages; Which time? the time when the Internet was new.*

PRACTICE IDEA: SPEAKING

Write on the board: *I like to shop when . . . .* and *I like to shop at stores where . . . .* Have students complete the sentences to make true statements about themselves. Then have them work in pairs to ask each other about their statements using *why* or *why not*:

> A: *I like to shop when I have a lot of money.*
> B: *Why?*
> A: *Because if I find something I like, I can buy it.*

EXERCISE 8 pages 193–194

🕐 Time: 10–15 min

Answers: 1. when; **2.** where; **3.** Ø/when; **4.** when; **5.** where; **6.** when; **7.** where; **8.** when; **9.** Ø/when; **10.** where; **11.** when

---

PRACTICE IDEA: SPEAKING

Have students retell conversations with an older person who used/did something that was new during their time (e.g., a navigation system in a car, a cell phone, a microwave, wrote a research paper on a computer). Have students work in pairs and use Exercise 8 as a model. Ask a few volunteers to share their stories with the class.

EXERCISE 9 pages 194–195

🕐 Time: 10–15 min

Answers will vary.

EXERCISE 10 page 195

🕐 Time: 10–15 min

Answers will vary.

7.6 *Whose* in Adjective Clauses, page 195

🕐 Time: 15–20 min

1. Review *whose*. Have students go back to the reading on page 192 and underline all of the *whose* phrases. Write a few of the phrases from the reading on the board, such as … *Deron Beal, whose idea was to protect the environment . . . .* Ask: *What question does* whose *answer here?* (tells about possession, who the idea belonged to) Review the difference between *whose* and *who's* (contraction for *who is*).

2. Ask: *What possessive pronouns can* whose *stand for?* (*his, her, its, their*) *What other type of word can it stand for?* (possessive form of a noun) Elicit examples and write them on the board (e.g., Barbara's, Tim's).

3. Have students review the diagrams and explanations carefully. Write this additional example on the board: *I have intelligent friends. Their e-mails are full of mistakes.* With the class, write a combined sentence with *whose + noun* (e.g., *I have intelligent friends whose e-mails are full of mistakes.*).

4. Ask: *Can you use* whose + noun *as the object of the adjective clause in the example?* (no) Redirect students' attention to *whose + noun* as object in the chart. To help students understand the use, point out that *be* (in *are full of mistakes*) is intransitive or linking and does not take objects. Write on the board: *She is here. You drove her car.* Elicit a combined sentence with

whose + noun as object. (*The person whose car you drove is here.*) Say: *We can use* whose + noun *as the object in this sentence because* drove *is a transitive verb.*

5. To help clarify for students how to form *whose + noun* phrases as objects of an adjective clause, point out that the adjective clause reverses the normal word order in a sentence: V DO ⟶ DO V.
Write on the board:

$$V= drove\ DO = her\ car$$
$$DO = whose\ car\ (you)\ V = drove$$

Elicit additional examples of V DO phrases and have volunteers come to the board and convert them to *whose + noun* adjective clauses.

ADDITIONAL PRACTICE

Provide a list of transitive verbs with *whose + noun* objects. Have students work in pairs and make sentences or phrases with adjective clauses. Have pairs exchange their work for feedback. Ask several pairs to share their work with the class.

EXERCISE 11 page 196

🕐 Time: 5–10 min

Answers:

1. A person whose basement was flooded needs new furniture.
2. A person whose radio broke needs a new one.
3. A person whose daughter is in the school orchestra needs a violin.
4. A person whose bicycle was stolen needs one to get to work.
5. A person whose new apartment is small wants to give away a lot of books.
6. A person whose laptop doesn't work anymore needs a new one.
7. A person whose children are grown now wants to give away their toys.
8. A person whose kids are starting school needs two backpacks.

EXERCISE 12 page 197

🕐 Time: 10–15 min

Answers: 1. whose tablet I bought; **2.** whose vacation rental I found online; **3.** whose computer I bought online; **4.** whose profile picture I don't like; **5.** whose picture I received by e-mail; **6.** whose names I accidentally deleted; **7.** whose picture you see on my page; **8.** whose class we're taking

7.7 Adjective Clauses after Indefinite Pronouns, page 197

🕐 Time: 5–10 min

1. Draw students' attention to the list of indefinite pronouns in the top section of the grammar chart. Ask: *Why are these called indefinite pronouns?* (because they don't name a specific person or thing)
2. Have students review the examples and explanations in the grammar chart. Point out that indefinite pronouns are used to make broad or general statements.

EXERCISE 13 pages 197–198

🕐 Time: 5–10 min

Answers: 1. (that) I have gotten; **2.** (that) I need/(that) I needed; **3.** (that) I've bought/(that)I bought; **4. a.** who uses, **b.** (that) I know; **5.** (that) you sent; **6.** (that) you told; **7.** (that) you saw; **8.** who rents; **9.** who wants; **10.** who has

READING

Tim Berners-Lee, page 199

PRE-READING

🕐 Time: 10–15 min

1. Have students look at the photo and read the title.

Ask: *Who is Tim Berners-Lee?* (the man in the photo)

2. Have students look briefly at the reading. Ask: *What is the reading about? How do you know?* Have students use the title and photo to make predictions.

3. Pre-teach any vocabulary words your students may not know, such as *vision, creator, credits, cables,* and *wisdom.*

4. Activate students' prior knowledge about Berners-Lee. Have students turn to the Lesson 7 opener on pages 180–181. Ask: *What did Berners-Lee say?* and have a volunteer read aloud the quote. Ask: *Had you heard of Berners-Lee before this lesson? What did you know about him?* Have students share their information in small groups. Have a student from each group share the group's information with the class.

READING GLOSSARY

vision: ability to imagine the future
creator: a person who creates
to credit: to express admiration for something well done
cable: strong, thick rope, usually made of many wires twisted together
wisdom: good sense learned from experience

EXPANDING ON THE READING

The topic for this reading can be enhanced with the following items:

1. Article on the development of the Internet
2. Article on the invention of the printing press
3. Timeline showing the increasing numbers of users on the Internet
4. Timeline of communication inventions, including the telephone, telegraph, television, Internet

READING CD 2 TR 5
🕐 Time: 10–15 min

After students have read the article, go over the answers to the Comprehension Check on page 200: **1.** F; **2.** F; **3.** T

ADDITIONAL COMPREHENSION QUESTIONS

Where was Berners-Lee born? (in England) *When was the first Web page introduced?* (1990) *What was Berners-Lee's vision?* (any person could share information with anyone else anywhere) *What was invented first: the Internet or the Web?* (the Internet) *How is the Web different from the*

Internet? (It connects information with links instead of cables.)

PRACTICE IDEA: LISTENING

Have students listen to the audio with their books closed. Ask a few comprehension questions (e.g., *When was Berners-Lee born?* [1955] *Where was Berners-Lee when he thought of the idea of the World Wide Web?* [working in Switzerland] *Who is he compared to?* [Johannes Gutenberg] *Why?* [because they both made it possible for people everywhere to share knowledge]). Repeat the audio if necessary. Have students open their books, read along as they listen to the audio, and check their answers.

7.8 Nonessential Adjective Clauses, page 200

🕐 Time: 5–10 min

1. Review the meaning of *essential* (necessary) and *nonessential* (not necessary). Have students review the example sentences and explanations in the chart. Point out that commas signal that the information contained between them is not necessary to understand the main idea of the sentence.

2. Ask: *Do sentences with nonessential clauses always have two commas?* (no) *When is only one comma used?* (when the clause is at the end of the sentence)

3. Write on the board: *I went to the restaurant, which was a sushi bar, to pick up my friend.* Ask: *What is the basic meaning of the sentence?* (I went to the restaurant to pick up my friend.) *Is it necessary to know that it's a sushi bar to understand the meaning?* (no)

EXERCISE 14 page 200
🕐 Time: 5–10 min

Answers:

1. The first modern computer, which was called ENIAC, took up a lot of space.
2. ENIAC was created in 1942, when the U.S. was involved in World War II.
3. Personal computers, which were introduced in the 1970s, were smaller and faster than previous computers.
4. Berners-Lee, whose name is not widely recognized, made a great contribution to the world.

5. Bill Gates went to Harvard University, where he developed the programming language BASIC.

6. Bill Gates dropped out of Harvard to work with Paul Allen, who was his old high school friend.

7. Bill Gates and his wife Melinda set up the Bill and Melinda Gates Foundation, which helps people in need all over the world.

8. Jeff Bezos got money from his parents, who lent him $300,000 to start Amazon.

7.9 Essential vs. Nonessential Adjective Clauses, page 201

Time: 10–15 min

1. Have students cover the explanation column in grammar chart **7.9**. In pairs, ask students to look at the sentences in the first two sections of the chart and to decide which section presents nonessential adjective clauses (first section), and which presents essential (second). Then have students review the explanations. Have volunteers read each sentence aloud without the adjective clause, as suggested in the chart, as an aid to distinguishing between essential and nonessential adjective clauses.

2. Review the rest of the chart. Have students compare the (a), (b), and (c) sentences in the third section. Ask: *Why is the clause in (c) essential?* (You need to know that the computer is old to understand why it is slower than computers today.)

3. Draw students' attention to the Language Notes. Ask: *What kind of nouns are* unique? (proper nouns that name specific persons, places, and things) Elicit or provide additional examples and write them on the board (e.g., *The Writers House, Emory University, Macy's Department Store,* United Kingdom).

ADDITIONAL PRACTICE

Have students close their books and list the five criteria, or questions, for deciding if an adjective clause needs commas.

EXERCISE 15 page 202

Time: 5–10 min

Answers:

1. NC

2. My father, who texted me a few minutes ago, is sick.

3. NC

4. The Freecycle Network™, which was created in 2003,

helps keep things out of landfills.

5. NC

6. Berners-Lee, whose parents were very educated, loves learning new things.

7. NC

8. Meg Whitman, who ran eBay for 10 years, left the company in 2008.

9. Berners-Lee worked in Switzerland, where a physics laboratory is located.

10. The Windows operating system, which was developed by Microsoft, came out in 1985.

11. NC

12. NC

13. The Web, which is one of the most important inventions of the twentieth century, has changed the way people get information.

14. Bill Gates, who created Microsoft with his friend, became a billionaire.

15. Steve Jobs, who died in 2011, helped create the Apple computer.

16. NC

17. NC

PRACTICE IDEA: SPEAKING

Have students work in pairs to decide which items in Exercise 15 required commas and discuss why.

EXERCISE 16 pages 202–203

Time: 5–10 min

Answers:

1. eBay, which was started in Pierre Omidyar's house, is now a large corporation.

2. Tim Berners-Lee works at MIT, where he does research on artificial intelligence.

3. Pierre Omidyar, whose wife became part of the company, started eBay as a hobby.

4. eBay hired Meg Whitman in 1998, when more expert business knowledge was needed to run the company.

5. In 2008, eBay hired John Donahoe, who fired a lot of people.

6. E-mail, which was first created in 1972, did not become popular until the 1990s.

7. Pierre Omidyar, whose idea started to become popular, had to charge money for each sale.

8. Berners-Lee created the Web at a laboratory in Switzerland, where he was working in the 1980s.

9. Berners-Lee wrote a book called *Weaving the Web*, in which he answers questions about his project.

PRACTICE IDEA: WRITING

1. Have students write short sentences about themselves (e.g., *My family gets together on holidays. Our apartment is not big enough.*). Then add a nonessential clause (e.g., *My family, which is quite large, gets together on holidays. Our apartment, which is 900 square feet, is not big enough.*).

2. Encourage students to add clauses that add to the description of the subject.

3. Write model sentences on the board if needed.

7.10 Descriptive Phrases,
page 203

⏲ Time: 10–15 min

1. Have students cover the right side of the chart and look at the example sentences. Elicit from students how the bolded phrases in (b) sentences differ from those in (a) sentences (the relative pronoun is absent). Say: *When a relative pronoun can be removed, this is called* reducing. *Reduced adjective clauses are descriptive phrases.*

2. Elicit the four types of descriptive phrases in the chart. (past participle, present participle, noun/appositive, preposition)

3. Review the explanations and examples with the class.

4. Direct students' attention to the Language Notes. Point out that only adjective clauses with relative pronouns followed by *be* can be reduced (shortened). Ask: What *is an appositive?* (a phrase that defines a noun)

EXERCISE 17 page 204

⏲ Time: 10–15 min

Answers:

1. On eBay, people ~~who are~~ living in California can easily sell to people ~~who are~~ living in New York.

2. Google, ~~which is~~ a popular search engine, is used by millions of people.

3. Bill Gates, ~~who is~~ the founder of Microsoft, has set up a foundation to help others.

4. eBay takes a percentage of each sale ~~that is~~ made on its website.

5. Tim Berners-Lee, ~~who is~~ from England, now works at MIT.

6. MIT, ~~which is~~ located in Massachusetts, is an excellent university.

7. Berners-Lee developed the idea for the Web when he was working at CERN, ~~which is~~ a physics lab in Switzerland.

8. Berners-Lee's parents worked on the first computer ~~that was~~ sold commercially.

9. People ~~who are~~ interested in reading newspapers from other cities can find them on the Web.

10. The World Wide Web, ~~which is~~ abbreviated WWW, was first introduced on the Internet in 1991.

11. The Internet, ~~which was~~ designed in the 1970s, didn't attract casual users until Berners-Lee created the Web.

12. Some wealthy people signed a Giving Pledge, ~~which is~~ a promise to give away most of their money in their lifetime.

13. Pierre Omidyar, ~~who is~~ a billionaire, signed the Giving Pledge.

14. Computers ~~that are~~ sold today have much more memory and speed than computers ~~that were~~ sold 10 years ago.

15. Deron Beal, ~~who is~~ from Arizona, created The Freecycle Network™.

EXERCISE 18 pages 204–205

⏲ Time: 10–15 min

Answers:

1. Pierre Omidyar, whose father was a professor, came to the U.S. when he was a child.

2. Pierre Omidyar, (who is) from France, wrote his first computer program at age 14.

3. He lived in California, where he started his business.

4. Pierre Omidyar, who started eBay as a hobby in his home, saw a good use for computer technology.

5. *BusinessWeek*, (which is) a popular business magazine, named Meg Whitman among the 25 most powerful business managers.

6. Meg Whitman resigned from eBay in 2008, when she decided to go into politics.

7. John Donahoe, whom Omidyar hired in 2008, got the company out of decline.

8. Bill Gates, who dropped out of Harvard during his second year, started Microsoft at the age of 19.

9. Amazon, (which is) now the largest online retailer, began by selling books.

10. Jeff Bezos's parents, who had never heard of the Internet, invested money in Amazon.
11. Tim Berners-Lee is sometimes compared to Johann Gutenberg, who made books possible in the fifteenth century.
12. Berners-Lee, whose parents designed computers, was interested in using the Internet to share information.

PRACTICE IDEA: WRITING

Have students use information about famous people they know to make sentences similar to those in Exercise 18, using descriptive phrases. Have students share their sentences with a partner or the class.

EXERCISE 19 page 205

◔ Time: 10–15 min

Answers will vary.

PRACTICE IDEA: WRITING

Have students write sentences about people, institutions, or inventions they admire. Ask them to combine facts and opinions in their statements, such as: *I admire Tim Berners-Lee, who invented the World Wide Web.* / *I admire the Red Cross, which helps people after disasters.*

SUMMARY OF LESSON 7

◑ Time: 20-30 min

PART A PRONOUN AS SUBJECT, OBJECT, AND OBJECT OF PREPOSITION

Have students use the examples in the chart to make new statements. For each use, have students make a sentence with an essential adjective clause and one with a nonessential adjective clause (e.g., subject: *People who use Freecycle save money.* [essential] / *Tim Berners-Lee, who is English, invented the Web.* [nonessential]; object: *The computer that I use is slow.* [essential] / *I love my new computer, which is pink.* [nonessential]; object of preposition: *The person I loaned my book to returned it.* [essential] / *Kennedy, who(m) we read about, debated Nixon.* [nonessential]).

If necessary, have students review:

7.1 Adjective Clauses—Introduction (page 183)
7.2 Relative Pronoun as Subject (page 185)
7.3 Relative Pronoun as Object (page 187)
7.4 Relative Pronoun as Object of Preposition (page 190)
7.9 Essential vs. Nonessential Adjective Clauses (page 201)

PRACTICE IDEA: WRITING AND SPEAKING

Have students work in pairs and write sentences with essential and nonessential adjective clauses in formal and informal English (e.g., *This is the person I told you about.* [informal] / *This is the person about whom I told you.* [formal]).

PART B *WHERE* AND *WHEN*

Write cues on the board, such as: *Sellers/flea markets, Omidyar/computer programmer, Internet/1970, Freecycle/neighborhoods, Tim Berners-Lee/1955,* etc. Have students use the cues to talk about people and events in this lesson using *where* and *when* in essential and nonessential adjective clauses (e.g., *Sellers sold items in flea markets where they lived.* [essential] / *Omidyar started eBay, where you can sell to people everywhere.* [nonessential]; *Omidyar started eBay when he was a computer programmer.* [essential] / *Tim Berners-Lee was born in 1955, when most people had never heard of a computer.* [nonessential]).

If necessary, have students review:

7.5 Place and Time in Adjective Clauses (page 193)
7.9 Essential vs. Nonessential Adjective Clauses (page 201)

PRACTICE IDEA: SPEAKING

Divide students into small groups. Have groups brainstorm people and events they have read about in this lesson. When they are finished, have them discuss places and times connected to these people and events. Have each group appoint monitors to listen for essential and nonessential adjective clauses during the conversation. Have students from each group share their responses with the class and report their use of clauses.

PART C WHOSE + NOUN AS SUBJECT AND OBJECT

Have students use the examples in the chart to make new statements with essential and nonessential adjective clauses using *whose* + noun as subject and object (e.g., subject: *Beijing is a city whose shops attract many tourists.* [essential] / *Beijing, whose shops attract many tourists, is the capital of China.* [nonessential]; object: *I mailed a thank-you note to my sister whose encouragement helped me.* [essential] / *I mailed a letter to my sister, whose advice I wanted.* [nonessential]).

If necessary, have students review:

7.6   *Whose* in Adjective Clauses (page 195)

7.9   Essential vs. Nonessential Adjective Clauses (page 201)

PRESENTATION IDEA

To help students use *whose* + noun as subject/ object, write a few sentences on the board and have students convert them to *whose* + subject/ object phrases (e.g., subject: *His book is interesting →whose book is interesting*; object: *I reported his error → whose error I reported*). If needed, remind students that a *whose* + noun phrase as object reverses normal sentence order for verbs and direct objects: V DO → DO V.

PART D ADJECTIVE CLAUSE AFTER INDEFINITE COMPOUND

Write on the board a series of indefinite pronouns (e.g., *something, someone, everyone, everything, nothing, no one, anything*). Have students use them to talk generally about themselves, using sentences with adjective clauses (e.g., *I like everything that I got for my birthday.*).

If necessary, have students review:

7.7   Adjective Clauses after Indefinite Pronouns (page 197)

7.9   Essential vs. Nonessential Adjective Clauses (page 201)

PART E DESCRIPTIVE PHRASE

Dictate or write on the board a list of adjective clauses (e.g., *who was the inventor of the Web, that is made in China, which is used in the film industry, who appeared in silent films*). Have students reduce the clauses in essential and nonessential statements on any subject (e.g., *Berners-Lee, inventor of the Web, was born in 1955.*).

If necessary, have students review:

7.9   Essential vs. Nonessential Adjective Clauses (page 201)

7.10   Descriptive Phrases (page 203)

TEST/REVIEW

Time: 15 min

Have students do the exercise on page 207. For additional practice, use the Assessment CD-ROM with Exam*View®* and the Online Workbook.

Answers:

PART 1

1. that/which; **2.** who/that; **3.** when; **4.** with which; **5.** whose; **6.** Ø/that/which; **7.** about which; **8.** where; **9.** Ø; **10.** that/Ø; **11.** when/during which; **12.** that; **13.** where/in which; **14.** who; **15.** whose; **16.** that/Ø

PART 2

1. John Donahoe, who replaced Meg Whitman, saved eBay from decline.

2. In 2008, when John Donahoe came to work at eBay, many top people were fired.

3. NC

4. Amazon, an online retailer, was created by Jeff Bezos.

5. NC

6. NC

7. NC

8. NC

9. NC

10. Many people confuse the Web with the Internet, which was created in the 1970s.

11. NC

WRITING

PART 1 EDITING ADVICE

Time: 10–15 min

1. Have students close their books. Write the first few sentences without editing marks or corrections on the board. For example:

    I bought a used computer from a person what lives in another state.

    Everything what we learned about the Internet is interesting.

2. Ask students to correct each sentence and provide a rule or an explanation for each correction. This activity can be done individually, in pairs, or as a class.

3. After students have corrected each sentence, tell them to turn to page 208. Say: *Now compare your work with the Editing Advice in the book.* Have students read through all the advice.

PART 2 EDITING PRACTICE

◔ Time: 10–15 min

1. Tell students they are going to put the Editing Advice into practice. Ask: *Do all the shaded words and phrases have mistakes?* (no) Go over the examples with the class. Then do #1 together.

2. Have students complete the practice individually. Then have them compare answers with a partner before checking answers as a class.

3. For the items students had difficulties with, have them go back and find the relevant grammar chart and review it. Monitor and give help as necessary.

Answers: 1. C; **2.** who; **3.** C; **4.** C; **5.** parts that needed/ parts which needed; **6.** (that) I don't want; **7.** C; **8.** who lives; **9.** my friend was taking the picture; **10.** whose; **11.** that; **12.** whose class I'm taking; **13.** A person who/ Anyone who/Whoever

PART 3 WRITE ABOUT IT

◑ Time: 30–40 min

1. Tell students they are going to write a paragraph. Before students begin, have them think of three ways that computers and the Internet have made their life easier and simpler. Have students write a sentence or two about each way. Then have students write an introductory and a concluding sentence for their paragraphs. Have them then combine the sentences into a paragraph.

2. Ask students to list several websites or apps that they like and write notes about them. Elicit from students examples of adjective clauses they might include to describe how the sites/apps help or entertain them (e.g., *… which shows me how to get a new password, … where I can play a game for free*). Have students write a paragraph.

PART 4 EDIT YOUR WRITING

◔ Time: 15–20 min

Have students edit their writing by reviewing the Lesson Summary on page 206 and the Editing Advice on page 208. Collect for assessment and/or have students share their essays in small groups.

EXPANSION ACTIVITIES

1. Tell students these activities are about their opinions. Ask: *When do we say: Yes, but …?* (when we want to disagree politely) Have students complete their sentences which answer the questions individually. Then have them present their sentences to partners and agree or disagree with each other (e.g., *Yes, and …. or Yes, but ….*).

Have students work in groups. Elicit other inventions that changed the world and write them on the board (e.g., *the wheel, the nail, the compass, the light bulb, penicillin*). Either assign or have each group choose one or two inventions to discuss, deciding how the invention changed people's lives. Review with students language for agreeing, checking for agreement, and disagreeing (e.g., *I think so too. Are you sure that's right? I'm not sure I agree.*). Set a time limit for discussion. Have groups talk about their choices. If appropriate, have each group appoint a spokesperson who reports back to the class.

8 HELPING OTHERS

GRAMMAR CHARTS

LESSON OPENER

Have students look at the photo and read the caption. Ask: *Who are these people? What are they doing?* Have students read the quotation. Ask: *Do you agree?*

Background: Many Americans believe that giving time or money to a good cause helps others and yourself. Based on religious beliefs, British laws for charity, and ancient Greek philosophy, *philanthropy* became an integral part of America's culture very early. Since the 1600s, donations have aided communities and foreign countries; built schools, hospitals, churches, prisons, and libraries; and funded school lunches, relief and rescue operations, scholarships, civic projects, and art and cultural awards and grants. Today Americans give about $300 billion to charity, and 56% of adults and 59% of teenagers volunteer their time to organizations such as Girl Scouts or YMCA; soup kitchens for the homeless; care for the elderly; and walks, runs, and cycling for the sick.

H. Jackson Brown, Jr. is an author of a popular self-help book called *Life's Little Instruction Book*, which he originally wrote as advice for his son who was going to college. In the tradition of Benjamin Franklin, the book is a practical, humorous guide to how to succeed and be happy in life. Brown, who lives in Tennessee, was born in 1940.

CONTEXT

This unit is about helping others. Students will read about Andrew Carnegie, a wealthy industrialist and philanthropist; Joyce Koenig, an artist who raises money for children with cancer; Matel Dawson, a forklift driver who donated money for college scholarships; and Dan Pallotta, a Californian who organizes bike rides to raise money for AIDS.

1. Give students a few minutes to look through the lesson. Have them look at the photos and titles. How do they relate to the context?

2. Elicit the topics that will be discussed.

3. Have students discuss in pairs or small groups what they know about helping others, volunteering, and charitable programs.

GRAMMAR

Students will learn about infinitives and gerunds.

1. To activate students' prior knowledge, ask what students know about the "to" form of verbs and verbs that act like nouns.

2. Give several examples of sentences using infinitives and gerunds (e.g., *I can't wait to go on vacation. To learn is to teach. Giving is better than receiving. I tried studying all night, but it didn't help.*).

3. Have volunteers give additional examples and write them on the board.

`READING`

Andrew Carnegie, Philanthropist, page 212

PRE-READING

⏱ Time: 10–20 min

1. Have students look at the photo and read the caption. Ask: *What is this building?* (a library) *Whose funds were used to build it?* (Andrew Carnegie's)
2. Have students read the title and look briefly at the reading. Ask: *What is the main idea of the reading?* Have students make predictions.
3. Pre-teach any essential vocabulary words your students may not know, such as *industries, persuaded, contribution,* and *gospel.*
4. Ask: *Why was Carnegie a philanthropist?* Have students discuss in small groups and share their answers with the class.

READING GLOSSARY

industries: (businesses involved in) making and selling products
to persuade: to lead someone to believe or do something by argument or reasoning
contribution: a gift or donation
gospel: an idea that cannot be questioned

READING

⏱ Time: 10–15 min

After students have read the article, go over the answers to the Comprehension Check on page 213: **1.** T; **2.** F; **3.** T

CONTEXT NOTE

1. Andrew Carnegie was one of the industrialist giants during the nineteenth century who were both respected and criticized. Today, these industrialists are known as "Robber Barons" for their dubious business practices, and many of them, such as Carnegie, John D. Rockefeller, and J. P. Morgan, as philanthropists for the huge amounts of money they donated to charitable enterprises. Carnegie built libraries, Morgan patronized the arts, and Rockefeller funded biomedical research and the sciences. Ask students if they have similar people in their countries, whom people think do both bad and good. Have students work with a partner to discuss these people and how they have helped their countries. Try to pair students from the same culture. Ask a few pairs to share their information with the class.
2. Students might recognize other terms for successful industrialists, e.g., *tycoon* (from the Japanese word *taikun* or "great lord"), *business magnate,* or *captain of industry.* Have students share terms in their native languages for big businesspersons. Find out if the terms are native to the culture or borrowed from other languages.

ADDITIONAL COMPREHENSION QUESTIONS

How old was Andrew Carnegie when his family left Scotland? (thirteen) *In Carnegie's opinion, what was the key to a successful life?* (education) *What is* The Gospel of Wealth? (Carnegie's book about philanthropy for wealthy people)

8.1 Infinitives—Overview, page 213

🕐 Time: 10–15 min

1. Have students look at grammar chart **8.1**. Ask: *What is an infinitive?* (*to* + base form of a verb) Elicit several ways an infinitive is used (e.g., after certain verbs and adjectives, as subjects of sentences, after certain expressions that begin with *It*).

2. Have students look at the examples and explanations in the chart. Direct students' attention to the Language Notes. Ask: *In negative sentences with infinitives, where does* not *go?* (before the infinitive) *How do you form a passive infinitive?* (*to be* + past participle)

PRACTICE IDEAS: WRITING AND SPEAKING

1. Write on the board an additional example for each use of infinitives. Have students identify each use (e.g., *To be rich isn't enough* [infinitive as subject of sentence], *Carnegie needed to make money* [infinitive after certain verbs]). Write their answers on the board and review them as a class.

2. Provide stems for students to use to make statements with infinitives, such as: *I want …, I'm excited …, It's important …*. Write the stems on the board and have students practice making sentences in pairs. Ask several students to share their sentences with the class.

EXERCISE 1 pages 213–214 CD 2 TR 7

🕐 Time: 10–15 min

Answers: 1. to work; **2.** to find; **3.** to collect; **4.** to get; **5.** to finish; **6.** to think; **7.** to do; **8.** to continue; **9.** finish; **10.** to emphasize; **11.** to learn; **12.** to have; **13.** to help; **14.** to teach; **15.** To provide

---

PRESENTATION IDEAS

1. Before students listen to the audio, have them skim the reading for key ideas. Ask: *Where did Leslie Natzke start her program?* (in the United States) *Who is the program for?* (Nigerian girls) *What is the main purpose of Natzke's program?* (to educate/train the girls) *Why did Natzke want to help Nigerian girls?* (because she thought they were too young to marry and needed an education)

2. After students are finished skimming, have them close their books and listen to the audio. Ask additional comprehension questions, such as *What is Save the Children?* (an organization that says Niger is a bad place to be a mother) *What is Expanding Lives?* (Natzke's program)

8.2 Verbs Followed by an Infinitive, page 214

🕐 Time: 10–15 min

1. Have students look at grammar chart **8.2**. Review the explanation and example sentences.

2. Ask students to study the list of verbs in the Language Notes. Clarify any vocabulary students are unfamiliar with. Ask: *What can you observe about these verbs?* (some have the same type of meaning and can be categorized) Elicit and write on the board categories and then classify some of the words in the chart with students (e.g.,
   Feelings: expect, hate, hope, like, love, can't stand, …
   Desires: need, want, wish, would like, …
   Deciding: agree, choose, decide, …
   Plans and expectations: hope, intend, expect, learn, prepare, promise, start, …).

3. Elicit additional categories from students and classify the relevant verbs on the board. Ask students to provide example sentences using some of the verbs with infinitives.

EXERCISE 2 page 215
🕐 Time: 10–15 min
Answers: 1. to make; **2.** to follow; **3.** to help; **4.** to give away; **5.** to use; **6.** to get; **7.** to give away; **8.** to persuade; **9.** to provide

EXERCISE 3 page 215
🕐 Time: 5–10 min
Answers: 1. to work; **2.** to leave; **3.** to start; **4.** to build; **5.** to die; **6.** to get; **7.** to be given; **8.** to be educated; **9.** to have; **10.** to learn

EXERCISE 4 page 216
🕐 Time: 5–10 min
Answers will vary.

8.3 Object before Infinitive,
page 216

🕐 Time: 5–10 min

1. Have students look at the grammar chart. Elicit the definition of direct object. (noun that follows main verb and answers the question: [verb] *what?*)

2. Direct students' attention to the example sentences. Ask students to say what they observe about objects and infinitives. If students have difficulty, say: *The infinitive follows the object. It completes the meaning*

of the object: Carnegie wanted poor people to what? to have the same opportunities. Without the complement, the object has no meaning.

3. Review the rest of the chart. Draw students' attention to the Language Note. Provide several examples of your own using verbs from the list (e.g., *The library encourages people to donate books. My friends asked me to help.*). Clarify any vocabulary students are unfamiliar with. Ask volunteers to give sentences about themselves using the verbs, objects, and infinitives.

ADDITIONAL PRACTICE

Have students take a moment to study and memorize the list of verbs in the chart. When they have finished, have them close their books. Ask them to write as many of the verbs as they can remember. Give 1 point per correct word; a total of 18 points are possible. Have students share their scores with the class.

EXERCISE 5 pages 216–217
🕐 Time: 5–10 min
Answers: 1. him to use; **2. a.** them to think, **b.** them to sign; **3. a.** them to suffer, **b.** him to do, **c.** him to take; **4. a.** them to help, **b.** me to teach; **5. a.** me to volunteer, **b.** them to finish; **6. a.** me to buy, **b.** me to save; **7. a.** them to go, **b.** them to become

EXERCISE 6 pages 217–218
🕐 Time: 10–15 min
Answers: 1. him to teach the children good values; **2.** me to help others; **3.** them to not forget about other people; **4.** them to give to charity; **5.** them to be kind to others; **6.** you to work hard; **7.** us to give money to people in need; **8.** her to be generous; **9.** me not to be selfish; **10.** them to be polite

EXERCISE 7 page 218

⏱ Time: 5–10 min

Answers will vary.

> ### PRACTICE IDEA: SPEAKING
>
> After students complete Exercise 7, have them work in pairs to ask each other about their statements with *why* or *why not*, such as:
>
> A: *My parents wanted me not to be selfish.*
>
> B: *Why?*
>
> A: *Because I didn't want other kids to play with my toys.*

8.4 Causative Verbs, page 219

⏱ Time: 5–10 min

1. Have students cover the grammar chart. Say: *Tell me about something that someone got you to do. Tell me about something someone permitted you to do.* Give examples if necessary. Write students' answers on the board. Then say: *Verbs that show that something or someone causes us to do something are called* causative verbs.

2. Have students look at the grammar chart. Review the examples and explanations in the chart. Point out the use of the base form in the examples after *help, let, permit, allow, make,* and *have.* Point out the usage of the verb *have,* meaning *to give a job or task to someone.* Elicit or say that in this meaning *had* is similar in meaning to *made* or *told* but softer.

> ### PRESENTATION IDEA
>
> After students have reviewed the example sentences in the grammar chart, have them go back to the reading on page 212 and identify causative verbs followed by the infinitive and causative verbs followed by the base form. Have them identify each type of use referring to the explanations in the chart.

ADDITIONAL PRACTICE

Have students close their books. Write on the board a mix of causative verbs that are followed by the *to* form and the base form of verbs. Have students write a few sentences with the causative verbs and share their answers with the class. Provide feedback.

EXERCISE 8 pages 219–220

⏱ Time: 10–15 min

Answers: 1. a. to give, **b.** to donate; **2. a.** do, **b.** feel; **3. a.** drive; **4. a.** buy, **b.** to use, **c.** save, **d.** to give

EXERCISE 9 page 220

⏱ Time: 5–10 min

Answers: 1. to give; **2.** answer; **3.** tell; **4.** to contribute; **5.** pay; **6.** to volunteer; **7.** (to) send

8.5 Adjective plus Infinitive, page 221

⏱ Time: 10–15 min

1. Ask students to cover the grammar chart. Write on the board: *I'm proud to be … and I'm happy to be able to ….* Ask students to complete the statements about themselves and then ask volunteers to share their answers. Ask: *What can you observe about these sentences?* (all use *be* and have an adjective followed by an infinitive)

2. Have students look at the grammar chart. Review the examples and explanations in the chart.

3. Point out the adjective list in the Language Note. Clarify the meaning of any words students are not familiar with. Have students give a few examples of their own using the adjectives.

EXERCISE 10 page 221

⏱ Time: 10–15 min

Possible Answers: 1. to donate; **2.** to help; **3.** to do; **4.** to learn/to find out; **5.** to have; **6.** to ask; **7.** to help; **8.** to go; **9.** to bring/to give; **10.** to have; **11.** to have

> ### PRACTICE IDEA: SPEAKING
>
> Have students work alone to brainstorm five or six adjectives they think describe a relative, friend, or other person they know (e.g., *eager, willing, lucky*). Have students make notes and use the notes to describe this person to a group, using adjective + infinitive phrases in their descriptions.

EXERCISE 11 page 222

⏱ Time: 5–10 min

Possible answers: 1. to do; **2.** to get/to find; **3.** to work; **4.** to hire; **5.** to get/to find; **6.** stay; **7.** to save; **8.** to buy; **9.** to think; **10.** to go; **11.** to pay; **12.** to make; **13.** to think;

14. (to) learn; **15.** (to) clean; **16.** to make; **17.** feel; **18.** to be; **19.** (to) get; **20.** to be/to become; **21.** to give

READING
One Step at a Time, page 223

PRE-READING

🕐 Time: 10–15 min

1. Have students look at the photo, read the title, and skim the reading. Ask: *What is the reading about? How do you know?* Have students use the photo and title to make predictions.

2. Pre-teach any vocabulary words or phrases your students may not know, such as *one step at a time*, *combine*, *raise money*, and *fairs*.

3. Activate students' prior knowledge about how charity organizations raise money. Ask: *Do volunteers get paid for the work they do? How do charities raise money?* Elicit and write on the board a few ways, such as *telethons, asking for money through letters, campaigning, selling something (e.g., lemonade) and donating the proceeds.* Have students discuss the questions in pairs. Try to pair students from different cultures.

READING GLOSSARY

one step at a time: slowly and carefully; doing just one thing at a time (idiom)

to combine: to join together

to raise money: to ask people for money

fairs: trade exhibitions or events

EXPANDING ON THE READING

The topic for this reading can be enhanced with the following items:

1. A card or other item made and sold to raise money for charity

2. An article from the newspaper or a website about people who make things or sell their art for charity

---

READING ^{CD 2} _{TR 8}

🕐 Time: 10–15 min

After students have read the article, go over the answers to the Comprehension Check on page 223 **1.** T; **2.** T; **3.** F

ADDITIONAL COMPREHENSION QUESTIONS

What does the title of the reading refer to? (the camp, Joyce Koenig's way to raise money, and how to help the kids at the camp) *Why did Joyce start making the cards?* (because she didn't have a lot of money to donate) *Why did her friends seem unsure about helping her at first?* (They didn't think they could make art.) *How much money has Joyce made for the camp?* ($40,000)

PRACTICE IDEA: LISTENING

Have students close their books and listen to the audio. Tell them to write all the infinitive phrases they hear. Repeat the audio if necessary.

PRESENTATION IDEA

Discuss with students how art is used. Elicit ways that art is used to help people, such as for therapy, to create awareness, to teach people who cannot read, and to lift people's spirits. Write the ideas on the board. Ask: *What is your experience with art?* Have students discuss as a class what they know about how art can help people.

8.6 Infinitives as Subjects, page 224

🕐 Time: 10–15 min

1. Have students cover grammar chart **8.6**. Write on the board: *It is important for people to ….* Have volunteers complete the statement.

2. Have students review the example sentences and explanations carefully.

3. Point out the use of indirect objects with *take* and *cost* in the fourth section of the chart. Provide examples about yourself, such as *It didn't take me long to get here today; there wasn't much traffic.*

EXERCISE 12 page 224

⏱ Time: 5–10 min

Answers: 1. to; **2.** take; **3.** It's; **4.** for; **5.** To; **6.** costs, to; **7.** To

EXERCISE 13 pages 224–225

⏱ Time: 5–10 min

Answers will vary.

EXERCISE 14 page 225

⏱ Time: 5–10 min

Answers will vary.

EXERCISE 15 page 225

⏱ Time: 5–10 min

Answers:

1. It's a good thing to raise money for charity.
2. It isn't easy to raise one million dollars. / It's not easy to raise one million dollars. / It is not easy to raise one million dollars.
3. It takes a lot of money to fight disease.
4. It's everyone's responsibility to help poor people. / It is everyone's responsibility to help poor people.
5. It takes a lot of money to produce high-quality education.
6. It was Carnegie's dream to build libraries.
7. It's Joyce's goal to raise money for sick children. / It is Joyce's goal to raise money for sick children.
8. It will take time to fight disease in poor countries.

8.7 Infinitives to Show Purpose, page 226

⏱ Time: 5–10 min

1. Tell students the phrase *in order to* shows purpose and is a short form for *in order + to [base form of the verb]*.

Write the formula on the board. Review the examples and explanations in grammar chart **8.7** with the class.

2. Draw students' attention to the second section of the chart. Provide several examples of your own to illustrate shortening (e.g., *I bought the suit in order to wear it to my interview. / I bought the suit to wear it to my interview.*). Ask volunteers to provide examples about themselves.

EXERCISE 16 page 226

⏱ Time: 5–10 min

Possible Answers: 1. learn; **2.** build; **3.** get; **4.** get, get; **5.** help; **6.** raise; **7.** to work/to volunteer; **8.** to give

8.8 Infinitives with *Too* and *Enough*, page 226

⏱ Time: 5–10 min

1. Review *too* and *enough*. Say: *My shoes are size 7. Size 8 is too big, and size 6 isn't big enough.* If necessary, explain that *too* is generally more than necessary or not possible, *enough* is just right, and *not enough* is less than necessary or not possible.
2. Have students review the examples and explanations in the grammar chart. Point out the last section of the chart and the omission of infinitive phrases. Elicit or say that the phrase can be omitted because it has already been stated or implied. Write on the board: *I can't volunteer this summer because I'm too busy ~~to volunteer this summer~~.* Write on the board: *I don't have enough time to …, I'm not old enough to ….* Ask students to complete the sentences about themselves.

EXERCISE 17 page 227

⏱ Time: 5–10 min

Answers: 1. enough talent; **2.** too old to learn; **3.** easy to make; **4.** too long to make; **5.** enough time; **6.** talented enough; **7.** to make; **8.** too busy to help; **9.** too much work to do; **10.** enough time to help; **11.** enough money to buy

EXERCISE 18 page 227

⏱ Time: 10–15 min

Possible answers: 1. enough time; **2.** too many; **3.** too much time; **4.** too hot; **5.** well enough; **6.** too much

`READING`

Helping Others Get an Education, page 228

PRE-READING

⏱ Time: 5–10 min

1. Have students look at the photo and read the caption. Ask: *Who is this man?* (Matel Dawson)

2. Have students look briefly at the reading. Ask: *What is the reading about? How do you know?* Have students use the title and photo to make predictions.

3. Pre-teach any vocabulary words your students may not know, such as *investing, fancy, drop out, grateful, lifestyle,* and *shortly.*

4. Activate students' prior knowledge about philanthropy. Ask: *What other philanthropist have you read about? What is a philanthropist?* Have students discuss the questions in pairs. Try to pair students of the same culture. Have a few pairs share their answers with the class.

READING GLOSSARY

to invest: to put money into business ideas to make money

fancy: very expensive and fashionable

to drop out: to leave school permanently

grateful: thankful, appreciative

lifestyle: the manner in which one lives

shortly: soon; in a small amount of time

READING 🎧 CD 2 TR 9

⏱ Time: 10–15 min

After students have read the article, go over the answers to the Comprehension Check on page 228: **1.** T; **2.** F; **3.** T

ADDITIONAL COMPREHENSION QUESTIONS

Why was education important to Matel Dawson? (because he had to drop out of school to work) *What did Dawson donate his money for?* (college scholarships) *What did Dawson know about not having an education?* (It limits job possibilities.) *Where did Dawson learn about giving?* (from his parents)

8.9 Gerunds—Overview, page 229

🕐 Time: 10–15 min

1. Tell students that gerunds express actions as nouns. Have students look at grammar chart **8.9**. Ask: *How do you form gerunds?* (-*ing* form of a verb) *How are gerunds used?* (as subjects, direct objects, and objects of prepositions)

2. Review the examples and explanations in the chart. Direct students' attention to the Language Notes. Ask: *In negative sentences with gerunds, where does* not *go?* (before the gerund) *How do you form a passive gerund?* (*being* + past participle) *Are gerund subjects singular or plural?* (singular)

EXERCISE 19 page 229 🎧 CD 2 TR 10

🕐 Time: 10–15 min

Answers: 1. making; **2.** advancing; **3.** working; **4.** volunteering; **5.** providing; **6.** working; **7.** eliminating; **8.** being; **9.** getting; **10.** living; **11.** eating; **12.** providing; **13.** ending; **14.** spending; **15.** having; **16.** Doing

8.10 Gerunds as Subjects, page 230

🕐 Time: 5–10 min

1. Have students review the examples and explanation in the grammar chart.

2. Point out the use of the singular verb with gerunds as subjects, and remind students of the placement of *not* (before the gerund).

ADDITIONAL PRACTICE

Write several gapped sentences on the board, such as ___ *made Mr. Dawson happy.* ___ *wasn't important to him.* Ask questions to have students fill the gaps, such as *What made Mr. Dawson happy?* (giving money away) *What wasn't important to him?* (having a fancy car) Have students provide additional examples about themselves.

EXERCISE 20 page 230

🕐 Time: 5–10 min

Possible Answers: 1. Giving; **2.** Working; **3.** having; **4.** Getting; **5.** Having; **6.** Driving; **7.** Taking; **8.** Knowing/Feeling; **9.** Volunteering; **10.** Ending

EXERCISE 21 page 230

🕐 Time: 5–10 min

Answers will vary.

8.11 Gerunds after Prepositions and Nouns, page 231

🕐 Time: 5–10 min

1. Have students cover the explanation column of the grammar chart. Elicit the word order of the boldfaced words in the examples in the first three sections. Write the word order on the board: verb + preposition + gerund; adjective + preposition + gerund; verb + object + preposition + gerund. Ask: *What comes before the gerund?* (preposition)

2. Have students review the examples and explanations.

3. Draw students' attention to the list of phrases followed directly by a noun in the last section of the chart. Review the word order (verb + noun + gerund) of these expressions.

> ### PRACTICE IDEA: SPEAKING
> Have students work in small groups and talk about things they do/don't care about or spend money for, using gerund phrases. Write on the board: *I don't care about …* and *I don't spend money ….* When they are finished, ask several students to share their answers with the class.

EXERCISE 22 page 231

🕐 Time: 10–15 min

Answers: 1. about (making); **5.** to (providing); **7.** on (eliminating); **9.** in (getting); **12.** about (providing); **13.** in (ending)

EXERCISE 23 page 231

🕐 Time: 5–10 min

Answers: 1. driving; **2.** helping; **3.** giving; **4.** volunteering; **5.** quitting; **6.** having; **7.** building; **8.** creating; **9.** signing; **10.** making, selling; **11.** providing

8.12 Prepositions after Verbs, Adjectives, and Nouns, pages 232–233

🕐 Time: 5–10 min

1. Have students look at the grammar chart. Tell students not to spend too much time on each section of the chart. Ask: *What are the four categories of combinations in the chart?* (verb + preposition, verb + object + preposition, adjective + preposition, noun + preposition)

2. Tell students that the phrases in the chart and their uses are best learned by practice and repetition. Clarify words they are not familiar with and use them in a sentence. Have students provide examples of their own to demonstrate comprehension.

3. Draw students' attention to the Language Notes. Review the examples carefully.

PRESENTATION IDEAS

1. Divide students into four groups. Have each group review a section of the chart. Have groups practice making sentences with phrases from their section. Circulate and help groups as needed by providing one or two examples of your own (e.g., *I believe in working hard. I am proud of your progress.*). Then ask volunteers from each group to present sentences about themselves using the phrases.

2. Brainstorm ideas for memorizing the phrases and combinations in the chart. Write them on the board. Have students choose one method and apply it. Keep time, and after 5 or 6 minutes, stop them. Have students close their books and write all the phrases they remember. Then have students compare results as a class to see which method seems most effective.

3. Before presenting the grammar chart, have students underline phrases with prepositions and a gerund in the reading on page 228.

CONTEXT NOTE

A common, polite way to end a conversation is "I don't want to keep you from what you are doing" or "Don't let me keep you from finishing your work." Elicit similar examples from the class.

EXERCISE 24 page 234

🕐 Time: 10–15 min

Answers: 1. about having; **2.** for being; **3.** on working; **4.** watching; **5.** to having; **6.** in gardening; **7.** of having; **8.** about volunteering; **9.** working; **10.** at giving; **11.** for giving

EXERCISE 25 page 234

🕐 Time: 10–15 min

Answers will vary.

8.13 Verbs Followed by Gerunds, page 235

🕐 Time: 5–10 min

1. Tell students the chart is about verb-followed-by-gerund phrases. Say: *One of the most common is* go + *gerund, in which the gerund stands for an activity.*

2. Activate students' prior knowledge of activity terms. Ask: *Have you heard* go + *activity phrases before?* Elicit answers such as: *go + walking, shopping, running, camping,* and write them on the board.

3. Have students review the examples, explanations, and *go* + gerund phrases. Have them check to see if the phrases on the board are on the list.

4. Draw students' attention to the Language Notes and the footnoted definitions. Ask: *What do these sentences mean: I can't help feeling sad today* (have no control); *I can't stand it when people are late* (really don't like); *I don't mind if you turn the television on.* (it's okay); and *Don't put off your homework* (postpone).

PRACTICE IDEA: SPEAKING

Have students use the expressions with *go* in the chart to talk about themselves using the present perfect and simple past tenses (e.g., *I've never gone hunting. I went sightseeing when I was in New York last year.*).

EXERCISE 26 pages 235–236

🕐 Time: 10–15 min

Possible answers: 1. helping; **2.** getting/receiving; **3.** driving; **4.** living; **5.** working; **6.** getting/receiving; **7.** helping; **8.** working OR volunteering; **9.** making; **10.** getting/receiving; **11.** making; **12.** swimming

PRACTICE IDEA: WRITING

Have students create new statements making a contrast from the prompt and using one of the verbs from chart **8.13**. Model an example: *He didn't mind driving an old car; He couldn't stand driving an old car.* Have students exchange their work with a partner for feedback.

8.14 Verbs Followed by a Gerund or Infinitive, page 236

⏱ Time: 5–10 min

1. Have students look at the grammar chart. Review the examples and explanations.

2. Draw students' attention to the Language Note. Review the list of verbs that can be followed by either a gerund or an infinitive.

3. Have students make their own sentences with the verbs in the list and either a gerund or an infinitive (e.g., *I started to volunteer at the animal shelter a few years ago; I want to continue helping there after I retire.*).

PRESENTATION BOX

Have students cover the grammar chart. Write the eight verbs in the Language Note on the board. Elicit example sentences for the verbs and write them on the board. Then convert each gerund to an infinitive and each infinitive to a gerund and write the new sentences. Say: *These verbs can be followed by an infinitive or a gerund.*

EXERCISE 27 page 236

⏱ Time: 5–10 min

Answers:

1. Dawson's parents loved helping others.
2. They hated to see people suffer.
3. Dawson began to work when he was 19 years old.
4. He liked to give away money.
5. He continued working until he was 80 years old.
6. He preferred living in a small apartment.
7. He loved helping students get an education.

EXERCISE 28 page 237

⏱ Time: 10–15 min

Possible answers: 1. being/to be; **2.** to be/being; **3.** to work/working; **4.** to be/being; **5.** to look/looking; **6.** to work/working

8.15 Gerund or Infinitive as Subject, page 237

⏱ Time: 5–10 min

1. Have students cover grammar chart **8.15**. Ask students to provide examples of sentences with a gerund or infinitive as the subject; remind students that they studied these in grammar chart **8.6** on page 224 and grammar chart **8.10** on page 230. Write the examples on the board.

2. Have students review the grammar chart and check their sentences on the board. Direct students' attention to the second section. Ask: *Why is* to help others *a delayed subject?* (because it means the same thing as [is the referent of] the subject of the sentence, *It*)

EXERCISE 29 pages 237–238

⏱ Time: 10–15 min

Answers:

1. Helping others is wonderful.
2. Going to college costs a lot of money.
3. Working and studying at the same time is hard.
4. Helping students get an education is important.
5. Working in a factory is difficult.
6. Dying rich is a disgrace (according to Carnegie).
7. Helping others is satisfying.
8. Signing the Giving Pledge is a wonderful thing.

8.16 Gerund or Infinitive after a Verb: Differences in Meaning, page 238

⏱ Time: 5–10 min

1. Ask: *What was grammar chart* **8.14** *about?* (verbs that can be followed by a gerund or an infinitive with no difference in meaning) Say: *Chart* **8.16** *lists some verbs that do change meaning.*

2. Have students look at the grammar chart. Review the example sentences and explanations carefully.

3. Direct students' attention to the Language Note. To help students understand the difference in meaning with *try* in past and present, write this example on the board:

> A: *I tried calling my sister, but she wasn't home.*
> B: *Try calling her cell phone.*

Elicit or say that *try* in the first sentence means *experiment,* and *try* in the second sentence means *make an effort.*

PRESENTATION BOX

Have students cover the explanation column of the grammar chart. Review the examples with students. Ask students to try to figure out the differences in meaning between the examples with gerunds and the examples with infinitives.

EXERCISE 30 pages 238–239
🕐 Time: 10–15 min

Answers: 1. telling; **2.** hearing; **3.** meeting; **4.** to rest; **5.** to get; **6.** to pick up; **7.** to leave; **8.** to call/calling; **9.** to call/calling; **10.** to leave/leaving; **11.** to text/texting; **12.** to use; **13.** worrying; **14.** giving; **15.** to understand

PRACTICE IDEA: SPEAKING

Tell students that the mother in the conversation in Exercise 30 has a lot of advice for her son. Have students work in groups to make a list of the advice she gives him, and then add advice they think a person traveling a long distance should follow. Have groups share their advice with the class.

READING

AIDS Bike Rides, page 240

PRE-READING
🕐 Time: 5–10 min

1. Have students look at the photo and read the caption. Ask: *Who is in the photo?* (Dan Pallotta) *Where is he?* (in a park by a bike trail)

2. Have students read the title and look briefly at the reading. Ask: *What is the reading about? How do you know?* Have students make predictions.

3. Pre-teach any vocabulary words your students may

not know, such as *bike, round trip, ten-speed road bike,* and *twenty-four-speed mountain bike.*

4. Activate students' prior knowledge about raising money for charity. Ask: *What ways for raising money for charity have we discussed so far?* (volunteering, making cards to sell) *What kind of volunteering can you do?* (sample answers: helping kids, helping old people, taking food to families in need) Have students discuss the questions in pairs.

READING GLOSSARY

to bike: to ride a bicycle

round trip: a journey that starts and ends in the same place

ten-speed road bike: a bicycle with a choice of ten gears, for riding on paved roads

twenty-four-speed mountain bike: a heavier bicycle with a choice of twenty-four gears, for riding on dirt, rocky trails, etc.

EXPANDING ON THE READING

The topic for this reading can be enhanced with the following items:

1. A flyer, news article, or Web page listing volunteer opportunities

2. Newspaper or Web articles about bicycle rides, walks, or other charity fund raiser events involving exercise

3. Articles about other fund-raising trends, such as ribbons for breast cancer awareness or bracelets for cancer research

READING   CD 2 TR 11
🕐 Time: 10–15 min

After students have read the article, go over the answers to the Comprehension Check on page 240: **1.** F; **2.** T; **3.** F

ADDITIONAL COMPREHENSION QUESTIONS

What did Dan Pallotta do? (organized the first AIDS bike rides) *How many people participated in 9 years?* (182,000) *Where is Mimi Gordon from?* (Chicago) *Why was biking in Chicago different from biking in Los Angeles/San Francisco?* (Chicago is flat; San Francisco has hills and mountains.) *How much did she ride when she was in training?* (150 miles per week)

PRACTICE IDEA: LISTENING AND SPEAKING

Have students listen to the audio alone and then retell the main points of the article to a partner. Repeat the audio if necessary. Have students open their books, read along as they listen to the audio, and check their versions of the article.

8.17 Used To / Be Used To / Get Used To, page 241

🕐 Time: 5–10 min

1. Tell students this chart is about expressing regular past actions. Have students review the examples and explanations in the grammar chart carefully.

2. Point out the different meanings of *used to / be used to / get used to*. Point out the negative *didn't use to* in the first section of the grammar chart.

3. Ask students to provide examples of their own. Say: *What did you use to do that you don't do now? What is something you are used to doing now, and something you had to get used to when you came to the United States?* Write several examples on the board (e.g., *Natalia had to get used to living in an apartment.*).

4. Draw students' attention to the Pronunciation Note. Have students practice pronouncing *used to* correctly. Note that the final *–d* is pronounced in formal English.

PRESENTATION IDEA

After students have reviewed the example sentences in the grammar chart, have them go back to the reading on page 240 and identify which explanation applies to each boldfaced phrase in the reading.

EXERCISE 31 page 241

🕐 Time: 5–10 min

Possible Answers: 1. exercise once a week; **2.** drive/take the bus; **3.** think; **4.** ride; **5.** donate; **6.** spend/save

PRACTICE IDEA: SPEAKING

Have students take turns interviewing each other in pairs about their answers to Exercise 31 using *couldn't get used to*. For example:

A: *I used to have a full-time job. Now I work part time.*

B: *Why?*

A: *I couldn't get used to being away from my kids. Now I can spend more time with my children.*

EXERCISE 32 pages 241–242

🕐 Time: 10–15 min

Answers: 1. 'm not used to working/am not used to working; **2.** 'm not used to riding/am not used to riding; **3.** 's used to giving/is used to giving; **4.** was used to driving; **5.** 's used to helping/is used to helping; **6.** 'm not used to working/am not used to working; **7. a.** 'm not used to doing/am not used to doing, **b.** 's used to hearing/is used to hearing; **8.** 'm not used to riding/am not used to riding

EXERCISE 33 page 243

🕐 Time: 10–15 min

Answers: 1. are used to riding; **2.** I; **3.** I was; **4.** take; **5.** got used to; **6.** riding; **7.** riding; **8.** couldn't; **9.** get used; **10.** used; **11.** use

PRACTICE IDEA: SPEAKING AND WRITING

Have students work in pairs to tell each other about things they aren't used to and things they had a hard time getting used to. Ask students to give information they don't mind sharing. Then have students write a paragraph about their partners using the information they discussed. Collect the paragraphs and read them to the class. Have students guess which student is being described.

8.18 Sense-Perception Verbs,
page 244

🕐 Time: 5–10 min

1   Have students cover the chart. Ask: *What are the senses?* (sight, smell, hearing, taste, touch) Brainstorm with the class a list of sense-perception verbs. Say: *Tell me all the verbs you can think of that we use to talk about our senses.* Write the verbs on the board.

2. Review the chart. Elicit the meaning of *slight difference* (a very small difference) in the note at the top of the chart.

3. Have students look at the examples and explanations in the grammar chart. Ask: *What did you see people doing on your way to school today?*

EXERCISE 34 page 244

🕐 Time: 10–15 min

Answers: 1. walking; **2.** crying; **3.** take; **4.** tell; **5.** take; **6.** running; **7.** tell; **8.** say/saying; **9.** help/helping

SUMMARY OF LESSON 8

◐ Time: 20–30 min

PART A INFINITIVES AND BASE FORMS

Have students work in pairs to write a new question for each example in the chart, such as: *What did Matel Dawson want? What did his mother want him to do?* Have pairs ask and answer their questions using the examples as a model.

If necessary, have students review:

8.2   Verbs Followed by an Infinitive (page 214)

8.3   Object before Infinitive (page 216)

8.4   Causative Verbs (page 219)

8.5   Adjective plus Infinitive (page 221)

8.6   Infinitives as Subjects (page 224)

8.7   Infinitives to Show Purpose (page 226)

8.8   Infinitives with *Too* and *Enough* (page 226)

8.18 Sense-Perception Verbs (page 244)

PRACTICE IDEA: SPEAKING

Write phrases from the chart on the board (e.g., *It's fun for me …, She convinced me ….*). In pairs, have students make statements about themselves using the phrases.

PART B GERUNDS

In pairs, have students make statements about things they enjoy doing, don't like doing, avoid doing, or have a hard time doing (e.g., *I enjoy skiing. I avoid texting while I'm driving. I have a hard time talking to my brother.*).

If necessary, have students review:

8.10 Gerunds as Subjects (page 230)

8.11 Gerunds after Prepositions and Nouns (page 231)

8.13 Verbs Followed by Gerunds (page 235)

8.14 Verbs Followed by a Gerund or Infinitive (page 236)

PRACTICE IDEA: SPEAKING

Have students use gerunds to make statements about things that have been easy and things that have been hard in the United States (e.g., *Learning English has been easy. Making friends has been hard.*).

PART C GERUND OR INFINITIVE— DIFFERENCES IN MEANING

Have students make statements about themselves based on the examples in the chart (e.g., *I used to volunteer, but now I don't have time. I stopped to get coffee on the way to school today.*).

If necessary, have students review:

8.16 Gerund or Infinitive after a Verb: Differences in Meaning (page 238)

PRACTICE IDEA: SPEAKING

Have students work in pairs to make sentences contrasting *remember, stop,* and *try* followed by a gerund and an infinitive, using the models in the chart.

🕐 Time: 15 min

Have students do the exercise on page 247. For additional practice, use the Assessment CD-ROM with Exam*View*® and the Online Workbook.

Answers: 1. to have; **2.** to help; **3.** in helping; **4.** to read; **5.** play; **6.** to read; **7.** play; **8.** for helping; **9.** crying; **10.** crying; **11.** to leave; **12.** to cry/crying; **13.** learning/to learn **14.** ringing/to ring; **15.** picking; **16.** to taking; **17.** sleep; **18.** sleeping; **19.** To complete/In order to complete; **20.** do; **21.** to study; **22.** take; **23.** having; **24.** to help; **25.** to take; **26.** taking; **27.** watching; **28.** grow; **29.** Seeing; **30.** leave; **31.** Bringing

WRITING

PART 1 EDITING ADVICE

🕐 Time: 10–15 min

1. Have students close their books. Write the first few sentences without editing marks or corrections on the board. For example:

    He wants help other people.

    It's important be a charitable person.

2. Ask students to correct each sentence and provide a rule or an explanation for each correction. This activity can be done individually, in pairs, or as a class.

3. After students have corrected each sentence, tell them to turn to page 248. Say: *Now compare your work with the Editing Advice in the book.* Have students read through all the advice.

PART 2 EDITING PRACTICE

🕐 Time: 10–15 min

1. Tell students they are going to put the Editing Advice into practice. Ask: *Do all the shaded words and phrases have mistakes?* (no) Go over the examples with the class. Then do #1 together.

2. Have students complete the practice individually. Then have them compare answers with a partner before checking answers as a class.

3. For the items students had difficulties with, have them go back and find the relevant grammar chart and review it. Monitor and give help as necessary.

Answers: 1. C; **2.** to do; **3.** helping; **4.** me to help; **5.** working/work; **6.** to become; **7.** Ø; **8.** C; **9.** finding; **10.** C; **11.** making; **12.** feel; **13.** it's/it is; **14.** C; **15.** C; **16.** C; **17.** C; **18.** C; **19.** used to sleeping; **20.** to sleep; **21.** making; **22.** they used to make; **23.** C; **24.** them to be; **25.** becoming; **26.** to; **27.** C; **28.** to find; **29.** C; **30.** C

PART 3 WRITE ABOUT IT

🕐 Time: 30–40 min

1. Review the Andrew Carnegie quotation with the class. Make sure that the meaning is clear. Brainstorm descriptions with the class of a rich spirit and a poor spirit and write them on the board. Have students write a paragraph that clearly states their opinion and is supported by the experience and knowledge of the topic that they include.

2. Have students read the direction line. Make sure students understand the meaning of *enrich* (make rich or richer, either in money or in spirit). Elicit types of volunteering (e.g., helping old people, visiting sick people, giving out food at a shelter). Have students discuss volunteering with a partner and how/if it enriches one's life to generate ideas before they begin to write.

PART 4 EDIT YOUR WRITING

🕐 Time: 15–20 min

Have students edit their writing by reviewing the Lesson Summary on pages 245–246 and the Editing Advice on pages 248–249. Collect for assessment and/or have students share their essays in small groups.

EXPANSION ACTIVITIES

1. Ask: *What do you expect your teacher(s) to do? What do the teachers here expect you to do?* Brainstorm several answers. Write them on the board. Have students discuss the questions in small groups and share interesting answers with the class.

2. Tell students to interview a friend on the following topics. Have students complete these sentences and report the person's answers to the class.

    a. S/he worries about _____

    b. S/he's grateful to his/her parents
        for _____

    c. S/he has a good time _____

    d. S/he used to _____, but s/he doesn't do it anymore.

9 COMING TO AMERICA

GRAMMAR CHARTS

LESSON OPENER

Have students look at the photo and read the caption. Ask: *What do you see?* (the Statue of Liberty) *What does it represent?* (freedom) Have students read the quotation. Ask: *Do you agree?*

Background: Since the seventeenth century, people have been immigrating to America from all over the world. While immigrants come for many reasons, many have come to escape their countries. Since its beginning, the nation has stood for freedoms and possibilities that cannot be found in many other countries: to speak freely, to practice your religion, to participate in government, to make a living. By 2010, the number of immigrants rose to 40 million, with almost 14 million arriving between 2000 and 2010, the highest number of immigrants in a single decade in the nation's history. The impacts of the earliest immigrants on the country are still visible: in British architecture of government buildings, Spanish missions, French foods and plantation-style homes; Irish St. Patrick's Day celebrations; and communities of Italian, Polish, and other European nationalities. Increasingly in recent decades, the influence of newer populations is also being seen in advertising and media, as well as in government elections.

John F. Kennedy was the 35th president of the United States. While a senator, Kennedy authored *A Nation of Immigrants* (1958), a short history of immigration in the United States that analyzes the importance of immigration to the nation and influenced Kennedy to urge more liberal immigration laws, which were eventually passed in 1965.

CONTEXT

This unit is about coming to America. Students will read about patterns and statistics of immigration, refugee immigrants, unwilling immigrants, effects of immigration on the population, and a new type of immigrant: a foreign-adopted baby.

1. Give students a few minutes to look through the lesson. Have them look at the photos and titles. How do they relate to the context?

2. Elicit the topics that will be discussed.

3. Have students discuss in pairs or small groups what they know about immigration and its effects on a population, and about immigration in the United States.

GRAMMAR

Students will learn about adverbial clauses and phrases, sentence connectors (conjunctive adverbs), and *so/such that* for result.

1. To activate students' prior knowledge, ask what students know about adverbs, clauses, connectors, and *so/such that* or words that signal result or effect.

2. Give several examples of sentences with adverbial clauses and phrases, sentence connectors, and *so/such that* (e.g., *The Irish came because of a famine. After 1965, more Asians immigrated to the United States. However, it takes a long time to adopt a baby. In addition, adopting is expensive. The application process is so expensive many people cannot afford it.*).

3. Have volunteers give examples. Write the examples on the board.

EXPANDING ON THE CONTEXT

The context for this lesson can be enhanced with the following items:

1. Census data showing foreign-born population data over time
2. Magazine, newspaper, or online articles about refugees around the world
3. An editorial from a local newspaper about immigration issues
4. Photos showing immigrant influence in U.S. culture (e.g., architectural styles, restaurants, music)
5. Online U.S. and world population clocks

READING

A Nation of Immigrants, page 252

PRE-READING

⏱ Time: 15–20 min

1. Have students read the title of the article. Ask: *What is this article about?* (immigrants in the United States) Direct their attention to the bar graph. Ask: *What does the graph show?* (a big increase in foreign-born populations in the United States in 2010)
2. Have students look briefly at the reading. Ask: *What will the reading say about immigration in the United States? How do you know?* Have students make predictions.
3. Pre-teach any essential vocabulary words your students may not know, such as *takes in, face, diverse, unrest,* and *quadrupled.*
4. Activate students' prior knowledge of the topic. Ask: *Are immigrants in your country and in the United States the same nationalities? Why or why not?* Have students discuss in pairs or small groups and share their answers with class. Try to pair or group students from the same geographic areas. Before students begin their discussions, elicit the difference between *emigrate* (leaving one's country) and *immigrate* (coming to a new country).

READING GLOSSARY

to take in: to give shelter to
to face: to meet with; confront
diverse: varied; different from each other
unrest: discontent; uneasiness

to quadruple: to multiply by four

READING   CD 2 TR 12

⏱ Time: 10–15 min

After students have read the article, go over the answers to the Comprehension Check on page 253: **1.** T; **2.** T; **3.** F

ADDITIONAL COMPREHENSION QUESTIONS

How many foreigners does the United States usually take in every year? (almost one million) *Do Americans often ask each other about their family background?* (yes) *Who came to the United States to escape hunger?* (Irish and Chinese people) *Who came for work?* (Italians) *What did some Americans fear about immigration in 1910?* (the United States would lose its "American" identity)

EXPANDING ON THE READING

The topic for this reading can be enhanced with the following items:

1. Information on immigration and/or naturalization from the USCIS website
2. Newspaper, magazine, or online articles showing numbers and/or proportions of areas of origin for immigrants settling in the local area
3. A timeline showing the history of U.S. immigration

CONTEXT NOTE

The U.S. Census Bureau makes statistics available on the population of the United States, including information on immigrants and the foreign-born population in general. (*Foreign-born* means anyone born in another country.)

PRACTICE IDEA: SPEAKING

Have students who are comfortable with the topic share their knowledge and personal experiences with immigrants or foreign influence in the United States. For example, invite them to recount touring Chinatown, trying out ethnic foods, vacationing in historical cities, such as New Orleans or St. Augustine.

9.1 Adverbial Clauses and Phrases—Introduction,
page 253

🕐 Time: 10–15 min

1. Review the definitions of *adverb* (a word that modifies a verb, adjective, other adverb, or a group of words showing place, time, circumstance, manner, cause, degree), *clause* (generally: a group of words with a subject and a verb) and types of clauses (independent/main, dependent/subordinate), and *phrase* (a small group of related words). Note that *adverbial* can describe an adverb used as a word, clause, or phrase.

2. Have students cover the right side of their charts and look at the examples. Ask: *What can you observe about adverbials?* (They can modify an independent clause/complete sentence; they are located at the beginning or end of a sentence. Some are clauses, and some are phrases.) Ask volunteers to identify which are phrases and which are clauses.

3. Have students review the examples and explanations in the chart. Ask questions such as *Which words begin a contrast clause?* (even though) *A time clause?* (before) Clarify any vocabulary that students are unfamiliar with.

4. Draw students' attention to the Language Note. Emphasize the use of a comma when the dependent clause comes before the main clause.

ADDITIONAL PRACTICE

1. Write the following sentences on the board unmarked. Elicit from students the adverbials in the sentences. Have students underline the clauses once and the phrases twice.
   a. *I'm going to lunch <u>because I'm hungry.</u>*
   b. *<u>During the war,</u> people fled the country.*
   c. *My parents fell in love <u>when they met.</u>*
   d. *He gets up early <u>so that he can avoid bad traffic.</u>*
   e. *<u>Before you go,</u> please check the mail.*

2. Discuss with the class what the adverbials modify (a, c, d, e: main clause, b: *fled*) and what they show (a: reason; b, c, e: time; d: purpose)

3. Have students work in groups and make up additional sentences with adverbial clauses and phrases and mark them.

4. Ask a few students to write their sentences on the board. Have the class identify the adverb components and explain what and how they modify.

EXERCISE 1 pages 253–254
🕐 Time: 10–15 min

Answers: 1. because; **2.** even if; **3.** While; **4.** so that; **5.** After; **6.** Even though; **7.** because; **8.** When; **9.** since; **10.** because; **11.** until; **12.** because; **13.** unless; **14.** After; **15.** When; **16.** so that

EXERCISE 2 page 254
🕐 Time: 5–10 min

Answers: 1. R; **2.** Cd; **3.** T; **4.** P; **5.** T; **6.** Ct; **7.** R; **8.** T; **9.** R; **10.** R; **11.** T; **12.** R; **13.** Cd; **14.** T; **15.** T; **16.** P

9.2 Reason and Purpose,
page 255

🕐 Time: 10–15 min

1. Have students cover the grammar chart. Elicit adverbs they know that show reason and purpose. (*because, in order to/to, so that*)

2. Have students uncover the explanation column of the grammar chart. Have students locate and underline the words that show reason and purpose. (*because, because of, since, in order to, so that/so,* and *for*) Have students then review the example sentences. Point out the shortened forms of *in order to (to)* and *so that (so)*.

3. Ask volunteers to give sentences about themselves using *because, because of, since, in order to, so that,* and *for.* If needed, remind them to include a modal with *so that/so.*

4. Direct students' attention to the Language Notes. Review the use of the comma for *so* indicating result but not for *so* indicating purpose.

PRESENTATION IDEA

Write sentences with *because, because of, since, in order to, so that,* and *for* on the board (e.g., *I checked the TV in order to see the weather forecast. Because the weather was bad, class was canceled. I called my students to tell them. We were late, so we rushed to the meeting. He bought the stationery so he could write a letter.*). Ask students whether each sentence shows reason or purpose. Then review the grammar chart.

EXERCISE 3 pages 255–256

🕐 Time: 10–15 min

Answers: 1. (in order) to; **2.** because/since; **3.** So (that); **4.** Because of; **5.** so (that); **6.** because of; **7.** (in order) to; **8.** Because/Since; **9.** (In order) To; **10.** because; **11.** for

---

PRACTICE IDEA: SPEAKING

After students complete Exercise 3, have them work in pairs to match each item with an explanation in grammar chart **9.2** on page 255.

EXERCISE 4 page 256

🕐 Time: 5–10 min

Answers may vary. Possible answers: 1. so that; **2.** because/since; **3.** Because of; **4.** for/to get/to find; **5.** so (that); **6.** (in order) to; **7.** so (that); **8.** because/since; **9.** because/since; **10.** so (that); **11.** because of; **12.** Because/Since

---

PRACTICE IDEA: LISTENING AND SPEAKING

Ask two students to perform the conversation in Exercise 4 for the class (using their books, if needed). Have the rest of the class listen with books closed, and ask questions periodically in appropriate places (e.g., *Why did you move into a big house? Why don't you get home until after 6:00 p.m.?*). Allow both speakers to take turns answering (e.g., *My parents were coming …, Her parents were coming ….*).

EXERCISE 5 page 256

🕐 Time: 5–10 min

Answers will vary.

READING

The Lost Boys of Sudan, page 257

PRE-READING

🕐 Time: 15–20 min

1. Have students look at the photo with the map inset and read the title. Ask: *Where are the boys in the photo?* (Kenya) *Where are they from?* (Sudan) *How do you think they are feeling?* (Answers will vary.)

2. Have students look briefly at the reading. Ask: *What will the reading say about the boys?* Have students make predictions.

3. Pre-teach any essential vocabulary words your students may not know, such as *refugees, supermarket, palace,* and *homeland.*

4. Note the distance between Sudan and Kenya on the map. Ask: *What do you think happened on their journey?* Have students discuss in pairs or small groups and share their answers with the class.

READING GLOSSARY

refugees: persons who are leaving oppression, war, hunger, etc.

supermarket: a large store where food and general household items are sold

palace: the home of a king; a large and grand house

homeland: one's native country

READING 🎧

🕐 Time: 10–15 min

After students have read the article, go over the answers to the Comprehension Check on page 258: **1.** F; **2.** F; **3.** T

ADDITIONAL COMPREHENSION QUESTIONS

What made the boys leave Sudan? (their villages were attacked) *How old were they?* (between 4 and 12) *What did they eat on their journey to Ethiopia?* (leaves, roots, and wild fruit) *How long were they in refugee camps in Kenya?* (almost 10 years) *How many lost boys came to the United States?* (3,800)

EXPANDING ON THE READING

The topic for this reading can be enhanced with the following items:

1. Newsletter or donation solicitation from a refugee resettlement agency
2. Newspaper, magazine, or online articles on a recent refugee situation
3. Flyer or brochure from a local refugee service or refugee resettlement agency
4. Page from the website of the Office of the United Nations High Commissioner for Refugees
5. Online article on U.S. refugee resettlement or refugee assistance from the U.S. Department of State's Bureau of Population, Refugees, and Migration
6. Statistics on numbers of global refugees

CONTEXT NOTE

According to an early United Nations definition (1951), a refugee is a person who cannot return to his or her own country because of a "well-founded fear" of persecution based on race, religion, nationality, or membership in a social group. Today, the term also includes those who run from their country to escape famine, earthquakes, tsunamis, and war. There are at least 51.2 million refugees waiting for help in the world today.

9.3 Time Clauses and Phrases,
page 258

🕐 Time: 10–15 min

1. Have students look at the reading on page 257. Elicit and write on the board the time words: *when, while, until, during, for,* and *whenever*. Ask students to name other time words they know and write them on the board (e.g., *before, after, as, since, ever since*).
2. Have students look at the examples and explanations in the chart. Point out the differences in meaning and use.
3. Provide additional examples and write them on the board (e.g., *Ever since I moved to San Francisco, I've been interested in refugees. When I was visiting a friend, I met refugees from the tsunami in Thailand. While I was talking to them, I decided to volunteer to work in a refugee camp for the United Nations.*). Elicit the adverb clauses and time words, and their meanings or uses.

PRACTICE IDEAS: SPEAKING AND WRITING

1. Have students work in groups to identify how each time phrase in the reading on page 257 is used. Have groups share their answers with the class and be prepared to defend their explanations.
2. Have students work in pairs to make a timeline of the lives of the Lost Boys, based on information in the reading.

ADDITIONAL PRACTICE

Write on the board in two columns the list of time words in chart **9.3** and a mixed-up list of their uses. With books closed, have students match the two columns and write three sentences using *while, for,* and *until*. Have students exchange papers. Review answers as a class. Give 10 points for each correct answer or sentence, for a total of 100 points.

EXERCISE 6 pages 258–259

🕐 Time: 10–15 min

Answers: 1. when; **2.** for; **3.** During; **4.** for; **5.** during; **6.** while/as; **7.** while/when; **8.** While/As; **9.** until; **10.** Since; **11.** When; **12.** when; **13.** while; **14.** since; **15.** When/Whenever

EXERCISE 7 page 259

🕐 Time: 10–15 min

Answers: 1. When; **2.** When/Whenever; **3.** for; **4.** When/Whenever; **5.** When; **6.** during; **7.** When; **8.** While/As; **9.** until; **10.** Since/Ever since; **11.** since; **12.** for; **13.** While; **14.** during; **15.** until

EXERCISE 8 page 260

🕐 Time: 10–15 min

Answers will vary.

9.4 Using the *-ing* Form after Time Words, page 261

🕐 Time: 10–15 min

1. Ask students to cover the grammar chart. On the board, write: *The boys have been telling their story since they came to the United States.* Elicit the two clauses in the sentence. (*The boys have been telling their story; since they came to the United States*) Point out that the clauses have the same subject. Have students predict how to shorten the information. Say: *The subject is the same. Can the verb forms be the same?* (yes; can shorten *they came* to *coming*)

2. Have students look at grammar chart **9.4**. Review the example diagrams. Ask: *Why is a phrase with -*ing *called a participial phrase?* (because the *-ing* form is the present participle) Point out that the use of commas does not change when the *-ing* form is used, as in the second example.

EXERCISE 9 page 261

🕐 Time: 10–15 min

Answers:

1. While running from their homes, they saw many dangerous animals.
2. The Lost Boys went to Kenya before coming to the U.S.
3. While living in Kenya, they studied English.
4. Before coming to the U.S., the Lost Boys had never used electricity.
5. Peter Bul learned how to use a computer after coming to the U.S.
6. Before finding a job, Peter got help from the U.S. government.
7. Peter went to visit South Sudan after graduating from college.

8. While studying for his degree, Peter raised money for a school in South Sudan.

READING

Slavery—An American Paradox, page 262

PRE-READING

🕐 Time: 10–15 min

1. Have students look at the photo and read the caption. Ask: *Who are these people?* (slaves) *What are they doing?* (picking cotton)

2. Have students read the title and skim the reading. Ask: *What is the reading about? How do you know?* Have students make predictions.

3. Pre-teach any vocabulary words your students may not know, such as *slavery, agricultural, exhausting,* and *seeds.*

4. Activate students' prior knowledge about slavery in the United States. Ask: *Why did the South want to keep slaves? Do you think all Southerners believed in slavery?* Have students discuss the questions in groups. Ask volunteers to share their opinions with the class.

READING GLOSSARY

slavery: the state of being owned by another person and working for no money

agricultural: related to the science of growing food

exhausting: very tiring

seeds: parts of a plant that are put into the ground and grow into another plant

READING 🎧 CD 2 TR 15

🕐 Time: 10–15 min

After students have read the article, go over the answers to the Comprehension Check on page 263: **1.** F; **2.** T; **3.** F

ADDITIONAL COMPREHENSION QUESTIONS

Were there as many as 500,000 slaves in the United States? (yes) *How much did the Constitution say a slave was worth?* (three-fifths of a person) *What are two crops that were grown in the South?* (tobacco and cotton) *When did the African slave trade end?* (1808) *Why did it become popular again in the South?* (cotton became faster to produce)

EXPANDING ON THE READING

The topic for this reading can be enhanced with the following items:

1. Timeline of the history of the Civil War
2. Copy of the Declaration of Independence
3. Eyewitness accounts of slaving (e.g., Dr. Alexander Falconbridge, 1788)
4. Web or magazine articles on farming and slavery in the South

9.5 Contrast, page 263

⏲ Time: 10–15 min

1. Have students cover the chart. Review the meaning of *contrast* with the class. Elicit contrast signals that students know (*but, however, although, even though, anyway*).

2. Write sentences on the board, such as *I like French fries, but they are not healthy. I like my neighbor, even though, he is noisy. Discrimination is wrong, it still, happens.* Have the class predict whether the sentences are correct.

3. Have students look at grammar chart **9.5**. Review the examples and explanations. Clarify any vocabulary students are unfamiliar with. Draw students' attention to the last section in the chart. Point out that *still* and *anyway* emphasize or strengthen a contrast that has already been made.

4. Point out the Language Note and the use of *though* in informal spoken English and *while* to show contrast versus time.

5. To help students understand how to use contrast signals, ask: *Which contrast words or phrases begin dependent clauses?* (*even though, although*) *Begin phrases?* (*in spite of*) *How are they punctuated?* (comma after the end of a dependent clause or a phrase; no comma before *anyway* or *still*) Have the class check the sentences on the board against the chart. Review corrections as a class.

CONTEXT NOTE

1. Tell students that *spite,* when it occurs as a single word (i.e., *She did it for spite. He spited his mother by not doing his chores.*), means a desire to hurt, annoy, offend, thwart, and defy. In the phrases *in spite of* and *in spite of the fact,* the meaning of the word is closer to defiance or thwart, while something done *out of spite* means done because of hatred or just to be mean.

2. *Despite* is a synonym for *in spite of.*

ADDITIONAL PRACTICE

Have students identify the parts of speech that directly follow the contrast clauses and phrases in the chart. Point out that only a noun follows *in spite of.*

EXERCISE 10 pages 263–264

⏲ Time: 5–10 min

Answers: 1. Even though; **2.** although; **3.** In spite of the fact that/Even though; **4.** Although; **5.** In spite of the fact that

EXERCISE 11 page 264

⏲ Time: 10–15 min

Answers: 1. In spite of the fact that; **2.** In spite of; **3.** In spite of the fact that; **4.** in spite of the fact that; **5.** in spite of; **6.** in spite of; **7.** In spite of; **8.** In spite of the fact that; **9.** in spite of the fact that

🕐 Time: 10–15 min

Answers: 1. Even though; **2.** In spite of the fact that; **3.** Although; **4.** even though; **5.** in spite of; **6.** even though/although

The Changing Face of the United States, page 265

PRE-READING

🕐 Time: 10–15 min

1. Have students look at the photo and read the caption. Ask: *What is happening?* (Hispanic people are celebrating Cinco de Mayo.) *Where are they?* (Detroit)

2. Have students read the title, look at the bar graph, and skim the reading. Ask: *What is the reading about? How do you know?* Have students make predictions.

3. Pre-teach any vocabulary words your students may not know, such as *face, descendants, assume, policy, trend,* and *projected.*

4. To activate students' prior knowledge of statistical data, have them look at the bar graph. Ask: *What percentage of the population was Asian American in 2011? What percentage of the population will be African American in 2050? What do you think the percentages will be for all groups in 2100?* Have students discuss the questions and make predictions in small groups. Have groups share their predictions with the class.

READING GLOSSARY

face: the front part of a structure
descendants: people born into a certain family line
to assume: to believe to be true without knowing
policy: a rule or group of rules for doing business by industry and government
trend: general curve or pattern
projected: estimated, predicted

READING

🕐 Time: 10–15 min

After students have read the article, go over the answers to the Comprehension Check on page 266: **1.** F; **2.** F; **3.** T

ADDITIONAL COMPREHENSION QUESTIONS

When was the foreign-born population about 15%? (between 1890 and 1900) *When did Hispanics pass African Americans as the largest minority?* (2003) *Which group influenced the 2012 presidential election?* (Hispanics) *Why could the Hispanic population grow in spite of a change in immigration policy?* (because they have the highest birth rate)

PRACTICE IDEA: LISTENING

Have students close their books and listen to the audio. Ask additional statistical data comprehension questions, such as *What percentage of the populations of California and Texas is Hispanic?* (about 38%) *In 2012, what percentage of the voting population was Hispanic?* (10%) *What is the projected population for the United States in 2050?* (438 million) Repeat the audio if necessary.

EXPANDING ON THE READING

The topic for this reading can be enhanced with the following items:

1. Photos, flyers, or articles regarding a community event sponsored by a Hispanic, Asian, or African-American organization

2. Bilingual or multilingual signs and notices in grocery stores or other ubiquitous places

3. Videos about the importance of Cinco de Mayo

4. More information on population trends, projections, and numbers

---

9.6 Condition, page 266

🕐 Time: 15–20 min

1. Have students cover the grammar chart. Review the meanings of *if* and *condition* with the class (*if* is a condition, meaning "supposing that …," and signals causes or conditions; *conditions* are situations upon which other things may depend).

2. Have students look at grammar chart **9.6**. Review the examples and explanations carefully. Ask: *What kind of statements are these?* (cause, condition/result) Draw students' attention to the future tense meaning of the examples in the first two sections and to the present tense meaning in the third section. Point out the Language Note and use of the simple present in the condition clause of a future sentence.

Before beginning the chart review, help students understand the meaning of *if*. On the board, make two columns. In the left column, write:

1. If you register,

2. Even if you are going to be away on Election Day,

3. Unless you register,

In the right column, write:

a. you can't vote.

b. you can vote.

c. you can vote by absentee ballot.

Have students combine the phrases to make three statements (1b, 2c, 3a). Say: *If states conditions or situations that may or may not have to happen for something else to happen. In #1, the condition affects the result. In #2, the condition doesn't affect the result.* Ask: *What does* unless *mean in #3?* (if not) Write: *Unless you register = If you don't register.*

ADDITIONAL PRACTICE

Write prompts on the board, such as: *If I …, I will …; Even if I …, I won't …;* and *Unless I …, I won't …*. Have students work in pairs to provide examples about themselves from the prompts.

EXERCISE 13 page 266

⏱ Time: 5–10 min

Answers: 1. a. continues, **b.** will be; **2. a.** goes, **b.** will increase; **3. a.** are, **b.** will be needed; **4. a.** will get, **b.** increases; **5. a.** will be, **b.** continues; **6. a.** will forget, **b.** encourage

EXERCISE 14 pages 266–267

⏱ Time: 10–15 min

Answers:

1. Immigrants can't become American citizens unless they pass a test.

2. Visitors can't enter the U.S. unless they have a passport.

3. Immigrants will continue to come to the U.S. unless conditions in their native countries improve.

4. In the 1800s, Southern farmers couldn't prosper unless they found a new crop to grow.

5. Cotton production was going to be slow unless they had a machine to help.

6. Foreigners cannot work in the U.S. unless they have permission.

PRACTICE IDEA: SPEAKING

Have students talk about conditional situations in their own countries using the statements in Exercise 14 as a model. Try to pair students of the same or similar backgrounds. Ask several students to share their sentences with the class.

EXERCISE 15 page 267

⏱ Time: 5–10 min

Answers: 1. If; **2.** If; **3.** unless; **4.** unless; **5.** unless; **6.** If; **7.** if; **8.** unless

PRACTICE IDEA: SPEAKING

Ask students to discuss the situation the mothers are talking about in the exercise. If appropriate, ask students to share their experiences with children who are at home in two cultures.

PRACTICE IDEA: WRITING

Have students brainstorm and write a list of ways immigrant children can learn about or remember their parents' cultures and languages. Have students use *if* and *even if* in their statements.

EXERCISE 16 page 268

⏱ Time: 5–10 min

Answers will vary.

PRACTICE IDEA: WRITING

Have students divide into pairs to describe an imaginary student at their level who is learning to speak English. Have students use statements from Exercise 16 as a basis for the description. Have each pair write their description. Collect the papers and read them at random to the class. Have the class vote for the most realistic characterization. Alternatively, to save time, have students work in small groups.

🕐 Time: 5–10 min

Possible Answers: 1. the weather is cold; **2.** your accent isn't perfect; **3.** you make (grammar) mistakes; **4.** you don't have to pay rent OR they don't charge you for rent; **5.** you're an American/you're an American resident/OR you're a resident

`READING`

Adopting a Baby from Abroad,
page 269

PRE-READING

🕐 Time: 10–15 min

1. Have students look at the photo and read the caption. Ask: *What is happening?* (A woman is holding her adopted baby.) *Where is the woman from?* (United States) *What country is she in?* (China)

2. Have students look briefly at the reading. Ask: *What is the reading about? How do you know?* Have students use the title and photo to make predictions.

3. Pre-teach any vocabulary words your students may not know, such as *adopting, couples, complicated,* and *stable.*

4. Activate students' prior knowledge about adoption and adopting foreign-born babies. Ask: *Do you know anyone who has adopted a baby? A foreign-born child? How did they do it?* Have students share their information in pairs. Try to pair students from the same country or region. Have a few students share their information with the class.

READING GLOSSARY

to adopt: to take legal responsibility for acting as parents to a child

couple: two people who are married, living together, or on a date

complicated: difficult

stable: calm; undisturbed

EXPANDING ON THE READING

The topic for this reading can be enhanced with the following items:

1. Websites about domestic or international adoption

2. Sections of the U.S. Citizenship and Immigration Services website on international adoption

3. Videos or other anecdotes and stories from parents or children who have been involved in foreign-born adoption

READING

🕐 Time: 10–15 min

After students have read the article, go over the answers to the Comprehension Check on page 270: **1.** T; **2.** F; **3.** T

ADDITIONAL COMPREHENSION QUESTIONS

Why do Americans adopt foreign babies? (because they have to wait too long for an American baby) *How many foreign-born babies were adopted in 2009?* (13,000) *What is the USCIS?* (United States Citizenship and Immigration Services) *How much does an international adoption cost?* ($44,000 on average)

> ### PRACTICE IDEA: LISTENING
>
> Have students close their books and listen to the audio. Tell them to write all the words and phrases they hear that connect two sentences. Repeat the audio if necessary. Then have students open their books and read along as they listen to the audio.

CONTEXT NOTE

Adopted children sometimes refer to the women who gave birth to them as their biological mothers or birth mothers. Generally, adopted children refer to their adoptive parents as their parents.

9.7 Sentence Connectors,
page 270

🕐 Time: 5–10 min

1. Review the meaning of *connector* with the class (something that joins things together). Point out the function of *sentence connectors* defined in the top section of the chart and the footnote that these are also called conjunctive adverbs. Ask: *How do they differ from clauses?* (clauses may modify another clause in a single sentence)

2. Have students skim the chart. Ask: *How many types of connectors are listed? What are they?* (five [and a half]: contrast, add information, ordering, result/conclusion, emphasize preceding statement [and may introduce a surprise])

3. Review the examples and explanations in the chart. Direct students' attention to the last section. Elicit or clarify that *for example* emphasizes by giving details or proof of the previous statement. Point out that sentence connectors connect two separate sentences.

4. Draw students' attention to the Punctuation Note. Point out that connectors can be used to combine two sentences into one if a semicolon is used.

PRESENTATION IDEA

As a class, ask students to identify the ideas being connected in the examples in the chart.

EXERCISE 18 page 271

🕐 Time: 5–10 min

Answers: 1. However; **2.** Furthermore/Moreover; **3.** As a result; **4.** However; **5.** For example; **6.** In addition; **7.** Nevertheless; **8.** Moreover; **9.** First, Furthermore; **10.** As a result/For this reason; **11.** However; **12.** As a result; **13.** However; **14.** Nevertheless; **15.** Therefore/As a result; **16.** However; **17.** However; **18.** Moreover/Furthermore; **19.** Consequently; **20.** In fact

EXERCISE 19 pages 272–273

🕐 Time: 5–10 min

Answers will vary.

PRACTICE IDEA: SPEAKING

After students complete the exercise, have them work in pairs to use the items in the exercise as models to talk about themselves, using *It is/was important for …. Therefore, ….* and *It is/was important for…. However, ….* Have each pair share a few answers with the class.

9.8 *So … That / Such … That,*
page 273

🕐 Time: 5–10 min

1. Have students skim the chart and say what the chart covers. (*such … that, so… that, so many/few … that, so much/little … that*) Ask: *What is* so/such … that *used to show?* (result; also, the degree or amount of something)

2. Review the explanations and examples in the grammar chart. If necessary, for the third and fourth sections, review count nouns (nouns for items that can be counted and take a plural ending such as *-s* or *-es*) and noncount or mass/abstract nouns (nouns for items that cannot be counted individually and do not take a plural ending).

3. Draw students' attention to the Language Note. Elicit the situations in which informal and formal speech are used. (informal: among friends and family, in everyday public interactions; formal: in work situations, with colleagues, before a group, and with people of authority or position)

4. Elicit from students the meaning of *so/so that* they learned earlier in the lesson. (to show purpose) If necessary, review the appropriate sections of grammar chart **9.2** on page 255.

EXERCISE 20 page 274

🕐 Time: 5–10 min

Answers: 1. so many; **2.** such a; **3.** so; **4.** so many; **5.** so; **6.** so much; **7.** so many, so much; **8.** such a; **9.** so; **10.** so few; **11.** so little

EXERCISE 21 page 274

🕐 Time: 5–10 min

Answers will vary. The connectors used should be: 1. so; **2.** so; **3.** such a; **4.** such a; **5.** so many; **6.** so little

SUMMARY OF LESSON 5

🕐 Time: 20–30 min

PART A WORDS THAT CONNECT A DEPENDENT CLAUSE OR PHRASE TO AN INDEPENDENT CLAUSE

Draw students' attention to the abbreviations. Have students cover page 275. Provide cues based on the examples in the chart (e.g., *Because my mother doesn't understand English, ...*; *I exercise in order to ...*). Have students complete the statements orally or in writing.

If necessary, have students review:

9.1 Adverbial Clauses and Phrases—Introduction (page 253)

9.2 Reason and Purpose (page 255)

9.3 Time Clauses and Phrases (page 258)

9.5 Contrast (page 263)

9.6 Condition (page 266)

PART B WORDS THAT CONNECT TWO INDEPENDENT CLAUSES

Have students write pairs of connected sentences about one of the issues they have studied in this lesson (immigration, refugees, slavery, immigration patterns, adoption), using connectors from the chart.

If necessary, have students review:

9.7 Sentence Connectors (page 270)

PART C WORDS THAT INTRODUCE RESULT CLAUSES

Write on the board the cues: *so ... that, so many / few / much / little ... that*, and *such a/an ... that*, and *such ... that*. Have students work in pairs to ask and answer questions about their countries.

If necessary, have students review:

9.8 *So ... That / Such ... That* (page 273)

🕐 Time: 15 min

Have students do the exercise on page 277. For additional practice, use the Assessment CD-ROM with Exam*View*® and the Online Workbook.

Answers: 1. for; **2.** to; **3.** to; **4.** so; **5.** For example; **6.** so that; **7.** In fact; **8.** In addition/Furthermore; **9.** Although; **10.** since; **11.** Even though; **12.** In fact; **13.** In spite of; **14.** Because; **15.** However; **16.** Furthermore; **17.** However; **18.** Until; **19.** In spite of the fact that; **20.** because of; **21.** until; **22.** Although

WRITING

PART 1 EDITING ADVICE

🕐 Time: 10–15 min

1. Have students close their books. Write the first few sentences without editing marks or corrections on the board. For example:
   She came to the United States for get a better education.
   Because his country was at war, so he left his country.

2. Ask students to correct each sentence and provide a rule or an explanation for each correction. This activity can be done individually, in pairs, or as a class.

3. After students have corrected each sentence, tell them to turn to page 278. Say: *Now compare your work with the Editing Advice in the book.* Have students read through all the advice.

PART 2 EDITING PRACTICE

🕐 Time: 10–15 min

1. Tell students they are going to put the Editing Advice into practice. Ask: *Do all the shaded words and phrases have mistakes?* (no) Go over the examples with the class. Then do #1 together.

2. Have students complete the practice individually. Then have them compare answers with a partner before checking answers as a class.

3. For the items students had difficulties with, have them go back and find the relevant grammar chart and review it. Monitor and give help as necessary.

Answers: 1. to; **2.** C; **3.** Even though/Although; **4.** Therefore, ; **5.** (in order) to; **6.** C; **7.** coming; **8.** would be; **9.** C; **10.** In addition/Furthermore/Moreover; **11.** (in order) to; **12.** C; **13.** class because; **14.** so that we could get together; **15.** C; **16.** Ø; **17.** such a; **18.** C; **19.** However/Nevertheless; **20.** so; **21.** save; **22.** Ø

PART 3 WRITE ABOUT IT

🕐 Time: 30–40 min

1. Have the class brainstorm problems and challenges that immigrants and refugees can face when they first arrive in the United States. Write them on the board. Encourage students to recall what they have learned in this lesson about immigrants and refugees and to think about conditions, results, purposes, time, etc. Have students write a paragraph.

2. Before students begin to write, encourage them to discuss with a partner what they experienced when they arrived in the United States. Tell them to think of types of assistance they received and the people or agencies that provided it. Have students write a paragraph about their experiences.

PART 4 EDIT YOUR WRITING

🕐 Time: 15–20 min

Have students edit their writing by reviewing the Lesson Summary on pages 275–276 and the Editing Advice on page 278. Collect for assessment and/or have students share their essays in small groups.

EXPANSION ACTIVITIES

1. Have students survey their neighbors or friends to ask what they do/don't like about their city. Have them write a brief list of statements to be completed, such as: *I like the …., Even though …., The … is so … that ….* Have students report their results to the class.

2. Ask students to interview a few immigrants about their experiences coming to America. Have students retell the stories or anecdotes in groups. Have groups share the most interesting stories with the class.

10 CHILDREN

GRAMMAR CHARTS

LESSON OPENER

Have students look at the photo and read the caption. Ask: *What do you see in the photo?* (children at a window) *What is each child doing? Why?* (Answers will vary.)

Background: Theories about children have changed a great deal, especially in the United States. In the past, children were seen as "adults-in-training." Only over many years did parents begin to show children much affection or pay attention to their development. In the twentieth century, however, childhood became a major focus of parents and of science. Today, studies research every phase of childhood, examining physical, neural, emotional, psychological, intellectual, and social development. But scientists and parents still debate what makes children as they are and what they become: is it DNA or is it environment that causes them to be reckless, to be kind, to be criminals, or to be geniuses?

Margaret Mead was an American cultural anthropologist who investigated the question of nature versus nurture in a field study of Samoans. The result was a scientifically controversial but popular work, *Coming of Age in Samoa* (1928), which included implications for raising American children. Mead's work helped change the course of parenting to focus on nurture and made her famous. Mead died in 1978.

CONTEXT

This unit is about children. Students will read about early childhood development, the teenage brain, Dr. Benjamin Spock and changes in parenting approaches, as well as the children's program *Sesame Street*.

1. Give students a few minutes to look through the lesson. Have them look at the photos and titles. How do they relate to the context?
2. Elicit the topics that will be discussed.
3. Have students discuss what they know about child development, parenting, and children's TV programs in pairs or small groups.

GRAMMAR

Students will learn about noun clauses.

1. To activate students' prior knowledge, ask what students know about noun clauses.
2. Give several examples of sentences with noun clauses (e.g., *I realize that I worry too much about my children. My mother said, "Eat everything on your plate." She told me that she will always love me. Many kids say their favorite TV show is* Sesame Street.).
3. Have volunteers give examples. Write the examples on the board.

EXPANDING ON THE CONTEXT

The context for this lesson can be enhanced with the following items:

1. Article about the role of music and art in a baby's life
2. Visual history of children's toys
3. List of American parents' top worries
4. History of children's TV programming
5. Summary of parenting theories
6. Magazine or Web article on latest research into child brains

Early Childhood Development,
page 282

PRE-READING
🕐 Time: 10–20 min

1. Have students look at the photo and read the caption. Ask: *What is happening in the photo?* (a baby's brain is being measured) *What kind of information will the test provide?* (measurements of brain activity involving speech and the ability to learn syntactically)

2. Have students read the title and look briefly at the reading. Ask: *What is the main idea of the reading?* Have students make predictions.

3. Pre-teach any essential vocabulary words your students may not know, such as *syntactically, classical, infants, hardly,* and *stimulating.*

4. Ask: *Should parents try to increase their baby's intelligence? Why or why not?* Have students discuss in pairs or small groups and share their answers with the class.

READING GLOSSARY

syntactically: with respect to syntax or the way words and phrases combine to form sentences
classical: related to 18th century European music
infants: babies from birth to 1 year of age
hardly: barely; very small amount
stimulating: increasing energy or activity

READING   CD 2 TR 18
🕐 Time: 10–15 min

After students have read the article, go over the answers to the Comprehension Check on page 283: **1.** F; **2.** T; **3.** T

ADDITIONAL COMPREHENSION QUESTIONS

Does talking to infants increase their language ability? (yes) *What can harm a baby for life?* (not talking to or holding them) *What happens to the brain of a baby who has not been touched very much?* (It develops to be 20 to 50% smaller than normal.) *Is overstimulation good for babies?* (no)

EXPANDING ON THE READING

The topic for this reading can be enhanced with the following items:

1. List of best classical pieces for babies
2. Video clips about infant visual stimulation and development
3. Web article on how to raise a smart baby
4. Timeline of infant development

CONTEXT NOTE

Preschool usually means a school for children who are 2 to 4 years old. Some preschools are full-day programs; others are half a day or three mornings a week. In most preschools, children learn to play together and develop social skills, do projects and artwork, play outside, and take a nap. At age 5, most children begin kindergarten.

10.1 Noun Clauses, page 283
🕐 Time: 10–15 min

1. Have students look at grammar chart **10.1**. Elicit the definition of a clause. (a group of words that has a subject and a verb) Ask: *How would a noun clause function in a sentence?* (like a noun)

2. Have students review the example sentences in the chart. Diagram one or two of the sentences on the board (e.g., *Parents know* | *that kids need a lot of attention. I hope* | *that our children will be successful.*). Ask: *What can you observe about the function of the noun clause?* (It is acting as direct object of the main verb.) Have students identify the main verbs in the examples. Point out that *so* can replace a noun clause in a short answer.

3. Direct students' attention to the Language Notes. Elicit the meaning of *feel* as "think" or "believe." Ask volunteers to use it in a sentence.

ADDITIONAL PRACTICE

Have students work in pairs to unscramble mixed-up sentences. Compare answers as a class.

a. We know smart that he is and he very learns quickly.
b. Today young babies realize a lot of love mothers need that and attention.
c. The language increases their ability that study shows talking to babies.

d. Experts it is not good that warn to overstimulate babies.

e. I'm parent sure going you are that to be a wonderful.

Answers:

a. We know that he is smart and he learns very quickly.

b. Today young mothers realize that babies need a lot of love and attention.

c. The study shows that talking to babies increases their language ability.

d. Experts warn that it is not good to overstimulate babies.

e. I'm sure that you are going to be a wonderful parent.

EXERCISE 1 page 284
🕐 Time: 5–10 min

Answers: 1. Do you know that; **2.** I didn't realize that; **3.** I'm not so sure; **4.** I think that; **5.** don't forget that; **6.** I hope; **7.** I predict that; **8.** I hope so

---

PRACTICE IDEA: LISTENING

Have students first listen to the audio alone. Ask a few comprehension questions (e.g., *What is the topic of the conversation?* [parenting, infant/baby stimulation]. *Do both speakers feel strongly that parents should play music for their babies?* [no]). Repeat the audio if necessary. Then have students open their books and read along as they listen to the audio.

EXERCISE 2 page 284
🕐 Time: 5–10 min

Possible Answers: 1. a baby's early experiences; **2.** children don't spend enough time; **3.** it's important to play; **4.** reading to babies/talking to babies; **5.** kids who hardly play/kids who aren't touched

EXERCISE 3 pages 284–285
🕐 Time: 5–10 min

Answers will vary.

EXERCISE 4 page 285
🕐 Time: 5–10 min

Answers will vary.

EXERCISE 5 page 285
🕐 Time: 5–10 min

Answers will vary.

The Teenage Brain, page 286

PRE-READING
🕐 Time: 10–20 min

1. Have students look at the photo and read the caption. Ask: *What is happening?* (A teenage boy is learning to drive.) *What do you imagine the boy is thinking?* (Answers will vary.)

2. Have students read the title and look briefly at the reading. Ask: *What will the reading be about? How do you know?* Have students make predictions.

3. Pre-teach any essential vocabulary words your students may not know, such as *risks, accelerator, brake, behind the wheel, roller coaster,* and *sensation.*

4. Ask: *Do you think teenagers take risks? If so, how?* Have students discuss in small groups and share their answers with class.

READING GLOSSARY

risks: chances; dangers of losing something important

accelerator: a device (usually a floor pedal) that increases the speed of an engine

brake: a device that stops a wheel from turning

behind the wheel: driving a vehicle (idiom)

roller coaster: an amusement ride in which small cars travel fast on a hilly track

sensation: physical feeling

READING
🕐 Time: 10–15 min

After students have read the article, go over the answers to the Comprehension Check on page 287: **1.** T; **2.** F; **3.** F

ADDITIONAL COMPREHENSION QUESTIONS

Why is sixteen a magic number for American teenagers? (They can get their driver's license.) *How many teen deaths occur in car crashes?* (one in three) *What are scientists using to study the teenage brain?* (scans) *What is a teenager's brain compared to?* (a car with weak brakes) *Why can't Professor Steinberg stand driving fast?* (because he no longer needs to seek thrills)

PRACTICE IDEA: WRITING

Divide the class into writing groups and one research group. Have the research group skim the reading on page 286 and write key ideas and details. At the same time, have the other groups write a brief summary of the reading, with books closed. When students are finished, have a member of each group read their summary to the class for feedback from the researchers.

PRACTICE IDEA: SPEAKING

Have students discuss in pairs their own experiences as teens and any risks they took. When students are finished, have some pairs share their experiences with the class.

10.2 Noun Clauses as Included Questions, pages 287–288

⏱ Time: 10–15 min

1. Ask students to close their books. On the board, write: *What is her name? Where is she from? Is she a student? Does she work here?* Elicit students' help to write: *I don't know what her name is. I don't know where she is from. I don't know if she is a student. I don't know if she works here.* Ask students if they can figure out the rules for including the questions in longer sentences and elicit their predictions.

2. Have students look at the grammar chart. Review the examples and explanations in the chart carefully. Review with students the list of phrases used before included questions. Provide a few examples of your own (e.g., *I'm not sure whose pen this is. Can you tell me if there is day care available here?*). If possible, have volunteers provide examples.

3. Draw students' attention to the Language Notes. Note that *or not* is generally not added in formal speech or writing. Discuss with students when to convert a question to a statement in addition to being more polite/less direct (to give information that answers someone's question).

PRESENTATION IDEAS

1. While presenting the Language Notes, have students go through the chart and identify the purpose of converting each example question to a statement (e.g., To be polite: *Please tell me what app I can use. I'd like to know who bought the app.* To give information that answers someone's question: *The app can tell you if the teenager is driving too fast. Scientists want to know why a teenager takes risks.*).

2. After students have reviewed the example sentences, have them go back to the reading on page 286 and identify the explanation that applies to each boldfaced noun clause in the reading.

PRACTICE IDEA: SPEAKING

Have students write a simple question about a service (e.g., a school, a children's program, a bus or train schedule, the location of an office or facility). Collect the questions and read them to the class one at a time. Have students convert them to more polite questions using an included question.

EXERCISE 6 pages 288–289
⏱ Time: 10–15 min
Answers: 1. where; **2.** if/whether; **3.** why; **4.** if/whether; **5.** how much; **6.** if/whether; **7.** what; **8.** how many; **9.** what; **10.** how; **11.** if/whether; **12.** who; **13.** where; **14.** whether; **15.** when/if/whether

EXERCISE 7 page 289

Time: 5–10 min

Answers: 1. who has an app to check their teenager's driving habits; **2.** what happens if teenagers text while driving?; **3.** how many teenagers are involved in accidents each year; **4.** who invented this app; **5.** which parents use this app

EXERCISE 8 page 289

Time: 5–10 min

Answers: 1. when your sister will get her driver's license; **2.** why teenagers are so careless?; **3.** why scientists are studying the teenage brain; **4.** when teenagers can get their driver's license in this state; **5.** when the brain is fully developed

EXERCISE 9 page 290

Time: 5–10 min

Answers: 1. how scientists study the brain; **2.** why teenagers take risks; **3.** when you got your driver's license; **4.** how new technologies affect driving habits; **5.** how Professor Steinberg studies the teenage brain

EXERCISE 10 page 290

Time: 5–10 min

Answers: 1. if teenagers drive too fast; **2.** if/whether teenagers understand the risk; **3.** if/whether your son's cell phone has this app; **4.** if/whether you drove carefully when you were a teenager; **5.** if/whether the brain develops completely by the age of twenty

EXERCISE 11 pages 290–291

Time: 5–10 min

Answers: 1. where you are going; **2.** why you need to use the car; **3.** what time you will come back home; **4.** if/whether there is going to be another teenager in the car (or not); **5.** how many kids are going to be in the car; **6.** if/whether your friend has permission from his parents (or not); **7.** where your friend lives; **8.** if/whether I ever met this friend (or not)

PRACTICE IDEAS: WRITING

1. Have students work in groups. Have each student write a simple *wh-* question with *be* or an auxiliary verb (e.g., *Where is the post office? Who brought the cookies?*). Then have students write their names on the paper and pass their questions to other students. Refer students to the list of phrases in grammar chart **10.2** on page 287. Have each student use the phrases to convert the questions that he or she has received into included questions using the first student's name (e.g., *Juan needs to know where the post office is. Mariana would like to know who brought the cookies.*).

2. Have students work in groups. Have each student write a simple *wh-* question with *do, does,* or *did* and a *yes/no* question with an auxiliary verb or *be*. Then have students pass their questions to another student. Refer students to the list of phrases in grammar chart **10.2** on page 287. Have each student convert the questions that he or she has received into included questions using the first student's name (e.g., *Josef wants to know when the semester ends. Luisa wonders if there is going to be a class party.*).

1. Have students work in threes to role-play. Have Students B and C in each group close their books. Have Student A (playing a shy student, a new student, or a student on the telephone) direct questions from Exercises 6–11 to Student B. Have Student B convert the question to an included question and Student C (playing an informed student) answer the question:

   > A (to B): *Where is the teacher from?*
   >
   > B (to C): *She'd like to know where the teacher is from.*
   >
   > C (to B): *He's from Los Angeles.*

   Have students switch roles several times during the activity.

2. Have students work in threes to role-play. Have Student A play a parent and whisper a question about his or her teenager's driving or infant child to Student B. Have Student B play a second parent and convert the question to an included question. Have Student C play a psychologist and answer the question:

   > A (to B): *Why does my son drive too fast?*
   >
   > B (to C): *She'd like to know why her son drives too fast.*
   >
   > C (to B): *He drives too fast because teenagers like to take risks.*

   Have students switch roles throughout the exercise.

10.3 Question Words Followed by an Infinitive, page 291

🕐 Time: 10–15 min

1. Have students cover the chart. Tell students this chart is about how to shorten included questions. Write on the board: *Which computer should I buy?* Have a volunteer convert the question to an included question with *I don't know* (e.g., *I don't know which computer I should buy.*). Elicit predictions from the class on how to shorten the statement. Write ideas on the board.

2. Have students look at grammar chart **10.3**. Review the examples and explanations in the chart.

3. Draw students' attention to the Language Notes and phrases often used with infinitives. Then, with the

class, check students' predictions on the board against the chart.

ADDITIONAL PRACTICE

Have students provide several example sentences of their own with the phrases in the chart. Divide students into pairs and have them brainstorm problems, things they often forget, things they want to know, etc., and then make statements (e.g., *I don't know what I should do about my car; it needs new tires and I don't have the money. / I can't decide if I should let my sister borrow my car; she drives too fast.*).

EXERCISE 12 page 292

🕐 Time: 5–10 min

Answers: 1. to get; **2.** to do; **3.** to compare; **4.** to begin; **5.** to write; **6.** to make; **7.** to chat; **8.** to do

Dr. Benjamin Spock, page 293

PRE-READING

🕐 Time: 10–15 min

1. Have students look at the photo and read the caption. Ask: *What is the man doing?* (playing gently with his baby)

2. Have students read the title and skim the reading. Ask: *What is the reading about? What makes you think so?* Have students make predictions.

3. Pre-teach any vocabulary words your students may not know, such as *expert, hug,* and *kiss.*

4. Activate students' prior knowledge about Dr. Spock and parenting theories. Ask: *Have you heard of Dr. Benjamin Spock? What are some theories about parenting newborn babies?* Have students discuss the questions and make predictions in pairs. Try to pair students from the same country or region. Have pairs share their predictions with the class.

READING GLOSSARY

expert: a master at something; an authority

to hug: to put one's arms around someone

to kiss: to touch with the lips to show that one likes or loves someone or something

READING 🎧 CD 2 TR 21

🕐 Time: 10–15 min

After students have read the article, go over the answers to the Comprehension Check on page 294: **1.** F; **2.** T; **3.** F

ADDITIONAL COMPREHENSION QUESTIONS

How many copies has Dr. Spock's book sold? (over 50 million) *How was Dr. Spock's childcare theory different?* (He was supportive of parents; he said to smile at, talk to, and gently play with your baby.) *Who was the child care expert before Dr. Spock?* (Dr. John Watson) *How old was Dr. Spock when he died?* (94) *How many times did he revise his book?* (seven times)

PRACTICE IDEA: LISTENING

Have students close their books and listen to the audio. Tell them to write all the exact words of Dr. Spock that they hear. Repeat the audio if necessary.

EXPANDING ON THE READING

The topic for this reading can be enhanced with the following items:

1. Copy of Dr. Spock's book *Dr. Spock's Baby and Child Care*
2. Advice column on caring for young children from a newspaper, magazine, or website
3. List of differences between new and older editions of Dr. Spock's book

10.4 Exact Quotes, page 294

⏱ Time: 10–15 min

1. Have students cover up grammar chart **10.4**. Tell students this chart explains exact quotes. Elicit the definition of *quotes* (repetition of someone's words with no changes). Say: *Dr. Spock had good ideas.* Write the sentence on the board. Ask the class: *How do you indicate an exact quote in English?* Ask a volunteer to come to the board and rewrite the sentence as an exact quote.

2. Have students look at the chart. Review the example sentences and explanations. If necessary, go over the meanings of *inverted* and *split*.

3. Direct students' attention to the Punctuation Note. Point out that end punctuation goes inside the quotation marks. With the class, make any necessary corrections to the sentence on the board.

PRESENTATION IDEA

Discuss with students situations in which we would want or need to quote someone (e.g., notable words; as evidence, support, or proof of an idea or theory; to cap or conclude a point or essay with memorable words).

CONTEXT NOTE

Learning to quote is a skill which is important to master to succeed in academics. The skill requires learning when to quote, whom and what to quote, how much to quote, and the way to incorporate quotes into your writing. Note to students that in their essays and papers they will be expected to quote when necessary but to use quotations to support their own ideas. Generally, a paper should consist of no more than about 15% quoted material; the rest should be students' own ideas.

ADDITIONAL PRACTICE

Provide students with a list of unpunctuated quotes (e.g., *Dr. Spock said smile at your baby and I agree. The child supplies the power said Dr. Spock but the parents have to do the steering. Abraham Lincoln began his speech fourscore and seven years ago…. Hamlet's question was to be or not to be. If opportunity doesn't knock said one comedian build a door. As the novelist J. D. Salinger pointed out how do you know you're going to do something, until you do it?*). Have students work in pairs to punctuate the sentences as exact quotations in their own languages and then convert them to quotations in English. Try to pair students from the same country or region. When they are finished, ask several pairs to share their conversions with the class.

EXERCISE 13 pages 294–295

⏱ Time: 10–15 min

Answers:

1. Watson said, "Never hug or kiss your children."
2. Watson said, "Give your children a pat on the head if they have made an extraordinarily good job of a difficult task."
3. Dr. Spock said, "You know more than you think you do."
4. "I wanted to be supportive of parents," said Dr. Spock.
5. "Parents can dramatically influence systems in their child's brain," wrote child psychologist Margot Sunderland.
6. "To reduce violence in our society," said Dr. Spock, "we must eliminate violence in the home and on television."

7. "Adolescence is a period of significant changes in brain structure and function," wrote Dr. Steinberg.

8. Parents sometimes ask, "What is wrong with teenagers? Why do they take so many risks?"

9. "This process of maturation, once thought to be largely finished by elementary school, continues throughout adolescence," wrote David Dobbs in a *National Geographic* article.

10.5 Exact Quotes vs. Reported Speech, page 295

⏱ Time: 10–15 min

1. Review the exact quotes and reported speech in the grammar chart carefully. Point out that reported speech changes some words but uses words as close in meaning to the original as possible. Draw students' attention to the paraphrased ideas in the reported speech examples.

2. Point out the Language Notes. Discuss situations in which students would choose to use exact quotes instead of reported speech, and vice versa.

ADDITIONAL PRACTICE

After students have reviewed the grammar chart, have them convert the quotations in Exercise 13 to reported speech. Before beginning, brainstorm with the class synonyms for some of the terms in the quotes and write them on the board.

EXERCISE 14 page 295

⏱ Time: 10–15 min

Last week my daughter's teacher called me at work and told me that my daughter had a fever and was resting in the nurse's office. I told my boss that I needed to leave work immediately. He said that it would be fine. As I was driving my car on the highway to the school, a police officer stopped me. She said that I was driving too fast. She said that I had been going ten miles per hour over the limit. I told her that I was in a hurry because my daughter was sick. I said I needed to get to her school quickly. I told the police officer that I was sorry, that I hadn't realized I had been driving so fast. She said she wouldn't give me a ticket that time, but that I should be more careful in the future, whether my daughter was sick or not.

PRACTICE IDEAS: SPEAKING

Have students use the story in Exercise 14 as a model to tell a partner about a similar incident that happened to them. Ask a few students to share their stories with the class.

10.6 The Rule of Sequence of Tenses, page 296

⏱ Time: 15–20 min

1. Have students look at the grammar rule at the top of the chart. Say: *A past act cannot come before a present or future action. So the rule means to apply logic, to use correct tenses to show the true times of actions in your sentences.*

2. With the class, review the exact quote and reported speech examples in the first section of the chart one at a time. Point out that in each example, the verb in the noun clause in the reported speech moves back one tense. Clarify any unfamiliar vocabulary. Note that there are exceptions to the rule, which will be covered in chart **10.8**.

3. Review the modals that change form and the modals that do not change form in the second and third sections of the chart.

4. Direct students' attention to the Language Notes. Take time reviewing the differences between quotes and reported speech.

CONTEXT NOTE

The rule of the sequence of tenses is also used more broadly for any sentence with clauses or multiple actions, so that the sequence of events stated in the sentence flows correctly from past → present → future.

ADDITIONAL PRACTICE

Have students use the checklist of differences in the Language Notes of grammar chart **10.6** to explain how to change the sentences in Exercise 13 to reported speech. If students have previously converted the sentences to reported speech, have them use their converted sentences to explain what they did. When students are finished, have them exchange papers with a partner and compare answers.

EXERCISE 15 page 297

 Time: 10–15 min

Answers: 1. I was the love of her life; **2.** I would always be her baby; **3.** I had an easy life compared to his; **4.** they had had a much harder life; **5.** they wanted me to be happy; **6.** I had to listen to my teacher; **7.** I could be anything I wanted if I studied hard; **8.** they didn't want me to make poor choices; **9.** he (had always been/was always) a good student; **10.** they would always love me; **11.** I should follow my dreams; **12.** I could get my driver's license when I was sixteen; **13.** I should have studied harder

10.7 *Say* vs. *Tell,* page 298

 Time: 10–15 min

1. Write on the board: *She said that she has one child. She told me that she has one child.* Ask: *How are these sentences the same?* (both reported speech) *How are they different?* (1: *said,* no indirect object; 2: *told,* indirect object [*me*])

2. Have students review the examples and explanations in the grammar chart. Point out that *say* is used in exact quotes.

3. Elicit or explain that *say* and *tell* are often used interchangeably but are not exact synonyms. Say: *The verb* say *implies only one speaker; the verb* tell *implies a speaker and a listener.* Tell *automatically takes an indirect object while* say *can have an indirect object added but with the full form* (to/for ….).

4. Direct students' attention to the Language Notes. Review other verbs used in reported speech that do/do not take indirect objects.

5. Ask volunteers to give sentences about things someone has said or told them using *say, tell,* and other verbs from the Language Notes.

EXERCISE 16 page 298

 Time: 10–15 min

Answers: 1. told; **2.** said; **3.** said; **4.** told; **5.** said; **6.** said; **7.** said; **8.** told; **9.** told; **10.** told; **11.** said; **12.** told

EXERCISE 17 pages 299–300

 Time: 5–10 min

Answers:

1. Lisa said that she needed to put the kids to bed.

2. Lisa told her son that she would read him a story.

3. Lisa and Paul said that they would take their kids to the park the (next/following) day.

4. Lisa said that the children had gone to bed early the night before.

5. Lisa and Paul said that their son wanted them to read him a story.

6. Lisa told the teacher that her son's name was Tod.

7. Tod told his mother that he didn't want to go to bed.

8. Tod told his teacher that he could write his name.

9. Lisa told Tod that he had to go to bed.

10. Tod told his father that he couldn't sleep.

11. Paul told Tod that he didn't want to argue with him.

12. Paul told Tod that he should have studied harder for his math test.

13. Tod told his friend that his grandmother would buy him a toy.

14. Tod told his friend that he loved his new bicycle.

15. Lisa said that she had never read Dr. Spock's books.

16. Tod told his father that he wanted to watch a program on TV.

10.8 Exceptions to the Rule of Sequence of Tenses, page 300

 Time: 10–15 min

1. Have students cover grammar chart **10.8**. Ask the class to say as much as they can about the rule of sequence of tenses. Make notes on the board about the rule. When students have said all they can, say: *Here are some exceptions to the rule of sequence of tenses.*

2. Write examples from the chart on the board. Elicit the exceptions to the rule of sequence of tenses. Note especially that when repeating speech immediately after it was said, the rule isn't usually followed.

3. Have students look at the chart. Review the example sentences and explanations carefully.

EXERCISE 18 pages 300–301

 Time: 10–15 min

Answers: 1. wanted; **2.** would; **3.** needed; **4.** were; **5.** could; **6.** watch; **7.** needed; **8.** wanted; **9.** will/would; **10.** ate/had eaten; **11.** shouldn't eat; **12.** have

ADDITIONAL PRACTICE

Have students work in pairs and identify the explanation for each choice of verb in Exercise 18. Have students compare answers as a class.

10.9 Reporting an Imperative, page 301

🕐 Time: 5–10 min

1. Ask: *What did Dr. Spock tell parents to do? What did Dr. Watson tell parents not to do?* Elicit several answers; write them on the board using the infinitive (e.g., *Dr. Spock told parents to be natural. Dr. Watson told parents not to kiss their children.*). Say: *These statements are imperatives or commands. How are the sentence forms alike?* (verb + infinitive)

2. Have students review the examples and explanations in the grammar chart. Point out the placement of *not* for a negative. Elicit the verb used with each type of imperative.

CONTEXT NOTE

Imperatives can be considered rude and disrespectful if used in the wrong context. Direct imperatives are not used when speaking to someone older or in a position of authority above your own. For example, if your boss drops a pen during a meeting, you would not say, "Don't pick that up. I'll get it." Instead, a softener is applied: "Let me get that for you." People on equal terms—at home, work, or school—can also be offended by direct imperatives. Common softeners include *let, please, would/could.*

ADDITIONAL PRACTICE

Review with students interactions in which they might tell someone to do something (e.g., their children, a good friend, a subordinate at work) and ask someone to do something (e.g., an acquaintance, a coworker, a store or office employee). Have students work in small groups and develop lists of commands for two or three situations. Have groups share their commands with the class.

EXERCISE 19 pages 301–302

🕐 Time: 5–10 min

Answers:

1. The mother told her kids to study for their test.
2. The son asked his mother to give him a cookie.
3. She told the babysitter not to let the kids watch TV all day.
4. The girl asked her father to buy her a doll.
5. The mother told her kids to eat their vegetables.
6. The father told his daughter to help him in the garage.
7. The girl asked her parents to take her to the zoo.
8. The dentist told the boy to brush his teeth after every meal.

9. I told my parents not to spoil their grandchildren.
10. The girl asked her mother to comb her hair.
11. The father told his daughter to do her homework.
12. The father told his teenage daughter not to come home late.
13. The father told his teenage son to drive safely.

PRACTICE IDEA: WRITING

Have students write examples of their own about things their parents told or asked them to do, or told or asked them not to do.

10.10 Using Reported Speech to Paraphrase, page 302

🕐 Time: 5–10 min

1. Have students review the examples and explanations in the grammar chart. Elicit or say the definition of *paraphrase:* to reword the main idea or gist of a statement or passage, using synonyms as substitutes for key terms.

2. With the class, identify the main idea of each quote. Guide students through the choice of synonyms in each paraphrase (e.g., *Dr. Spock said, "You know more than you think you do." You = parents, more than = enough,* implied topic = *trust*).

PRACTICE IDEAS: WRITING AND SPEAKING

Have students write sentences reporting questions they were asked recently in a job interview, in a social situation, or by a family member. Have students share their reported questions in groups and then answer them by reporting paraphrased responses. Encourage group members to ask follow-up questions, such as *How did you answer that question? What did you tell her?*

EXERCISE 20 page 303

🕐 Time: 5–10 min

Answers: 1. said; **2.** would; **3.** said; **4.** she; **5.** couldn't; **6.** told; **7.** would; **8.** her; **9.** told; **10.** to read; **11.** her; **12.** she; **13.** had seen; **14.** tell; **15.** don't/didn't; **16.** was; **17.** was; **18.** to call; **19.** them; **20.** had to; **21.** they; **22.** would; **23.** had started; **24.** couldn't; **25.** not to; **26.** was; **27.** they; **28.** didn't; **29.** me; **30.** had forgotten;

31. they; **32.** would; **33.** me; **34.** the following; **35.** didn't; **36.** wasn't; **37.** I; **38.** would; **39.** my; **40.** told; **41.** didn't/don't; **42.** will/would

CONTEXT NOTES

1. Teenagers in the United States often babysit for their neighbors. Babysitters stay with children while the parents are out for the evening, or during the day while parents are at work (when school is not in session). The parents usually pay babysitters by the hour. Laws about the age at which children may babysit are different in each area, and families should check the law before using a teenage or preteen babysitter.

2. The word *babysitting* applies to taking care of children of all ages, not just babies. The word has been expanded to include *house-sitting* (taking care of someone's house while they are away) and *pet-, cat-,* or *dog-sitting* (taking care of someone's pets).

PRACTICE IDEAS: LISTENING AND SPEAKING

Have students retell the anecdote in Exercise 20 to a partner. Have partners ask questions, such as *Who did the babysitter babysit for last month?* (a family that lives near her) *Had the babysitter babysat before?* (no) *Who is Danielle?* (the 3-year-old girl)

READING

An Innovation in Kids' TV, page 304

PRE-READING

🕐 Time: 10–15 min

1. Have students look at the photo and read the caption. Ask: *Who is in the photo?* (Joan Cooney and *Sesame Street* characters)

2. Have students read the title and look briefly at the reading. Ask: *What is the reading about? How do you know?* Have students use the title and photo to make predictions.

3. Pre-teach any vocabulary words your students may not know, such as *producers, documentary,* and *emotions.*

4. Activate students' prior knowledge about *Sesame Street.* Ask: *Did you watch* Sesame Street *as a child? What kinds of programs do you think are good for young children?* Have students discuss in pairs.

READING GLOSSARY

producers: people or companies that fund and present entertainment

documentary: a film or TV program based on facts and historical records

emotions: feelings such as love, hate, happiness, or sorrow

EXPANDING ON THE READING

The topic for this reading can be enhanced with the following items:

1. Biography of Jim Henson and the Muppets
2. History of *Sesame Street*
3. List of top educational shows for children in the United States
4. Facts about educational TV for children in the United States (e.g., FCC Guide) and around the world

---

READING

🕐 Time: 10–15 min

After students have read the article, go over the answers to the Comprehension Check on page 305: **1.** F; **2.** T; **3.** F

ADDITIONAL COMPREHENSION QUESTIONS

How many countries show Sesame Street? (120) *Why did Joan Cooney create the program?* (to educate and entertain young children at the same time) *What did Jim Henson do?* (He created the Muppets.) *When did producers realize that kids needed to express their feelings?* (after the events of September 11, 2001) *Why does* Takalani Sesame *have a puppet who is HIV-positive?* (to deal with children's fears of AIDS)

10.11 Noun Clauses after Past-Tense Verbs,
page 305

🕐 Time: 5–10 min

1. Have students review the example sentences and explanation in the grammar chart.

2. Provide several examples of your own with one of the main clause verbs listed in the grammar chart in the past tense (e.g., *I thought that my daughter would like this babysitter. When they were 13 or 14, my kids realized that they could make money by babysitting.*).

ADDITIONAL PRACTICE

Divide students into small groups. Have each group take a section of the reading on page 304 and identify the noun clauses after past-tense verbs. Have them report their findings to the class (e.g., *There were four cases in paragraph 2. The past-tense verbs were …. The noun clauses were ….*).

EXERCISE 21 page 305

🕐 Time: 5–10 min

Answers: 1. *Sesame Street* would be such a popular program; **2.** early education could be fun; **3.** small children were watching a lot of TV; **4.** she could help kids prepare for school; **5.** kids didn't have the attention span to watch a one-hour program; **6.** kids had become fearful after September 11; **7.** they should address kids' fears; **8.** their kids could learn at home; **9.** he would write a book about babies; **10.** he could help parents feel more comfortable; **11.** he wanted to help parents; **12.** they could trust themselves; **13.** his book would become so popular; **14.** I could use an app to check my son's driving habits

10.12 Noun Clauses as Reported Questions,
page 306

🕐 Time: 10–15 min

1. Have students cover the grammar chart. Ask students to suggest several questions they might ask about *Sesame Street.* Write the questions on the board as exact quotes (e.g., *"How many countries show the program?" "How long does the program last?" "Who created it?" "Does it address kids' fears and feelings?"*).

2. Tell students that the grammar rules for reported questions are similar to the grammar rules for included questions, which they studied earlier in the lesson. Have students look at the grammar chart. Review the examples and explanations in the chart carefully. Help students identify the patterns in each of the sections of the chart.

3. Draw students' attention to the Language Notes. Point out that the exceptions to the rule of sequence of tenses apply to reported questions as well.

4. Ask volunteers to come to the board and convert the questions on the board into reported speech. Provide feedback and make corrections as a class.

ADDITIONAL PRACTICE

1. Have students close their books. Write a question from each section of chart **10.12** on the board. Ask: *Which questions do you use* if *or* whether *with when you convert them to reported speech?* (Yes/No questions) *Which questions have the subject and verb inverted in reported speech?* (Wh- questions) If students have difficulty, revisit the relevant section of the chart.

2. Divide the class into pairs. Have a list of questions ready. Go around the room one pair at a time, asking one student of each pair a question. Have partners ask: *What was the question?* Have students report the question to their partner in reported speech. When you have completed a turn around the room, repeat the process, posing a question to the opposite student of each pair, etc. Provide feedback when needed.

EXERCISE 22 pages 306–307

🕐 Time: 5–10 min

Answers: 1. if/whether I had seen the September 11 episode; **2.** how much TV my kids watched; **3.** if/whether they liked *Sesame Street* (or not); **4.** why this show was so popular; **5.** if/whether he had ever seen the show (or not); **6.** how long *Sesame Street* had been on TV; **7.** if/whether she liked Big Bird (or not); **8.** if/whether Jim Henson was still alive (or not); **9.** how *Sesame Street* handled/handles scary situations; **10.** if/whether *Sesame Street* had/has made any changes in the past forty-five years (or not); **11.** if/whether the Muppets would hold kids' attention (or not); **12.** if/whether *Sesame Street* had been the first educational TV program for kids (or not); **13.** how long *Sesame Street* would last

---

PRACTICE IDEA: WRITING

Have students write several additional questions a producer might ask before agreeing to show an educational TV program for young children. Provide the cue: *The producer should ask ….*

EXERCISE 23 pages 307–308

🕐 Time: 5–10 min

Answers: 1. I wanted; **2.** if I should; **3.** wanted; **4.** if I could; **5.** I wanted; **6.** would; **7.** I had; **8.** whether/if; **9.** knew; **10.** had; **11.** would; **12.** if I would; **13.** if/whether; **14.** would have; **15.** whether or not; **16.** wanted

EXERCISE 24 pages 308–309

🕐 Time: 5–10 min

Possible answers: 1. would be; **2.** if; **3.** would give; **4.** would make; **5.** what; **6.** would be; **7.** would work/would be working/would be busy; **8.** would find/would meet; **9.** would meet; **10.** was; **11.** didn't know; **12.** how; **13.** would treat; **14.** if/whether; **15.** could; **16.** would be; **17.** could; **18.** were; **19.** was; **20.** were; **21.** didn't want/didn't allow/didn't let; **22.** was

EXERCISE 25 page 309

🕐 Time: 5–10 min

Answers will vary.

SUMMARY OF LESSON 10

◑ Time: 20–30 min

PART A DIRECT STATEMENTS OR QUESTIONS VS. SENTENCES WITH AN INCLUDED STATEMENT OR QUESTION

Have students work in pairs and talk about themselves. Have Student A make direct statements about himself or herself and give imperatives. Have Student B write Student A's exact words on separate cards or slips of paper, and add *Speaker:* (*Student A's name*) and *Writer:* (*Student B's name*). Then have students reverse roles. Collect the slips and put them in a bag or container. Have students take three slips at random from the container. Have students take turns making a sentence with an included statement, question, or direction, using the original speaker's name (e.g., *Isabella said that her son is available to babysit. Hashim asked if Trung could recommend a good dentist.*).

If necessary, have students review:

PRACTICE IDEA: WRITING

Have students prepare sentences and questions as previously. Encourage students to be creative. After students take slips or cards from the container, have them write a sentence with an included statement or question for each slip or card, mentioning the writer's name as previously. Collect for assessment.

PRACTICE IDEA: SPEAKING

Have small groups perform question/answer sessions about the people and ideas they have read about in this lesson. If necessary, brainstorm ideas with the class and write them on the board as cues (e.g., *Joan Cooney, documentary producer/ educational TV for kids; Dr. Benjamin Spock, child care/parents should trust themselves*). Elicit and write on the board ways to use noun clauses (e.g., as included questions, exact quotes, reported speech, paraphrasing). Have some group members repeat/restate ideas and others ask questions about them. Have members reverse roles.

PART B PUNCTUATION WITH NOUN CLAUSES

Collect a variety of sentences from the lesson, including split quotations, uses of *say* versus *tell*, exact quotes and reported speech (e.g., *"More than anything else," said Dr. Spock, "children want to help." Dr. Spock said, "Trust yourself." The mother asked, "Why is the baby crying?" "Why is he crying?" asked the father. The teacher asked me what my name was. She told me that her son was a good driver. He said that he loves children. He said that he wants to have more children.*). Rewrite them without punctuation on the board. Have students punctuate the sentences. Collect for assessment.

If necessary, have students review:

10.2 Noun Clauses as Included Questions (pages 287–288)

10.4 Exact Quotes (page 294)

TEST/REVIEW

🕐 Time: 15 min

Have students do the exercise on page 311. For additional practice, use the Assessment CD-ROM with Exam*View®* and the Online Workbook.

Answers:

1. what to do
2. if/whether I should go to college or not
3. (that) she had the same problem when she was my age
4. if/whether I had ever heard of this program
5. (that) I hadn't
6. (that) she had lived with an American family for a year
7. that her English had improved a lot
8. how much this program would cost me
9. (that) I would earn about $200 a week
10. if/whether the work was very hard
11. (that) it was
12. (that) it was very rewarding
13. (that) I was thinking about going to the U.S. for a year
14. not to go
15. (that) I was too young
16. that I didn't have any experience
17. (that) I had babysat our neighbors' kids
18. (that) they would agree
19. (that) I wouldn't be accepted
20. not to worry
21. (that) I would e-mail them almost every day
22. what (I had) to do
23. if/whether I had to wait for them at school
24. while the kids were in school, I could take ESL classes
25. (that) I didn't have enough money to pay for school
26. that they would pay for my classes
27. (that) we would stay in touch
28. (that) I've become more mature
29. if/whether this experience is for everyone

WRITING

PART 1 EDITING ADVICE

🕐 Time: 10–15 min

1. Have students close their books. Write the first few sentences without editing marks or corrections on the board. For example:

   I know what she is a good driver.

   I don't know how fast is he driving.

2. Ask students to correct each sentence and provide a rule or an explanation for each correction. This activity can be done individually, in pairs, or as a class.

3. After students have corrected each sentence, tell them to turn to page 312. Say: *Now compare your work with the Editing Advice in the book.* Have students read through all the advice.

PART 2 EDITING PRACTICE

🕐 Time: 10–15 min

1. Tell students they are going to put the Editing Advice into practice. Ask: *Do all the shaded words and phrases have mistakes?* (no) Go over the examples with the class. Then do #1 together.

2. Have students complete the practice individually. Then have them compare answers with a partner before checking answers as a class.

3. For the items students had difficulties with, have them go back and find the relevant grammar chart and review it. Monitor and give help as necessary.

Answers: 1. that; **2.** C; **3.** C; **4.** would; **5.** asked me if/ whether I could; **6.** told me to call; **7.** not to; **8.** had done; **9.** told me/said; **10.** C; **11.** C; **12.** if I could; **13.** C; **14.** if/ whether I had gotten; **15.** C; **16.** it was; **17.** C; **18.** Ø; **19.** C; **20.** C; **21.** that OR Ø; **22.** tell me/say; **23.** why; **24.** C; **25.** I should/to; **26.** C; **27.** C; **28.** C

PART 3 WRITE ABOUT IT

🕐 Time: 30–40 min

1. Elicit advice parents often give their children. Make a list on the board. Then have students decide which particular advice from their parents they're going to write about. Have them write a few ideas about this advice and how it has helped them and then discuss it with a partner. Have students write their composition.

2. Ask them if they remember an incident from childhood when a teacher or parent particularly helped or encouraged them. Have students brainstorm experiences and make notes about what happened. Have students write a paragraph about their experiences.

PART 4 EDIT YOUR WRITING

🕐 Time: 15–20 min

Have students edit their writing by reviewing the Lesson Summary on page 310 and the Editing Advice on page 312. Collect for assessment and/or have students share their essays in small groups.

EXPANSION ACTIVITIES

1. Tell students to interview a classmate, coworker, or neighbor about his or her childhood. Have them find out about this person's family, school, house, activities, and toys. Then have them tell the class what this person said, using reported speech.

2. Tell students to interview a friend, coworker, or neighbor who has a child or children and ask these questions: *What's the hardest thing about raising a child? What's the best thing about raising a child?* Have students report this person's answers to the class.

11 SCIENCE OR SCIENCE FICTION?

GRAMMAR CHARTS

11.1 Unreal Conditionals—Present (page 317)

11.2 Implied Conditionals (page 322)

11.3 Real Conditionals vs. Unreal Conditionals (page 325)

11.4 Unreal Conditionals—Past (page 328)

11.5 Wishes (page 331)

LESSON OPENER

Have students look at the photo and read the caption. Ask: *What do you see?* (the *Curiosity* rover on Mars) *What is happening?* (The rover is exploring Mars.) Have students read the quotation. Ask: *Do you agree?*

Background: The interaction of science and science fiction has been noted frequently for many years. As recently as 2012, NASA's Mars Exploration Program paid tribute to science fiction author Ray Bradbury. Bradbury's *The Martian Chronicles* (1950) tells a story of humans colonizing Mars that Michael Meyer, lead scientist for the Mars Exploration Program, acknowledged had "truly inspired" them to explore the planet. To honor the author, the scientists named the *Curiosity*'s landing site on Mars the Bradbury Landing. In other famous instances, Simon Lake attributed his designs of the first submarines to French author Jules Verne, whose *Twenty Thousand Leagues Under the Sea* also inspired Sir Ernest Shackleton's exploration of the South Pole and Jacques Cousteau's exploration of the oceans. And finally, H. G. Wells, who predicted atomic bombs, invisibility masking, and a fourth dimension, sparked the imagination of numerous scientists through *The Time Machine* and *The War of the Worlds* to consider the possibility of actual time travel and of meeting extraterrestrials.

Carl Sagan, to whom the quote is attributed, was an American astronomer who directed the Laboratory for Planetary Studies at Cornell University. Dedicated to exploring the universe, Sagan authored several commercial works that stirred the public's imagination. Sagan's many accomplishments included creating the first message sent into space, authoring the science fiction novel *Contact* and *Cosmos: A Personal Voyage*, an award-winning TV series (1980) that addressed questions such as the origin of life and Earth's place in the universe.

CONTEXT

This unit is about science and science fiction. Students will read about time travel, exploring Mars, life 100 years ago, and the science of aging.

1. Give students a few minutes to look through the lesson. Have them look at the photos and titles. How do they relate to the context?

2. Elicit the topics that will be discussed.

3. Have students discuss what they know about the relationship between science and science fiction in pairs or small groups.

GRAMMAR

Students will learn about unreal conditionals and wishes.

1. To activate students' prior knowledge, ask what students know about unreal conditionals in the past and the present, as well as stating wishes.

2. Give several examples of sentences with unreal conditionals and wishes (e.g., *If astronauts go to Mars, they will land on the Bradbury Landing. If you were on Venus, you would be very hot. If you had lived 100 years ago, you wouldn't have had a microwave. I wish that I could time travel.*).

3. Have volunteers give additional examples and write them on the board.

EXPANDING ON THE CONTEXT

The context for this lesson can be enhanced with the following items:

1. Magazine, news, or Web articles about the history of the U.S. space program
2. Science fiction books, magazines, movie synopses, or comic books
3. TV program listing summarizing episodes of science fiction programs
4. Science fiction predictions that have become reality
5. Video on life in the early twentieth century (e.g., *The 1900 House*)
6. Predictions on human longevity

`READING`

Time Travel, page 316

PRE-READING

⏱ Time: 15–20 min

1. Have students look at the photo and read the caption. Ask: *What is in the illustration?* (a wormhole) *What do you think a wormhole is?* (a hole or tunnel in outer space that some people believe connects two very distant places)
2. Have students read the title and look briefly at the reading. Ask: *What will the reading about? Why do you think so?* Have students make predictions.
3. Pre-teach any essential vocabulary words your students may not know, such as *fantasy, dimensions,* and *stationary*.
4. Activate students' prior knowledge of time travel. Ask: *Have you read any stories about time travel? Would you travel through time? Why or why not?* Have students discuss in pairs or small groups and share their answers with class.

READING GLOSSARY

fantasy: the product of a creative imagination; a type of fiction

dimensions: measurements of something in one direction (e.g., length, width)

stationary: not moving or able to be moved

READING

⏱ Time: 5–10 min

After students have read the article, go over the answers to the Comprehension Check on page 317: **1.** T; **2.** F; **3.** T

ADDITIONAL COMPREHENSION QUESTIONS

What is the fourth dimension? (time) *Who proved that time travel is possible?* (Albert Einstein) *What did Einstein say about time and motion?* (time changes with motion) *What is the twin paradox?* (an example Einstein used to show that time travel can happen) *How long would it take to reach the nearest star?* (80,000 years)

EXPANDING ON THE READING

The topic for this reading can be enhanced with the following items:

1. Synopses of *The Time Machine* by Jules Verne and *A Wrinkle in Time* by Madeleine L'Engle
2. Article on the development of Einstein's relativity theory
3. Simplified illustration or cartoon of relativity theory
4. Video of mini-biography of Albert Einstein
5. Online articles about wormholes

PRACTICE IDEA: LISTENING

To practice listening skills, have students first listen to the audio alone. Ask a few comprehension questions (e.g., *Who is H. G. Wells? Which is faster: a clock that is moving or not moving? Who are Nick and Rick? How fast can rockets go today?*). Repeat the audio if necessary. Then have students open their books and read along as they listen to the audio.

CONTEXT NOTE

Students will often come across an allusion to Albert Einstein in everyday conversations in the United States. In popular culture today, Einstein frequently represents advanced intelligence and difficult-to-understand ideas. His name is often used in jest to refer to someone who is very intelligent (an Einstein) or not very intelligent (She or he's no Einstein).

11.1 Unreal Conditionals— Present, page 317

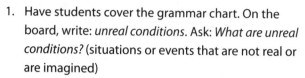

🕐 Time: 10–15 min

1. Have students cover the grammar chart. On the board, write: *unreal conditions*. Ask: *What are unreal conditions?* (situations or events that are not real or are imagined)

2. Give several examples of your own and write them on the board (e.g., *If I had more time, I'd get more exercise and I'd be in better shape. If I were you, I'd get a degree in business.*).

3. Have students carefully review the examples and explanations in the grammar chart. Clarify any vocabulary students are not familiar with. Draw students' attention to the use of a past form with *if*, the use of *were* in unreal *if* clauses, and the use of *What if* to propose a hypothetical idea. Say: *The verb in the* if *clause has a past form, but it does not have a past meaning.* Tell students that it is important not to confuse the past form with a past meaning; the examples are about an unreal condition in present, not past, time.

4. Draw students' attention to the note on word order in the last section.

CONTEXT NOTE

The verb *was* is often used instead of the subjunctive *were* in conversational English to express unreal conditions (e.g., *If time travel was possible, …*), but should not be used in formal or informal English with personal pronouns (e.g., *if* + I [*If I was you, ….*]).

PRESENTATION IDEA

Have students underline *if* clauses with unreal conditions in the reading on page 316 before they look at the grammar chart. Ask students for their observations on the rules for unreal conditions with *if* clauses.

EXERCISE 1 page 318 🎧 CD 2 TR 24

🕐 Time: 5–10 min

Answers: 1. a. were, **b.** would be; **2. a.** were, **b.** could; **3. a.** would be, **b.** brought; **4. a.** brought, **b.** would be; **5. a.** would be changing, **b.** brought; **6. a.** Would it be, **b.** tried

PRESENTATION IDEA

Have students close their books and listen to the audio. Ask comprehension questions, such as *What is the topic of the conversation?* (if dinosaurs were alive today; bringing back extinct species) *What could scientists use to bring back dinosaurs if it weren't so old?* (dinosaur DNA) Repeat the audio as needed. Then have students open their books and complete Exercise 1.

EXERCISE 2 pages 318–319

🕐 Time: 5–10 min

Answers: 1. could; **2.** would you clone; **3.** 'd clone; **4.** could; **5.** 'd have; **6.** died; **7.** wouldn't have; **8.** would want; **9.** had; **10.** produced; **11.** would be; **12.** could; **13.** could; **14.** would be interfering; **15.** could; **16.** would you clone; **17.** 'd clone; **18.** took; **19.** 'd be able to; **20.** didn't show; **21.** decided; **22.** would be living; **23.** 'd have; **24.** wouldn't have; **25.** were; **26.** 'd be

EXERCISE 3 pages 320–321

🕐 Time: 10–15 min

Answers: 1. a. would you do, **b.** were, **c.** were, **d.** 'd try; **2. a.** could, **b.** would you do, **c.** had, **d.** would drive; **3. a.** could, **b.** would you come, **c.** 'd come, **d.** 'd only come back; **4. a.** could, **b.** would you want, **c.** 'd want; **5. a.** could, **b.** 'd make, **c.** 'd probably make, **d.** 'd be; **6. a.** could, **b.** would you do, **c.** 'd go; **7. a.** would you do, **b.** could travel, **c.** 'd go, **d.** would you go, **e.** 'd go, **f.** 'd be able to; **8. a.** would be, **b.** could, **c.** didn't die, **d.** would be, **e.** wouldn't be, **f.** were, **g.** 'd never find

PRACTICE IDEAS: SPEAKING

1. Have pairs of students choose one of the conversations in Exercise 3. Ask them to write two additional sentences to continue the conversation. Have volunteers present their conversations to the class.

2. Have students work in pairs to create conversations with *if* clauses and unreal conditions. Pairs should use one or more of the conversations in Exercise 3 as a model. Have pairs perform their conversations for the class. Have the class vote on the most original or funniest conversation.

EXERCISE 4 page 321

🕐 Time: 5–10 min

Answers will vary.

PRACTICE IDEA: SPEAKING

After students complete Exercise 4, have them work in pairs to ask each other about their statements with *why* or *why not*:

A: *If I could travel to the past or the future, I would travel to the past.*

B: *Why would you travel to the past?*

A: *Because I would like to meet my grandmother.*

EXERCISE 5 page 322

🕐 Time: 5–10 min

Answers: 1. a. could, **b.** would walk; **2. a.** could, **b.** 'd tell/ would tell; **3. a.** 'd be/would be, **b.** could; **4. a.** had, **b.** would go; **5. a.** 'd attend/would attend, **b.** had; **6. a.** were, **b.** wouldn't worry/would not worry; **7. a.** 'd have/would have, **b.** were; **8. a.** didn't have/did not have, **b.** wouldn't be/would not be; **9. a.** were, **b.** 'd have to/would have to; **10. a.** told, **b.** wouldn't believe/would not believe

---

PRACTICE IDEAS: WRITING

1. Have students use the sentences in the exercise as a model to write their own imagined thoughts at different ages. Then have them read their sentences to the class. Have the class guess the age.

2. Have students use the sentences in the exercise as models to write the thoughts (using *if* clauses) of a famous person (*If I weren't the president, I could go outside by myself.*). Then have them read their sentences to the class. Have the class guess the identity of the "famous person."

EXERCISE 6 page 322

🕐 Time: 10–15 min

Answers will vary.

11.2 Implied Conditionals,
page 322

🕐 Time: 10–15 min

1. Tell students this chart is about implied conditionals. Elicit the definition of *implied* (giving information without stating it directly). On the board, write: *implied conditionals* (conditionals that are not directly stated) and the definition underneath.

2. Have students look at the examples and explanations in the grammar chart. Ask: *What is missing in each of the examples?* (the *if* clause) Say: *In each example, the* if *clause is implied, not stated (said).* Provide several additional examples (e.g., *I would never ask my parents for money. Would you?*). Ask volunteers to provide examples of their own.

CONTEXT NOTE

Several phrases with *if* or implied *if* are commonly used to show a strong opinion, such as *I wouldn't … if you/he/ she were the last man/woman/person on Earth. / I wouldn't trade … for a million dollars. / I wouldn't do … in a million years. / If they could see me now …. / I'll … if it's the last thing I do!*

ADDITIONAL PRACTICE

1. Have students share with the class a few things they'd like to do, would love to do, and would never do.

2. Have students work in pairs and use exaggerated unreal conditional statements (e.g., *I wouldn't … in a million years, If it's the last thing I do, I'll ….*). Ask several students to share their answers with the class.

EXERCISE 7 page 323

🕐 Time: 10–15 min

Answers: 1. a. Would, **b.** Would, **c.** be, **d.** wouldn't be, **e.** 'd, **f.** could tell/could warn, **g.** 'd be, **h.** would be; **2. a.** 'd, **b.** 'd, **c.** learn; **3. a.** Would, **b.** 'd want, **c.** 'd, **4. a.** 'd, **b.** would, **c.** 'd like/'d love; **5. a.** Would, **b.** want, **c.** wouldn't, **d.** would be, **e.** would be; **6. a.** want/'d want, **b.** would/could see

READING
Exploring Mars, page 324

PRE-READING
🕐 Time: 15–20 min

1. Have students read the caption and look at the photo. Ask: *What do you see?* (the planet Mars) *What is another name for Mars?* (the Red Planet)

2. Have students read the title and look briefly at the reading. Ask: *What will the reading be about? How do you know?* Have students make predictions.

3. Pre-teach any essential vocabulary words your students may not know, such as *fascinated, climate, geology, distance,* and *radiation*.

4. Activate students' prior knowledge of Mars. Ask: *Can you describe Mars? Where is it? What is it like?* Have students discuss in pairs or small groups and share their answers with the class.

READING GLOSSARY

fascinated: very interested in
climate: the type of weather that a place has
geology: the scientific study of Earth through its rocks, soil, etc.
distance: amount of space between two points
radiation: sending out of waves (of light, heat, etc.)

READING CD 2 TR 25

🕐 Time: 10–15 min

After students have read the article, go over the answers to the Comprehension Check on page 325: **1.** T; **2.** T; **3.** F

ADDITIONAL COMPREHENSION QUESTIONS

What planet is closest to Earth? (Mars) *Are astronauts who go to Mars called Martians?* (no) *What is* Curiosity? (a rover that is exploring Mars) *Why can't people and supplies be sent to Mars on the same spaceship?* (They would make the spaceship too heavy.) *What would happen if astronauts miss their chance of return from Mars?* (They would not be able to return to Earth.)

EXPANDING ON THE READING

The topic for this reading can be enhanced with the following items:

1. Magazine, newspaper, or Web articles about the Mars rovers
2. Pictures, time lines, and other information on lunar and planetary exploration from NASA
3. Web pages on Mars exploration, space in general, and research from NASA
4. Photos of Mars
5. A description of Mars from Ray Bradbury's *The Martian Chronicles*

CONTEXT NOTE

Travel to Mars and invasion of Earth by Martians, or creatures from Mars, are popular subjects for science fiction books and movies. In 1938, a famous radio broadcast of the story *The War of the Worlds*, written by H. G. Wells and performed by Orson Welles, convinced millions of listeners that creatures from Mars had attacked Earth.

11.3 Real Conditionals vs. Unreal Conditionals, page 325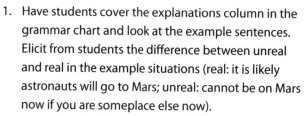

🕐 Time: 10–15 min

1. Have students cover the explanations column in the grammar chart and look at the example sentences. Elicit from students the difference between unreal and real in the example situations (real: it is likely astronauts will go to Mars; unreal: cannot be on Mars now if you are someplace else now).

2. Have students look at the explanations in the grammar chart and give example sentences of their own. If necessary, have students go back and review grammar chart **11.1** on page 317.

ADDITIONAL PRACTICE

Have students match the boldfaced *if* clauses in the reading on page 324 to the appropriate explanations in the grammar chart.

EXERCISE 8 pages 325–326

Time: 5–10 min

Answers: 1. a. get, **b.** 'll apply; **2. a.** go, **b.** 'll go, **c.** 'll go, **d.** don't have to; **3. a.** start, **b.** won't be able to put, **c.** tell, **d.** will ruin; **4. a.** find, **b.** can borrow, **c.** look, **d.** 'll probably find; **5. a.** google, **b.** 'll find, **c.** find, **d.** 'll write

---

PRACTICE IDEA: WRITING

Have students write pairs of sentences of their own using real and unreal conditions. Have students use the models:

> *If I …, I'll ….*
> *If I were …, I would ….*

EXERCISE 9 page 326

Time: 10–15 min

Answers: 1. is; **2.** solve; **3.** will happen; **4.** passes; **5.** will she get; **6.** is; **7.** can ask; **8.** could go; **9.** 'd go/would go; **10.** could go; **11.** 'd bring/would bring; **12.** left; **13.** would not come/wouldn't come; **14.** 'd miss/would miss; **15.** couldn't see/could not see; **16.** go; **17.** 'll visit/will visit; **18.** go; **19.** have; **20.** 'll watch/will watch; **21.** 'll record/will record

---

PRACTICE IDEAS: SPEAKING

1. Have students use the conversations in Exercise 8 as models to create short conversations on similar subjects.

2. Have students role-play a conversation about unreal conditions with a famous science fiction author or scientist. Have Student A play an interviewer and Student B play the famous person. Have Student A ask Student B what he or she would change about his or her life or world if he or she could, and why. Then have students reverse roles.

Life One Hundred Years Ago,

page 327

PRE-READING

Time: 10–15 min

1. Have students look at the photo and read the caption. Ask: *Who are these people?* (a vendor and two boys) *What year is it?* (about 1912)

2. Have students read the title and skim the reading. Ask: *What is the reading about? How do you know?* Have students make predictions.

3. Pre-teach any vocabulary words your students may not know, such as *rapid, antibiotics, pneumonia, influenza,* and *tuberculosis.*

4. Activate students' prior knowledge about life 100 years ago. Ask: *What was life like in your country 100 years ago?* Have students discuss the questions in pairs. Try to pair students from the same country or region. Ask volunteers to share their opinions with the class.

READING GLOSSARY

rapid: very fast, quick
antibiotics: a type of medicine that fights off disease-causing microorganisms
pneumonia: a serious viral or bacterial disease of the lungs
influenza: a contagious illness spread by viruses; flu
tuberculosis: a contagious lung disease

READING   CD 2 TR 26

Time: 5–10 min

After students have read the article, go over the answers to the Comprehension Check on page 328: **1.** F; **2.** F; **3.** T

ADDITIONAL COMPREHENSION QUESTIONS

How many Americans graduated from high school around 1900? (6%) *How much did a factory worker make?* (about 20 cents per hour) *Which diseases caused most deaths?* (pneumonia, influenza, and tuberculosis) *Did most homes have seven or more people living in them?* (No, only 20% did.)

PRACTICE IDEA: LISTENING

Have students close their books and listen to the audio. Tell them to write all the phrases they hear with *would have*. Repeat the audio if necessary.

CONTEXT NOTE

The word *circa* means *at, in, of*, or *approximately* and is used to give general dates to material whose specific dates are unknown.

11.4 Unreal Conditionals— Past, page 328

🕐 Time: 10–15 min

1. Ask students to cover the chart. On the board, write: *Life 100 years ago: If we had been alive 100 years ago, we would/wouldn't have ….* Ask volunteers to complete the statement with their own ideas, saying the entire sentence. Say: *This is an example of a past unreal conditional. How do you know it is unreal?* (If we are alive now [and are not yet 100 years old], we could not have been alive 100 years ago.)

2. Have students look at the grammar chart. Review the examples and explanations.

3. Draw students' attention to the Language Notes. Pronounce each of the examples in the chart using fast, informal pronunciation (*would've, woulda*). For #2, tell students that the very informal use of *would have known* instead of *had known* is often heard but is not considered correct and is not appropriate for formal conversation or writing.

ADDITIONAL PRACTICE

Have students complete a sentence about life 1,000 years ago: *If I had been living 1,000 years ago, I would/wouldn't have ….*

🕐 Time: 5–10 min

Answers: 1. a. had worked, **b.** would have earned; **2. a.** 'd had/had had, **b.** would have been born; **3. a.** 'd been/had been/were, **b.** would have worked; **4. a.** 'd lived/had lived, **b.** wouldn't have finished/would not have finished; **5. a.** wouldn't have had/would not have had, **b.** 'd lived/had lived/'d been living/had been living; **6. a.** would have been, **b.** 'd lived/had lived/'d been living/had been living; **7. a.** had needed, **b.** would have traveled

CONTEXT NOTE

Theodore Roosevelt became president of the United States in 1901 when President William McKinley was assassinated. He was 42 years old and the youngest president in U.S. history. Roosevelt had been a cowboy and a war hero, and he was a popular president. He is remembered for his conservation and national forest projects, and for making famous the proverb, "Speak softly and carry a big stick."

EXERCISE 11 page 329

🕐 Time: 5–10 min

Answers: 1. had been; **2.** would have been; **3.** 'd gone/had gone; **4.** would have majored; **5.** would have taken; **6.** would have gotten; **7.** 'd gotten/had gotten; **8.** would have quit; **9.** would have had; **10.** would have worked; **11.** would have had; **12.** wouldn't have had/would not have had; **13.** 'd grown/had grown; **14.** would have been

EXERCISE 12 page 329

🕐 Time: 5–10 min

Answers will vary.

The Science of Aging, page 330

PRE-READING

🕐 Time: 10–15 min

1. Have students look at the photo and read the title of the reading. Ask: *What do you see in the photo?* (a young man riding on a bicycle past an old man) *How is the photo connected to aging?* (The young man is bigger and stronger than the old man, and they're going in different directions.)

2. Have students skim the reading. Ask: *What is the reading about? How do you know?* Have students make predictions.

3. Pre-teach any vocabulary words your students may not know, such as *elderly person, ratio,* and *luck.*

4. Activate students' prior knowledge of aging. Ask: *What happens when we age?* Have students discuss the question in small groups. Have groups share their answers with the class.

READING GLOSSARY

elderly person: an old person
ratio: a relationship between two numbers
luck: chance or fortune

READING CD 2 TR 27

🕐 Time: 5–10 min

After students have read the article, go over the answers to the Comprehension Check on page 331: **1.** T; **2.** T; **3.** F

ADDITIONAL COMPREHENSION QUESTIONS

What group of people are scientists studying to find out about longevity? (centenarians) *Who is more likely to live longer: a woman or a man?* (a woman) *How is research on aging different now?* (Scientists are looking for genes that protect us instead of for genes that cause diseases.) *Who is Salvatore Caruso?* (a centenarian from Italy)

EXPANDING ON THE READING

The topic for this reading can be enhanced with the following items:

1. Time line of the aging process

2. Magazine or Web article about aging

3. Photos of a person going through the stages of aging

4. Study results on centenarians in the United States

11.5 Wishes, page 331

🕐 Time: 10–15 min

1. Ask: *What are things that you cannot or may not ever have but still want?* Write students' answers on the board. Say: *These are things you would wish for.* Elicit a few wishes expressed in the reading on page 330 (e.g., elderly people wishing for the memory of a young person, scientists wished they could find the gene for diseases) and write them on the board.

2. Have students look at Part A of the chart. Review the example sentences and explanations. In Part A, point out the forms for stating a wish (*wish* + [*that*] noun clause), noting the contrasting tenses between the main and noun clauses. Draw students' attention to the method for shortening the wish clause by stating only the auxiliary verb and the use of *would* to convey a complaint. Direct students' attention to the Language Note on the substitution of *was* for *were*.

3. Have students review Part B. Direct students' attention to the Usage Note. Tell students that the very informal use of *would have* + past participle instead of *had* + past participle is often heard but is not considered correct and is not appropriate for formal conversation or writing.

PRESENTATION IDEAS

1. Have students match the phrases with the boldfaced *wish*, either on the board or in the reading on page 330, to the appropriate explanations in the grammar chart.

2. Have students make wish statements using the list of things on the board that they want but cannot or may not ever have.

CONTEXT NOTE

Traditions related to wishing include wishing when you see the first star of the evening, wishing when you see a falling star, and making a wish before you blow out the candles on your birthday cake. Students may be interested in the old saying, "If wishes were horses, beggars would ride."

EXERCISE 13 page 332

🕐 Time: 5–10 min

Answers: 1. could stay; **2.** could live; **3.** had; **4.** lived; **5.** didn't have/did not have; **6.** were; **7.** were; **8.** could sleep; **9.** were

EXERCISE 14 pages 333–334

🕐 Time: 10–15 min

Answers: 1. a. wouldn't say, **b.** 'd teach, **c.** wouldn't make; **2. a.** 'd do; **3. a.** 'd show, **b.** 'd send; **4. a.** would find. **b.** 'd cure; **5. a.** 'd take, **b.** 'd get

EXERCISE 15 page 334

🕐 Time: 5–10 min

Answers will vary.

PRACTICE IDEA: SPEAKING

Have students talk about things they wish their friends or family would do. Ask several students to share their sentences with the class.

PRACTICE IDEA: WRITING

Have students work in groups and develop a list of wishes that people in different situations might make (e.g., a student, an astronaut on Mars, an elderly person, a driver stuck in a traffic jam, a child in a candy store). Have groups exchange lists for feedback on their writing.

EXERCISE 16 page 334

🕐 Time: 5–10 min

Answers: 1. had cloned; **2.** 'd paid/had paid; **3.** hadn't become/had not become; **4.** 'd brought/had brought; **5.** 'd lived/had lived; **6.** could have known; **7.** 'd asked/had asked

EXERCISE 17 page 335

🕐 Time: 5–10 min

Answers will vary.

EXERCISE 18 pages 335–336

🕐 Time: 5–10 min

Answers: 1. a. had, **b.** 'd had/had had; **2. a.** were, **b.** would find; **3. a.** weren't/were not, **b.** had, **c.** would find; **4. a.** were, **b.** had; **5. a.** could, **b.** could, **c.** 'd known/had known/could have known; **6. a.** could have gone; **7. a.** had, **b.** 'd had/had had; **8. a.** 'd come/had come, **b.** 'd told/had told, **c.** were, **d.** had

EXERCISE 19 pages 336–337

🕐 Time: 5–10 min

Answers: 1. would visit; **2.** 'd visited/had visited; **3.** 'd lived/had lived; **4.** were; **5.** were; **6.** 'd stop/would stop; **7.** 'd married/had married; **8.** 'd eat/would eat/ate; **9.** 'd listen/would listen; **10.** had; **11.** 'd gotten/had gotten

SUMMARY OF LESSON 11

🕐 Time: 20–30 min

PART A UNREAL CONDITIONALS—PRESENT

Provide a series of cues and have students make statements about themselves using unreal conditions in the present (*would visit, could travel, even if/could know, If I were you, would do, would think,* etc.).

If necessary, have students review:

11.1 Unreal Conditionals—Present (page 317)

> ### PRACTICE IDEA: SPEAKING
>
> Have students work in pairs to ask each other questions about unreal conditions in the present. Model the activity: *If you spoke English perfectly, what would do? If you were in your country right now, what would you be doing?*

PART B UNREAL CONDITIONALS—PAST

Write sentence stems on the board and have students complete them to talk about unreal conditions in the past (e.g., *If I had been alive in 1900, …. / If I had gotten up on time, …. / If I had known you were home, ….*).

If necessary, have students review:

11.4 Unreal Conditionals—Past (page 328)

> ### PRACTICE IDEA: SPEAKING
>
> Have students discuss in small groups what life would have been like in the early twentieth century. Have them make statements such as: *I wouldn't have had a microwave. I probably wouldn't have graduated from high school. If I had been a child, I might have worked in a factory.* If needed, have students brainstorm ideas and write them on the board as cues.

PART C REAL POSSIBILITIES—FUTURE

Have students make statements about their plans for the future (e.g., *If I do well in this class, I'll take a higher level class next year. If we have a party, I'll bring my guitar.*).

If necessary, have students review:

11.3 Real Conditionals vs. Unreal Conditionals (page 325)

> ### PRESENTATION IDEA
>
> Have students work in pairs and describe what might happen to astronauts who go to Mars. Have them write several statements. Collect for assessment.

PART D WISHES

Have students state wishes: one about the present, one about the future, one as a complaint or wish for a change in another person/situation, and one about the past (e.g., *I wish we were at the beach. I wish I could live forever. I wish my sister would stay out of my room. I wish I hadn't eaten so much last night.*).

If necessary, have students review:

11.5 Wishes (page 331)

TEST/REVIEW

🕐 Time: 15 min

Have students do the exercise on pages 339–341. For additional practice, use the Assessment CD-ROM with Exam*View*® and the Online Workbook.

Answers: 1. c. would; **2.** d. become; **3.** a. were; **4.** b. could; **5.** a. would be; **6.** a. weren't; **7.** d. took; **8.** b. paid; **9.** b. would visit; **10.** a. knew; **11.** a. could; **12.** d. would have asked; **13.** b. had taken; **14.** d. had served; **15.** c. had cloned; **16.** c. would find; **17.** b. had; **18.** d. did; **19.** a. had seen; **20.** c. would be

WRITING

PART 1 EDITING ADVICE

🕐 Time: 10–15 min

1. Have students close their books. Write the first few sentences without editing marks or corrections on the board. For example:
   If I will be on Mars, I would look for life-forms.
   The teacher would has helped you with your science project if you had asked her.

2. Ask students to correct each sentence and provide a rule or an explanation for each correction. This activity can be done individually, in pairs, or as a class.

3. After students have corrected each sentence, tell them to turn to page 342. Say: *Now compare your work with the Editing Advice in the book.* Have students read through all the advice.

PART 2 EDITING PRACTICE

🕐 Time: 10–15 min

1. Tell students they are going to put the Editing Advice into practice. Ask: *Do all the shaded words and phrases have mistakes?* (no) Go over the examples with the class. Then do #1 together.

2. Have students complete the practice individually. Then have them compare answers with a partner before checking answers as a class.

3. For the items students had difficulties with, have them go back and find the relevant grammar chart and review it. Monitor and give help as necessary.

Answers: 1. C; **2.** had; **3.** C; **4.** 'd continue/would continue; **5.** 'd/had; **6.** 'd/would; **7.** C; **8.** C; **9.** were; **10.** C; **11.** could; **12.** didn't have/did not have; **13.** C; **14.** C; **15.** 'd/would; **16.** C; **17.** would've/would have; **18.** were; **19.** have; **20.** C; **21.** 'll share/will share; **22.** 'd come/had come; **23.** C; **24.** C; **25.** 'd say/would say

PART 3 WRITE ABOUT IT

🕐 Time: 30–40 min

1. Have students brainstorm advantages and disadvantages of cloning. Write their ideas on the board. If necessary, have students review grammar chart **11.1** on page 317 and use the conversation in Exercise 1 on page 318 as a model. Have students write a paragraph.

2. Have students brainstorm important decisions they made in the past and what their lives would be like if they hadn't made this decision. Have them discuss ideas with a partner. Then have students write a paragraph.

PART 4 EDIT YOUR WRITING

🕐 Time: 15–20 min

Have students edit their writing by reviewing the Lesson Summary on page 338 and the Editing Advice on page 342. Collect for assessment and/or have students share their compositions in small groups.

EXPANSION ACTIVITIES

1. Tell students to ask a native speaker of English their ideas about the world. Tell them to ask: *What do you think would make the world a better place? What would make the world a worse place?* Have them report this person's answers to the class.

2. Tell students to rent one of these movies: *Cocoon, Sleeper, Back to the Future, AI (Artificial Intelligence), Contact, Kate and Leopold,* or *The Time Machine.* Have them write a summary and bring it to class to share. Have students discuss the movies they watched in groups or post summaries around the room for everyone to read. If some students are unable to rent and view a movie at home, consider bringing one of the movies to class to view together to complete the activity.